THEY CALL IT DIPLOMACY

PETER WESTMACOTT was a British diplomat for
more than forty years. He began his career in Iran
and rose to become ambassador to Turkey, France
and finally the United States, where he represented
the UK during the second term of President
Barack Obama and Vice President Joe Biden
between 2012 and 2016.

PETER WESTMACOTT

THEY CALL IT DIPLOMACY

FORTY YEARS *of* REPRESENTING BRITAIN ABROAD

An Apollo Book

First published in the UK in 2021 by Head of Zeus Ltd
This paperback edition first published in the UK in 2022 by Head of Zeus Ltd,
part of Bloomsbury Publishing Plc

9 7 5 3 1 2 4 6 8

A catalogue record for this book is available from
the British Library.

ISBN (PB): 9781800240971
ISBN (E): 9781800240988

Typeset by Adrian McLaughlin

Printed and bound in Great Britain by
CPI Group (UK) Ltd, Croydon CR0 4YY

Head of Zeus Ltd
5–8 Hardwick Street
London EC1R 4RG
WWW.HEADOFZEUS.COM

In memory of my parents, Ian and Patricia,
who made it all possible.

Contents

Foreword

Diplomats often write memoirs, sometimes very well. When I left the British Diplomatic Service at the beginning of 2016 after four years as ambassador in Washington, I was asked on a number of occasions to write about my life and career. I had served longer than any other British diplomat in modern times and was fortunate to have done so in fascinating and important countries at key moments in their and our history. But I hesitated. What, I asked myself, was the point?

In the end I decided that there was one, or perhaps three. First, to consider whether, in an age of instant communication, social media, special envoys and mass data – of which more had been created in the two years between 2015 and 2017 than in the entire history of mankind – the world still needed professional diplomats.

Second, to try and explain what we did, apart from consume Ferrero Rocher chocolates (which we didn't). In early 2016, after my stint in Washington, I spent three months as a fellow at Harvard University's Kennedy School of Government. There I found the brilliant, hard-working and earnest students less interested in the foreign policy lessons I was dying to share with them than in answers to more practical questions like: what sort of person becomes a diplomat? How do you join the foreign service? What does successful diplomacy look like?

Third, I wanted to tell a story showing what British diplomacy has been able to achieve, because my experience has been the exact opposite of the view of those Brexiteers who hold that being part of the European Union (EU) caused the UK to surrender its ability to conduct its own foreign policy and that only with Brexit would we be able to rediscover a global role.

Underlying it all was my sense that, in a Brexit and Trumpian world, those of us who care about international relations and relationships were going to have to work harder to maintain a semblance of international order along with respect for truth and the rule of law; and, in the British case, to ensure that the UK remained a player commensurate with the relationships, knowledge and understanding we had acquired over the centuries of some of the world's most complex and challenging geostrategic problems. The trauma of the Covid-19 pandemic, in which there was far less international cooperation than there had been even twelve years earlier when we wrestled with the global financial crisis, only strengthened that view.

Perhaps there is a fourth reason. After almost forty-four years doing my best to defend party lines, I am free, within reason, to say what I think.

I

Beginnings

I joined the Foreign and Commonwealth Office (FCO), as it was still known when I wrote these words, in 1972 at the age of 21, fresh out of university. I had little idea what it was, and even less of what the rest of the world looked like. We hadn't travelled as a family when I was young – times were hard in 1950s Britain and food stamps and petrol rationing were part of life in the small village of Edington in Somerset where I was born (in my parents' downstairs bedroom) and spent the first ten years of my life.

There was no television, no car and no refrigerator in those early years. At the age of 40 my father – not that unusually for people of his generation who had been in the thick of war and come through it physically, at least, unscathed – gave up a promising career in the Royal Navy, went to theological college and became a clergyman in the diocese of Bath and Wells in south-west England. He spent three years as a curate in Weston-super-Mare and then a further twenty as vicar of Long Ashton outside Bristol.

He set aside his early retirement lump sum to pay for

my two older brothers and me to go to Taunton School. It helped the finances when, to his disbelief, I won a scholarship covering half the fees. I was immediately streamed into the arts rather than science side of the school and left, four years later, without having taken a single lesson in physics, biology, chemistry or zoology.

Those of us studying arts subjects had to do an obligatory one-afternoon-a-week general science course. When I once asked our long-suffering teacher if we could do something useful like learn about the internal combustion engine rather than fool around with a Bunsen burner, so that we would know how to fix the kind of second- or third-hand car many of us aspired to own once we had passed our driving test, I was told that practical science wasn't part of the syllabus.

I wasn't a big reader and struggled with history lessons, which I recall as mainly memorable for having my side-burns tugged sharply, and painfully, upwards by the teacher whenever he didn't get the answer he wanted. Perhaps not surprisingly, I found myself concentrating on languages, which I enjoyed, and wondering what other cultures and countries were really like.

At the age of 15 I left Britain for the first time and took myself off for three weeks to Northeim, a small town in Lower Saxony, part of what was then West Germany, to stay with a family, learn some German and begin finding out.

I went by ferry and train, feeling pleased with the progress I had made until I discovered that in Hanover I had got on the express train to Munich rather than the stopping train that visited all stations on the same route. A kindly guard took pity on the terrified English schoolboy with halting German and told me to get off at the next big town and take the local train back up the line. There were no mobile phones in those days, of course, so I worried that the family who had come to meet me might give up when I was not on the right train. Fortunately, the local train arrived before the one I should have taken from Hanover and all was well.

In Northeim, I sometimes went to the local high school, or Gymnasium, with my host, a very kind schoolboy of my age, and helped with English conversation classes. On other days I went travelling with his father, a salesman for industrial bakery equipment who tried – to his son's distress – to tell me that Hitler had done the world a service by gassing millions of Jews. At least the experience was good for my German. I remember in particular being taken to visit the beautiful medieval university town of Göttingen, which wasn't far away, and the nearby, heavily guarded border with East Germany, with its menacing watchtowers every few hundred yards along the frontier that then separated free, democratic West Germany from the communist East.

In my last year at school, like other leavers, I signed up for career weekends arranged by potential employers. I joined one generously arranged at Fanhams Hall, a grand house near Ware in Hertfordshire, by what was then Westminster Bank. At the end, when asked to write an assessment of the weekend, I did so but also cheekily asked whether the bank would like to find me a job in France for the nine months I would have spare between school and university. I was staying on for an extra term after taking my A levels to sit the Oxford University entrance exam and liked the idea of speaking some French and earning a little money.

To my surprise, they agreed and sent me a return air ticket to Lyon. I had flown before, once, in a small biplane linking Cornwall to the Isles of Scilly. But I still remember gazing out of the window of the Boeing 707 at the amazing cloud formations we flew over. Heaven knows why British Airways put such a large plane on such a short route but it added to my sense of wonder.

I spent the first half of 1969 working at the Westminster Foreign Bank in Lyon – and witnessing the end of Charles de Gaulle's political career when he resigned in April after losing a referendum he never needed to hold. Dangerous things, referenda, as my French political friends reminded us, to no avail, half a century later. For several months I traded English conversation classes for a bedroom in the flat of Bruno Charmetant and his family in Caluire on the out-skirts of Lyon. The weekends we spent restoring a cottage they had bought on the edge of Beaujolais country. It helped enormously with my construction vocabulary, my do-it-yourself (or '*bricolage*') skills and my appreciation of the wines of Morgon, Gigondas and Fleurie. But I fear Bruno's English didn't advance as rapidly.

Having passed the entrance exam, and squeaked through what I still remember as an embarrassingly bad interview, I took up my place at New College, Oxford, in October 1969. There was no family connection. But that didn't stop Iris, the very welcoming wife of the warden, Sir William Hayter, remarking as she showed the new boys round on day one that she supposed I was there because of the stone carvings on the reredos of the college chapel executed by the nineteenth-century sculptor (and my ancestor) Sir Richard Westmacott. I had no idea that he had been given that commission, but for the rest of my time at the college – when I often went to the short evensong sung each day by the wonderful New College choir – I looked on the back wall of the chapel behind the altar with special affection.

I had been admitted to read French and German. Once there, I decided that Old French texts, Middle High German and linguistics were not for me. So I dropped the German and opted for a degree course combining Modern History with a European language – I chose French – and hoped my poor performance as a history student at school wouldn't drag me down too far.

My tutors warned that this new hybrid degree course – neither one thing nor the other – would end any aspiration I might have of pursuing an academic career. I had none, and felt I had come up with the perfect combination: for my history special subject I chose the French Revolution, and for French I chose the social history depicted in the novels of the nineteenth-century French author Honoré de Balzac.

I spent three fascinating and rewarding years at New College, and have believed ever since that those lucky enough to learn in an inspiring physical environment – six hundred years old in the case of New College, or brand new in the case of some iconic modern schools – have a head start in life. Two summers in a row I joined a party of students and fellows for a fortnight of 'reading and walking' at an old wooden chalet on the lower slopes of Mont Blanc which University College, Balliol and New College had co-owned for the previous seventy-five years. The chalet had no electricity or running water but it had a special atmosphere and rarely did anyone return home the worse for the experience or the survival cooking (we took it in turns to walk down the mountain to buy food and to prepare the meals).

At Oxford, I formed some lasting friendships but was too timid to tackle the – to me – frightening institution of the Oxford Union and high-profile societies and clubs frequented by those with more money and better connections than me. I found myself elected president of my Junior Common Room less because of any political activism on my part than because the candidates on the left and right were too polarizing for most of my fellow students.

In my last year, unsure how best to go about earning a living, I sought the advice of people I respected and whose judgement I trusted. My old Taunton School headmaster, John Rae – by then in charge of Westminster School – thought I should try the Foreign Office (people still hadn't got used to the addition in 1968 of the word 'Commonwealth' to its title, which changed again to Foreign, Commonwealth and Development Office in 2020). So did Warden Hayter, himself a former diplomat. Back then, when there were far fewer graduates coming onto the job market than there are today, those of us leaving university were almost spoiled for choice.

I knew nothing of diplomacy, though my grandfather had served in military intelligence in Brussels in the 1920s, pretending to be an entry clearance officer at the embassy, after serious injuries sustained at Ypres during the First World War had invalided him out of the army. Like so many others, my family had lost lives, limbs, property and much else during the two world wars and the Great Depression of the 1920s.

So I gave it a go. The application process began with a written Civil Service Selection Board examination common to all university graduates seeking to join the civil service. Passing that exam took you through to a second round comprising two days of written tests and interviews – one of which I remember involving a lot of questions about my relationship with my father, which made little sense until I realized afterwards that my interviewer had been a psychoanalyst. Then there was a third and final round, at which the FCO fielded its own panel of interviewers with a set of questions quite distinct from those put to candidates looking to join the Home Civil Service. Somehow, the examiners whittled the thousands of applicants down to twenty and eventually, after what seemed like a very long wait, I heard I had been accepted.

I hesitated between taking up the offer I had received from the FCO and joining an investment bank or an insurance company. Wrongly, I felt that the FCO would only give me one chance and that if I chose to go into finance, didn't like it, and wanted to switch to diplomacy later, I would not be allowed to do so. I thought the private sector would be far more accommodating if, after a few years of diplomacy, I decided to change horses. In fact, the FCO has always welcomed applicants with experience of other professions, but I didn't know that at the time.

William Hayter warned me that in his day the Foreign Office didn't pay salaries. He had heard that they did now. If I didn't have private means, he intoned, I might want to check that that was the case. I certainly did, since I had nothing in the bank. The answer, fortunately, was yes. The starting salary would be £1,530 a year – less than N. M. Rothschild & Sons were offering, but not deal-breakingly so. I took the plunge.

Forty years later when, as ambassador in Paris, I went to look him up, my old Lyonnais friend Bruno Charmetant claimed credit for my decision. He recalled driving me through the winding roads of the Haute-Loire one weekend in the summer of 1971 and me asking him what I should do with my life. Bruno had replied, he said, that I was useless – 'nul' – at business (my performance as a summer intern at Black & Decker, where he was commercial director, clearly hadn't impressed him) so I should try diplomacy instead.

I have no recollection of this conversation but perhaps part of me was already leaning that way. Telling the story clearly gave Bruno enormous pleasure so I didn't contest it.

At the end of August 1972 I found myself one of twenty new entrants joining the FCO, helping each other find our way round the intimidating corridors of the FCO's main building – Gilbert Scott's nineteenth-century Italianate statement of architectural grandeur in King Charles Street, London SW1.

Small events of no apparent consequence sometimes stick in the memory for a lifetime. I remember during my first weeks in the FCO a chance encounter in the corridor with Tony Parsons, the chairman of the final selection board that had admitted me to the FCO seven months earlier, and hearing this very senior under-secretary greet me with a cheery 'Hello, Peter. I'm glad you got in.' This grandee had remembered my face and name, and cared enough to make the new boy feel wanted.

After a short induction course, each new entrant was assigned to one of the FCO's three dozen 'geographical' or 'functional' departments. Chance determined that mine was to be Middle East Department (MED), where I would learn on the job as assistant desk officer for South Yemen and Oman. The array of talent and plain niceness I encountered amazed me. All my colleagues had already been on postings abroad and almost all would end up as senior heads of mission. Some of my fellow recruits joined convinced they would end up as a top ambassador, or as the Permanent Under-Secretary (PUS), the most senior civil servant in the office. But I doubt if I was alone in wondering whether I would ever be able to match the ability and self-confidence of my new colleagues, who, incidentally, could not have made me feel more welcome.

Before I had even crossed the threshold, I had a phone call from my future head of department, Patrick Wright (who himself went on to become PUS). I had cheekily asked for five days leave (including a weekend) to get married less than a month after I was due to join his team. Patrick was calling to say this was absurd. My heart sank. He had, he continued, been denied any time off when he had married his wife Virginia so I should get my marriage off to a decent start and take a fortnight. I put the phone down, amazed that my new boss should have taken the trouble to find my parents' number and call me up to deliver such a kind and understanding message.

The collegiality of the departments into which the FCO was organized, and the sense of belonging it gave to the twenty or thirty people in each one, was hugely reassuring to new recruits. It also engendered pride, teamwork and loyalty. When in later years departments were broken up into 'teams' and 'directorates', and there was no longer a culture of everyone bringing their mug to the head of department's PA's office for a few minutes at tea-time, something precious was lost. Those few minutes were time well spent, especially if they meant there was less need later for hours of painful counselling of lost, struggling souls.

In early 1973, not long after I joined, our intake went off for five days to Wilton Park, a fine country house on the South Downs in Sussex which now serves as the FCO's in-house conference centre. With us were a handful of new recruits from the six original member states of the European Economic Community (EEC), as it then was. The UK had joined on 1 January that year and the idea was to get young British diplomats used to the idea of EEC membership, and in the process build relationships with opposite numbers in other European capitals, of whom they would be seeing plenty in the years to come. It was a brilliant idea, and we all found the time we spent together enjoyable and useful. Unfortunately, the exercise wasn't repeated in future years. One of my modest achievements years later, when William Hague was foreign secretary, was to persuade him to reintroduce the same programme of joint training with young diplomats from other EU countries.

In several other respects I was fortunate in starting out in MED. We had a special relationship with Oman, since – not for the first time in that part of the world – Britain had been instrumental in putting the young sultan, Qaboos, on his throne two years earlier. His father had deliberately kept the sultanate in medieval conditions, which did not bode well for a peaceful succession. Qaboos had learned English in Britain, renting a modest room in the suburbs of London from a landlady whom he subsequently invited to Muscat for a month every year until she died. He went on to the Royal Military Academy at Sandhurst where he acquired a network of military relationships which stood him, and the servicemen who became his friends, in good stead for the rest of their lives. Those links, and the sultan's respect for the British special forces, were further strengthened by the role the British army played in helping him win the war against communist-backed rebels in Dhofar province in the south-west of his kingdom – a war which was still being fought when I joined MED in September 1972.

As late as 2018, the sultan, despite already suffering from a terminal illness, was still inviting a small group of retired British grandees from the worlds of defence, intelligence and finance to join him for an off-the-record dinner once a year. It was a much more intimate relationship than we had managed to maintain with the other Gulf states which we governed until Britain withdrew militarily from east of Suez in 1971 – partly because successive British governments have given those countries the impression that they only merit high-level attention when we need something from them, like a large arms contract. When the sultan died in January 2020, I was privately glad that The Prince of Wales, the prime minister and several other senior figures went to Muscat to offer condolences. No other government came close to showing such appreciation for the late sultan and his country.

We had history too in next-door South Yemen, the other country in my patch. Back then, there were two Yemens. One was the People's Democratic Republic, which was neither the people's nor democratic but had emerged from the bitter civil war between rival factions set off by Britain's announcement in 1966 that it was leaving the Aden Protectorate two years later. (We in fact left in 1967 – shades of the haste with which Lord Mountbatten had brought forward the partition of India twenty years earlier.) The other Yemen was the Yemen Arab Republic to the north, which was closely allied to Saudi Arabia.

Governance, development and the payment of pensions to former government servants of the Aden Protectorate were all part of what I found on my desk when I showed up for work in my new role.

2

Four years in Iran (1974–8)

Those formative months in MED gave me an early understanding of the baggage Britain had left behind in the region but also a taste for the Middle East which soon led to my decision to learn Persian.

The FCO was – and still is – renowned for the systematic way it trains its young diplomats in foreign languages. We were all expected to have adequate French, and to be able to learn enough Spanish, German or Italian to get by if we had to. But those who did respectably in the office's language aptitude test, and had the inclination, were given up to two years, depending on the difficulty of the language, to learn Mandarin, Japanese, Korean, Arabic, Russian or any other hard language necessary to communicate and understand what was going on in countries of importance to the UK. Then as now, whenever possible, we appointed as ambassadors diplomats who were both up to the job and had learned the language and the culture of the country earlier in their careers.

In my case, I saw enough of the Arab world and of my Arabist colleagues in my first months as a diplomat to realize that, fascinating as the geopolitics were, learning Arabic risked limiting me to a career which would rarely take me out of the region. So, instead of going for a language spoken in seventeen different countries, in Persian I chose one which was not only the key to understanding a people, civilisation and country with thousands of years of history but was also only spoken in two countries – Iran and Afghanistan. In the latter, the main official language, Dari, is in effect the same as Persian.

Persian, or Farsi as it is known in Iran, is not as difficult as Arabic or the East Asian languages, although reading, writing and getting to grips with the structure of some Persian words requires a rudimentary knowledge of Arabic. As an Indo-European language, Farsi is much closer to our European romance languages than, say, Turkish – which fools you into thinking it is going to be easier because Mustafa Kemal Atatürk, the founder of the Turkish Republic, decreed in the 1920s that the Ottoman script should be replaced by Latin letters and numbers. In fact, Turkish has more in common with Korean (and, oddly, Finnish) than any European language.

But learning Farsi was no walk in the park. I was sent off to London University's School of Oriental and African Studies (SOAS) for two terms. There, along with a small number of other diplomats, soldiers and would-be academics, I was taught by the formidable Professor Ann 'Nancy' Lambton, who had written numerous books about Iran, crossed the country on horseback disguised as a man, served in the British Embassy in Tehran during the Second World War, and incurred the displeasure of the shah for being critical of his land reform programme.

In the classroom, she was reputed to have reduced hardened special forces officers to tears. Back in 1964 she had written a seminal study of the Iranian branch of Shi'a Islam, known as 'Twelver' Shi'ism because of its attachment to the Twelfth, or Hidden, Imam, who disappeared in the ninth century and is expected by Shi'a Muslims to return one day and fill the world with justice and peace. Her book also explained the importance the Shi'a attached to creating the kingdom of God on earth and the risk this carries of bringing about violent revolution.

Perhaps she was mellowing by the time she took me on, and it may have helped that we played squash together (she usually won). Thirty-five years later, shortly after Nancy died at the age of 96, another of her former students, David Morgan, sent me the text of a talk he had given about her to the Royal Asiatic Society. It contained this passage: 'The language student she rated the best she had ever taught was a diplomat at the beginning of his career who took the course three years after I did. So far as I know, he is unaware that he holds this distinction (he is currently the British ambassador in Paris).' Having sat trembling in her classroom for two terms, feeling as inadequate as my classmates, I simply couldn't believe it.

One of the strengths of our system was the scope it gave young officers to build on what they learned in the classroom with a few months of 'immersion' in the local culture. But even in the relatively liberal 1970s it wasn't easy to find Iranian families who were able to take in as paying guests unaccompanied non-Muslim foreigners who wanted to be treated as part of the family. I was lucky enough to find a Christian family who lived modestly in the southern city of

Shiraz and were prepared to rent me a room and help with conversation classes. More formal tuition was provided at the British Council, which was then occupying the magnificent premises and garden of the former consulate general, built in the nineteenth century by the engineers of the Indian army and which the FCO had given up some years earlier.

Valuable as the lessons were, I was only too glad to supplement them with hours whiled away in the Shiraz bazaar learning about tribal rugs, visiting the breathtaking remains of the Achaemenid, Parthian and Sassanian civilisations which had left their traces across the province of Fars over the previous 2,500 years, and visiting the local Qashqa'i tribes in their tented villages.

More than forty years after leaving Iran, I still have a weakness for the natural dyes and designs – no two ever the same – of fine old Qashqa'i rugs hand-knotted by women living the kind of migratory tribal life now largely consigned to Iran's anthropological history.

I visited Isfahan, halfway between Tehran and Shiraz, whenever I had the opportunity, since it has the greatest collection of mosques and other Islamic treasures of any city in Iran. Looking at the gold- and turquoise-tiled domes of Isfahan's Friday Mosque, the Masjed-e Shah or any of the other great monuments of the Safavid era, I found myself wondering what it was about Shi'a Islam that led its architects to emphasize the external beauty of their buildings, and to make the areas of prayer open to the heavens, while those of the Sunni Ottoman Empire, most notably Sinan, chose to focus the minds and the gaze of the faithful on the interiors of the Sulaymaniyah, Sultanahmet (Blue), and other great mosques of Istanbul.

Istanbul's magnificent Haghia Sophia fell into neither category. Originally built as a Byzantine cathedral by Emperor Justinian in the sixth century, and for centuries the largest unsupported dome in the world, it only became a mosque after the fall of Constantinople in 1453. Atatürk made it into a museum in 1935, as a symbol of the new Turkish Republic's Western and secular orientation, a decision which President Recep Tayyip Erdoğan reversed in 2020 when Aya Sofya, as it is called in Turkish, once again became a mosque – to some local excitement but to the distress of Christian leaders around the world.

Isfahan was – and is – a city to which I also have a sentimental attachment. Thanks to Sir Denis Wright, a distinguished former British ambassador to Iran who was about to publish *The English Amongst the Persians*, I learned shortly before leaving the UK that one of my antecedents on my mother's side was a Persian-speaking surgeon called Andrew Jukes, who served as a doctor, translator and diplomatic representative of the East India Company in the Bushehr Residency on the Persian Gulf coast in the early nineteenth century. Jukes was on a mission to introduce smallpox vaccinations to rural Persia when he died of Asiatic cholera in Isfahan in 1821. He remains the only foreigner with a tombstone in the graveyard of what was then known as All Saviours Armenian Cathedral in the Isfahan suburb of Julfa, where it remains intact today. Jukes was also, I was sorry to discover, one of many foreign travellers to carve his name – quite elegantly – into the marble of the Gate of All Nations at Persepolis, Iran's most important and impressive archaeological site, when he visited in 1804.

Those months in Shiraz provided me with opportunities to meet people who could help me understand the local culture. One particular friend was Dr Hushang Ordubadi, a psychotherapist who taught at the local Pahlavi university. I was sometimes unnerved by the way he seemed to look through me and observe exactly what I was thinking or feeling. But I kept with me for many years his comment that Iranians would always follow a bold leader who knew where he was going as long as he remained '*chand qadam pish az havades*' ('a few steps ahead of events'). The shah, Mohammad Reza Pahlavi, lost his throne in 1979 when events left him behind.

Staff movements in Tehran meant that my language immersion was cut short and I ended up with nine rather than the scheduled twelve months of Farsi training. But there was a silver lining: arriving in Tehran to take up my first overseas posting as Third Secretary in the embassy's chancery in June 1974, the new ambassador turned out to be none other than my old mentor Tony Parsons.

He called me in on my first day to give me a job: take his Rolls-Royce and two silk carpets he had been given by a wealthy industrialist, Rahim Irvani of the Kafsh-e Melli shoe company, and return to the embassy with the Rolls-Royce but without the carpets or any damage to his personal relations with the donor. I returned a couple of hours later having achieved the first part of my mission, but not the second. However, I had learned an important lesson: in the Middle East, to return a gift is to cause grave offence. And since admiring someone else's possession automatically means it is offered to you as a gift, it is best to keep your admiration to yourself.

It was rare then, and it is rare now, to find people with such an exceptional mix of analytical brilliance, humility, integrity and what we now call interpersonal skills as Sir Anthony Parsons. But he was operating with one disadvantage: he was an Arabist, not a Persian expert, which led him, and others, to be very harsh on his performance when the British government failed to foresee that the shah's regime would come crashing down at the end of 1978.

As the young Persian-speaking political officer in the embassy, my role was to travel the country, talk to people, understand what was going on, explain it to my colleagues and to London, and do what I could to make people feel positively about my country.

Linguistic difficulties aside, Iran was a tough nut to crack. Although for hundreds of years there had been close relations between Britain and the Safavid and subsequently Qajar empires, Iranians knew that the UK had agreed with Russia at the beginning of the twentieth century to divide their country into zones of influence; and been responsible for helping put the Cossack Colonel Reza Shah on the throne in 1925. In 1941, when Britain felt he had become dangerously pro-German, we exiled him to South Africa and arranged for his son, Mohammad Reza, to take his place.

Iranians also knew that – with the Americans – we had made a significant contribution to the fall of Mohammad Mossadegh, their elected prime minister, in 1953.* By the

* In August 1953 the US and UK governments conspired to overthrow the government of Mohammad Mossadegh, with whom the Anglo-Iranian Oil Company (later BP) was in dispute over oil prices and production. The two governments had also become convinced that he had communist tendencies. After a false start, the coup succeeded in having Mossadegh

late 1970s, when Ayatollah Ruhollah Khomeini was threatening the survival of the Iranian monarchy, one of the jokes in Tehran was that if you lifted Khomeini's beard you would see '*sakht-e englis*' ('made in England') written underneath.

The shah didn't like the intelligence agencies of his allies frequenting mosques or talking to opposition groups. He believed they were there to help him combat the threat from communist groups – the Russians, after all, had set up a short-lived communist regime in Iran's north-west province of Azarbaijan at the end of the Second World War. So it was left to a small number of what were once called 'oriental secretaries' – people like me – in Western embassies to try and work out what was happening.

I took myself off to as many of the provinces as I could make the time to visit, often alone and driving myself. Even in the most remote parts of the country the roads were good. Local mayors, governors and heads of universities were welcoming and informative. Children went to modern schools in smart uniforms. People watched what they said to this inquisitive foreigner – the ubiquitous and much-feared intelligence organization, SAVAK, was never far away. But they never tried to interfere with my travels. And only at the beginning of 1978 did I begin to feel I might be travelling through a pre-revolutionary land.

Forty years later, when I was ambassador in Washington and the US still had no diplomatic representation in Tehran

---

arrested while the shah, Mohammad Reza Pahlavi, was confirmed in power. At a critical moment, the streets of Tehran were taken over by mobs paid in cash by the CIA team on the spot, led by the legendary Kim Roosevelt.

following the break in relations at the time of the 1979 revolution, I noticed how the US administration appreciated regular contact with British diplomats visiting from Tehran. Sharing the knowledge acquired by our own people on the ground in a country of such complexity and importance to US interests was a valuable contribution we were able to make to our side of Churchill's 'special relationship'.

In the mid-1970s, Iran was where everyone wanted to be. Western economies were in the doldrums, suffering from high inflation, interest rates and unemployment. Iran was newly rich, following the shah's decision to triple the price of oil on New Year's Eve 1973, and he was keen to drive forward a programme of modernization in partnership with Iran's Western allies. Investment bankers, oil company executives, conmen, fixers, arms salesmen, military training teams, civil engineers, educational specialists – everyone showed up.

There was also a huge influx of high-level visitors, including from the Royal family (always appreciated by the shah and his relatives). My role included putting together programmes and accompanying visitors on their out-of-town trips when a Persian speaker could come in handy. Taking my parents with me when I had to accompany The Queen Mother on an official visit to Isfahan, staying at the magnificent Shah Abbas hotel, was a highlight. Their contact with members of the Royal family had been limited to social events at the officers' mess in Malta when my father was stationed there in the early 1950s at the same time as Prince Philip (later The Duke of Edinburgh), whose wife, the then Princess Elizabeth, would visit whenever she could.

I left Iran in March 1978, less than a year before the revolution which was completed with Ayatollah Khomeini's triumphant return from France in February 1979, courtesy of an Air France Boeing 747. The British government was so scarred by its failure to foresee the collapse of the shah's Peacock Throne that the FCO took the unusual step of asking a former member of the Tehran embassy, Nick Browne, to carry out a post-mortem.

In the days before email, we didn't automatically copy all our internal reports to London, and most of the files kept in the embassy had to be destroyed when the revolution happened. This meant Nick had access only to documents available in London, and to people serving in the embassy at the time. Almost the only document he turned up foreseeing trouble was a paper I wrote in early 1978 following a visit I made to Tabriz after (at least) a dozen students were killed when the military put down a student protest in the local university. That, and a demonstration in the holy city of Qom a month earlier, had been sparked by the most unwise decision of someone in the shah's inner circle to place an article in *Ettela'at* newspaper on 7 January blaming Ayatollah Khomeini, exiled in Iraq, for all the unrest.

My note was not particularly bold or prescient. But it did say that, while I did not wish to sound alarmist, there were a number of distinct things – which I listed – going wrong, which, should they begin to coalesce, might bring the stability of the shah's regime into question. Nick highlighted the cautious tone of my conclusion as a symptom of the culture of an embassy that was reluctant to address unwelcome realities, but noted that at least someone had begun to hint at the possibility of trouble ahead.

I had adopted that cautious tone because I was still young and inexperienced and was basing my (tentative) judgement more on a hunch than on evidence. But Nick was right that the mission as a whole wasn't sure what was going on. We were also conscious that the shah would not look kindly on countries which regarded themselves as his close allies showing signs of beginning to lose confidence, or of hedging their bets; and we needed his business.

With dissidents fearful of the brutal reach of SAVAK, I found myself resorting to sending messages on scraps of paper by courier to fix meetings with people I wanted to talk to. A lawyer friend came to lunch one day towards the end of 1977 with his arm in plaster – it had, he said, been broken by SAVAK.

There were some potentially destabilizing things going wrong: bazaar merchants losing their monopolies to import sugar and other essentials; lawyers concerned about the lack of rule of law; rebellious students; fringe political parties (communist as well as Islamist); hitherto cowed clerics empowered by the decision of the authorities to blame the unrest on Khomeini; a public opinion encouraged by some of the shah's own, limited reforms to believe that they could ask for more; at times egregious corruption on the part of the shah's family and their cronies; and, finally, a concern that we had all been feeling for some years about the shah's increasing isolation and lack of an inner circle he would listen to, as its members either died or fell out of favour.

As the spring of 1978 turned to summer, the political temperature heated up. On 19 August there was a particularly tragic event in Abadan in the south-west which, with hind-sight, may have made the revolution inevitable. On the twenty-fifth anniversary of the 1953 coup against Prime Minister Mohammad Mossadegh, at least four hundred people died when attackers barred the doors to the Cinema Rex, doused the building in petrol and set fire to it. The government blamed radical Islamists, revolutionaries blamed SAVAK. Public opinion was outraged. Today it is generally believed that a pro-Khomeini group was responsible.

In September, six months after leaving Tehran, I ran into Tony Parsons outside the FCO in Whitehall. He was on mid-tour leave – the one time during their four-year overseas tours when diplomats were allowed a substantial, fare-paid break back in the UK. (These days, staff get an annual return airfare and are encouraged not to be away for such long periods.)

Knowing he had already been back for a good three months, and that the politics in Tehran were deteriorating, I asked Tony why he was still in London. He said people had given it careful thought but London felt that for him to return early from his leave might suggest we had lost confidence in the shah. When he did return, after almost four months away, he went straight to see the shah. He reported by cable that night that Iran's leader had lost the will to fight and it looked as though the game was over. The absence of the embassy's key man, at the key time, meant that the British government had failed to realize until very late in the day that we were losing a vital ally in the Middle East.

It was typical of the man that in his memoir, *The Pride and the Fall*, Parsons criticized himself for not having seen the revolution coming. Perhaps if he had been an Iran specialist as well as, or instead of, being an Arabist, and if he had been there throughout the difficult summer of 1978, he would have sensed the danger. But almost none of the so-called experts did; and if Parsons was to blame, so were those running the embassy in his absence, and perhaps those of us on his team who had failed to join the dots earlier.

On the other hand, revolutions tend to happen precisely because people don't see them coming. And in the case of Iran, there weren't many dots to join. The warning signs I had tentatively flagged were far from definitive; and I for one felt until quite late in 1978 that a determined stand by the shah, the military and his senior ministers, possibly including the distribution of small sums of money of the kind that had made such a difference on the streets of Tehran back in 1953, might have reversed the momentum of discontent. Today, in the light of what we now know of the ability of radical imams to mobilize support in the bazaar and the mosque, that feels unrealistic. But at the time the situation was not as clear-cut as some historians now claim.

Among Western governments, the French probably came closest to calling it right and seeing that the shah's days were numbered – perhaps because they had access to medical reports prepared by the shah's French doctors on his lymphoma and the effects treatment was having on his behaviour. But all Iran's partners and allies had an interest in believing – or at least hoping for – the best, given the state of the global economy and the acute need of many Western economies to take advantage of Iran's new-found oil wealth. 1978–9 was, after all, the 'winter of discontent' in Britain, marked by the widespread strikes and economic weaknesses which cost Prime Minister James Callaghan his job in the general election of May 1979.

Iranians – especially those who consider the revolution a national disaster – criticize US President Jimmy Carter's administration for having given conflicting messages to the shah at critical moments at the end of 1978 and beginning of 1979, and for himself being equivocal in his public remarks. There was also criticism of Western governments for not wanting to risk causing offence to the shah by telling him where he was going wrong before it was too late.

In his own way, Mohammad Reza Pahlavi did try and take some cautious steps towards political reform, for example by allowing the establishment of 'legitimate' political parties, such as the government-sponsored Rastakhiz (or 'Resurgence') Party. But as in France in 1789 and Russia in 1917, it was too little to buy off opponents who were only encouraged by the beginnings of a reform process and growing evidence that the object of their discontent wasn't prepared to commit mass murder to stay in power.

As the French historian Alexis de Tocqueville explained in *L'Ancien Régime et la Révolution* (*The Old Regime and the Revolution*) back in 1856, the most dangerous moment for autocrats is when they begin to reform, and when the plight of their subjects is beginning to improve. It's a lesson that has not been lost on the leaders of China, Islamic Iran and other repressive states in more recent times. As in France in 1789, Russia in 1917 and Egypt in 2011, so in Tehran in 1979 it was often brave, liberal activists who set the process in motion and took the greatest risks who became the first victims of the forces they had unleashed but found they could not control.

Would more genuine reform have allowed Iran to evolve into something akin to a constitutional monarchy? Possibly, if the shah had avoided other errors, curbed the excesses of his relatives and still had people around him who were able and willing to dispense unwelcome but necessary advice. But the evidence from elsewhere in the region suggests that it was the autocrats who brooked no dissent, like Saddam Hussein in Iraq, Hafez and then Bashar al-Assad in Syria, Muammar Qadhafi in Libya and Hosni Mubarak in Egypt (until the Americans disowned him), who survived best. For the shah, there was never the option of the Faustian pact the ruling Al-Saud family struck with the religiously conservative Sunni Ulema of their kingdom that allowed them free rein, and plenty of money, to export their fundamentalist form of Wahhabism to other Sunni countries in exchange for making no trouble at home.*

I am not sure even the shah realized the threat posed by Khomeini. The French were criticized at the time for granting Khomeini safe haven shortly before the end of 1978. But the first they knew of the ayatollah's decision to leave the holy city of Najaf in Iraq, where he had been living in exile since the 1960s, was when the duty officer at the Élysée Palace took a call from Orly airport on 8 October saying there was an old man with a long beard and a white robe

---

* Wahhabism is a conservative Islamic doctrine founded by Muhammad bin Abd al-Wahhab in the eighteenth century in the Najd region of what is now Saudi Arabia. It is largely interchangeable with Salafism. After Al-Wahhab made a pact with Muhammad bin Saud, founder of the dynasty which rules Saudi Arabia today, Wahhabism became the dominant strand of religious thinking in the region and, subsequently, Saudi Arabia's official form of Islam.

seeking to enter France on a tourist visa and saying he was Ayatollah Khomeini. President Valéry Giscard d'Estaing decided the shah should be asked if he wanted him sent back to Iraq. 'No', the shah replied, because he thought Khomeini would be a greater threat if he was returned to Najaf, and Saddam Hussein, against his will.

That may have been a misjudgement. Saddam Hussein and the shah had buried the hatchet in Algiers in 1975, in a deal which ended the boundary dispute over the Shatt al-Arab waterway between their two countries and, not for the first or last time in their tragic history, left the Iraqi Kurds high and dry. Saddam had little time for Shi'a theologians so he was unlikely to have allowed Khomeini to continue to make trouble at the shah's expense from Iraqi territory; and unlikely – unless the shah was complicit – to confer on him the martyrdom which could have unleashed a really violent revolution in next-door Iran.

Moreover, at that time Khomeini was still considered an outsider, even for the Islamic groups looking for a Shi'a-led revolution against the shah's government. There were few takers then for Khomeini's idea of bringing forward the perfect Islamic state which, under Shi'a theology, could only come into existence with the return of the Twelfth Imam, or Mahdi, who had disappeared in the ninth century. Few saw the risk that Khomeini meant what he had been preaching about *velayat al-faqih*, a concept which turned on its head traditional Shi'a theology that governance should be the responsibility of a secular state until the return of the Mahdi.*

---

* The concept first surfaced in a book co-authored by Khomeini in 1970.

Instead, the revolutionaries saw the opportunistic benefits of harnessing a firebrand whose sermons were beginning to be distributed throughout the bazaars of Iran's big cities on cassette tapes. Thanks to plenty of exposure through the international media – not least the BBC's World Service – which his flight to France had given him, just three months later Khomeini had forced the shah to flee his country. Khomeini returned himself to Tehran, in triumph, on 1 February 1979.

I am sometimes asked why the powerful and pampered military did not stand up for the monarchy more effectively. The main reason is that they were not ordered to by their commander in chief, the shah, who did not want a repeat of the massacre of civilians in Jaleh Square in Tehran in September 1978, when the army opened fire on demonstrators killing hundreds of civilians. The military were also shocked by the equivocal messages delivered by President Jimmy Carter, Implying that the United States was not at all sure that it would stand by its ally if the government did make a stand. Finally, there were doubts about the shah's own determination to fight to save his throne. In January 1979, he summoned back from London his widely-respected former ambassador to Spain, former brother-in-law, and former chief of the defence staff, General Fereydoun Djam, who had been relieved of his command some years earlier for telling the shah that he was too dependent on the United States. He wanted Djam to become minister of war.

Pending the return of the Twelfth Imam, it transfers all political and religious authority to the Shi'a clergy and makes all major decisions affecting the state subject to a supreme clerical jurist or 'faqih' – a role which Khomeini assumed for himself after Iran's 1979 revolution.

But when he began the conversation by telling Djam that he was on his way out of the country, the former general turned him down. The following week the shah left, just a fortnight before Khomeini's triumphant return.

It is often forgotten now, given the attention that has been paid in recent years to the military potential of Iran's nuclear programme, that in the mid-1970s the West – and the Soviet Union – had such confidence in the shah's peaceful intentions that we were falling over ourselves to help him develop a nuclear-powered electricity industry. During my time in Tehran, the Germans and subsequently the Soviets – after Kraftwerk Union got fed up with not being paid on time – were involved in constructing Iran's first nuclear power stations on the shores of the Persian Gulf at Bushehr. The French sold the shah a share in Eurodif, their uranium enrichment company. The Russians offered nuclear fuel, while we in Britain – no longer capable of offering nuclear reactors for export – proposed an ambitious training package led by Sir Walter Marshall, the charismatic director of the Atomic Energy Research Establishment at Harwell in Oxfordshire.

Marshall was a blunt, overweight, larger-than-life figure who made an impact. The Iranians respected his ability, and his directness. I regularly accompanied him to meetings with the head of Iran's Atomic Energy Organization, Akbar Etemad. I thought Marshall had blown it one evening when Etemad gave a dinner in his honour and Marshall, impressed by the decisiveness of his Iranian counterparts, said in his toast that he could see that there were clear advantages to government by dictatorship. There was a pause, and then everyone broke out laughing. His hosts knew that Marshall's heart was in the right place.

The late and legendary American reporter Arnaud de Borchgrave once told me that the shah had admitted to him in 1973 that the aim of his nuclear programme was to develop a weapons capability so he could help the West police the Gulf, following the UK's decision to withdraw from its military commitments east of Suez. Etemad records that, in response to his own direct question on the subject, the shah told him that building a nuclear weapon would guarantee Iran's international isolation. The foreign governments which were busy developing cooperative programmes with Etemad and his colleagues were glad to give his boss the benefit of the doubt.

Indeed, we were more than happy to accept the shah's argument that Iran's oil and gas reserves were too valuable a resource to be burned up unnecessarily producing electricity. At the time, no Western government seemed to fear that he was intending to develop nuclear weapons. Today, Iranian officials are adamant that they are not, and legally could not be, developing a nuclear weapons programme. But I have sometimes wondered during the intervening years whether we were missing something; and whether the ayatollahs, even more convinced of the need to take security seriously by the West's support for Saddam Hussein in the Iran–Iraq war (1980–88), didn't take a conscious decision to continue a weapons option first envisaged by the man they overthrew.

Since the early part of the sixteenth century, when the Safavid dynasty made it the country's official religion, Iran has adhered to the Shi'a branch of Islam, while most of the Arab world and the rest of South Asia has been Sunni. The Shi'a–Sunni schism goes back to the seventh century when there was disagreement over the succession to the Prophet Muhammad after the death of his son-in-law Ali; over the centuries, the Sunnis have regarded the Shi'a as inferior heretics. Successive (Sunni) Ottoman sultans and (Shi'a) Persian kings were nevertheless generally successful in keeping their religious differences under control.

The seizure of power in Iran in January/February 1979 by the Shi'a Ayatollah Khomeini, just a short distance across the Persian Gulf from the Sunni Wahhabists of Saudi Arabia, changed all that. In fact, 1979 was a turning point in the history of the Middle East. In Iran, the revolution set the country on a radical, intolerant, brutal path which threatened secularists and moderate Muslims, Sunni and Shi'a alike, throughout the region – as well as Western democracies and the state of Israel.

A few months later, Sunni Saudi Arabia lurched towards a fundamentalism of its own, following the seizure of the Grand Mosque of Mecca by Sunni fanatics during the annual Hajj pilgrimage. Seeing it as a warning that change was coming too fast, the monarchy reacted by turning Saudi society back towards a more literal and intolerant interpretation of Islam – an approach which remained largely unchanged until the tentative steps towards modernization begun by Crown Prince Mohammad bin Salman in 2017. A collision of some kind between the two increasingly hardline regimes on each side of the Gulf, one Shi'a and Persian, the other Sunni and Arab, was becoming inevitable.

Into this mix the same year came the Soviet invasion of Afghanistan, provoking the rise of an ultimately successful Sunni Mujahedin resistance movement, which forced the Soviets to leave after ten years of trying and failing to subdue the country.* The US and its allies had provided significant help, not least in the form of Stinger missiles, which the Mujahedin used to great effect to shoot down large numbers of Soviet military aircraft. Little did anyone realize that the Mujahedin would transform themselves into violent Islamic militias active in the Balkans and further afield; or that they would then splinter into different groups fighting for the future of Afghanistan, some nationalist like the Northern Alliance, others Islamist like the Pakistan-sponsored Taliban.

Theocratic Iran failed in its early attempts to export its revolution to neighbouring countries like (Sunni) Turkey. But it had considerable success at establishing itself as a major regional power, partly in line with a deliberate strategy of extending support to all Shi'a groups that it considered under threat, and partly opportunistically as other countries in the region descended into civil war, often helped by foreign military interventions. Too often these produced results far from those intended when the governments of the Soviet Union (later the Russian Federation), the US, Britain or Saudi Arabia chose to get involved.

---

* 'Mujahedin' is a term used throughout the Islamic world to designate those claiming divine authority for 'jihad', or religious war against non-Muslims. The Mujahedin-e Khalq (known as the People's Mujahedin Organization of Iran) was founded in Iran in the 1960s to oppose the shah's rule but is strongly opposed to the theocratic government which overthrew him. In Afghanistan, the Islamic resistance opposed to the Soviet occupation lasting from 1979 until 1989 were also known as the Mujahedin.

Today, Iran – or at least the powerful and largely autonomous Qods Force of the Revolutionary Guard – is involved in extending Iranian influence directly or through the use of proxies in Lebanon, Syria, Iraq, Yemen and even Afghanistan. We won't know for some time whether the assassination in January 2020 by means of a US drone strike of Qods Force commander General Qassem Soleimani inside the Baghdad airport security zone is going to change any of that. Soleimani was as much a political as a military influencer and will be hard to replace – not least because, for all the millions of mourners who took to the streets of Iran's cities when he was killed, Soleimani and his Qods Force had begun to over-reach and were felt by growing sections of Iranian public opinion to be wasting the country's scarce resources on unnecessary adventures abroad.

US public opinion cannot accept the repeated statements of the Iranian regime that it is determined to destroy Israel, and America remains scarred by the memory of fifty-two of its diplomats being held hostage in Tehran for 444 days from November 1979 until President Ronald Reagan was inaugurated in January 1981. It cannot forget or forgive Iran's involvement in terrorist outrages in later years which killed hundreds of US government personnel in Lebanon, Kenya and Tanzania. By the autumn of 2016, the game in Washington – as one senior Republican senator put it to me – was 'who could out-hate Iran'. So it only took the arrival at the White House in January 2017 of the Trump family, financially beholden to a number of wealthy Arab states and big Jewish donors, to see the formation of a powerful alliance of governments all with their own reasons to cut Iran down to size.

In May 2018 President Donald Trump carried out his threat to abandon the snappily named Joint Comprehensive Plan of Action (JCPOA), which placed stringent limits on Iran's ability to continue with its nuclear programme in exchange for the suspension of international sanctions. Negotiated by the five permanent members of the UN Security Council plus Germany (the P5+1), and facilitated by the EU's high representative for foreign and security policy, the deal was the high point of President Obama's international diplomacy – which was one of the main reasons why Trump had constantly railed against it.

Trump followed up his renunciation of the 2015 nuclear deal with the imposition of a series of additional sanctions against Iran, subsequently ruled illegal by the International Court of Justice in The Hague and strongly opposed by the other five governments which had signed the JCPOA. Although the Trump administration was nominally seeking a better deal than the JCPOA, the terms set out by his secretary of state, Mike Pompeo, were so non-negotiable that few were in any doubt that the real objective was regime change. For his then national security adviser, John Bolton, and for many others in Washington, the idea was to apply so much economic pressure that the Iranian people would rise up against their rulers. By early 2020, US neoconservatives were arguing that the US should be providing practical support to opponents of the regime to help them foment internal dissent.

Protests which broke out across the country at the end of 2017 were evidence that patience was wearing thin at grassroots level with the autocratic theocracy which had done so much to impoverish the country, pamper its own, and make Iran an international pariah. There were signs then of growing support among ordinary Iranians, increasingly aware through social media of the greed and corruption of the ruling elite, for the policies of incremental reform proposed by President Hassan Rouhani and his exposure of the secret slush funds being handed to religious organizations and the Revolutionary Guard.

Then came Trump's intervention. By the autumn of 2018, the additional US sanctions were adding significantly to the country's economic problems – rampant inflation, shortages and a collapsing currency. But US policy was weakening the hand of the pragmatists who negotiated the nuclear deal and saw it as a means of beginning to end Iran's isolation. Instead, it strengthened the hand of the Revolutionary Guard and other hardliners who have no interest in improving either the lot of the Iranian people or Iran's relations with the Western world but are only too happy to blame foreign enemies for all that is going wrong. When Joe Biden succeeded Donald Trump as President of the United States in January 2021, one of his top foreign policy priorities was to put the JCPOA back together again. Despite intensive negotiations in Vienna over the following months, the 'election' of the hardline jurist Ebrahim Raisi as Rouhani's successor in June 2021 was a clear sign that early progress was unlikely.

Engaging with Tehran is never easy – so many countries have historical baggage. But we should keep in mind that entrepreneurial young Iranians are more interested in making money through technology and trade than in the kind of murderous, suicidal jihad which led those young (Sunni)

Saudi and Egyptian hijackers to fly airliners into the World Trade Center, the Pentagon and the Pennsylvania countryside on 11 September 2001. Ironically, Tehran was the one Muslim, Middle Eastern capital in which spontaneous, candlelit vigils were held that night for the victims of the biggest act of terrorism to which America had ever fallen victim.

For all the repression and corruption apparent in Tehran today, Iranians are an Indo-European people whose language and culture are much closer to those of Europe than to those of their Turkic, Arabic and Central Asian neighbours, none of whom, like Iran, have the history and identity of a nation state – at times an empire – nearly 3,000 years old. Visiting Tehran in early 2018, I was amazed to hear a foreign ambassador who had wide experience of the Arab world comment, privately, that he felt there was more freedom of expression, and less theocracy, in Iranian society than in any of the neighbouring Arab countries he knew. And that Iran, despite the sanctions and the ayatollahs, was second only to Israel among the countries of the Middle East in terms of its entrepreneurialism and technological capability.

Back in the mid-1970s, living in Iran offered extraordinary possibilities for travel. My then wife Angie and I went camping with friends in the Valley of the Assassins, where in the eleventh century the Old Man of the Mountains, Hassan-e Sabah, was said to drug his followers with hashish – giving the world the word 'assassin' – before sending them out from his stronghold of Alamut to kill and pillage. We skied at 4,000 metres in the Alburz Mountains just north of Tehran. We visited the beautiful mosques and madrasas of the desert cities of Qom, Kerman, Kashan and Mahan, not to mention Bam, the ruined city built entirely of mudbrick, which was further devastated by an earthquake in 2003 killing twenty-six thousand people. And we visited the palaces and other monuments left behind by the different empires which had ruled the country during the previous 2,500 years.

There were also neighbouring countries to visit. Over the Easter holiday break of 1977, accompanied by a couple of friends, we drove our old Land Rover Dormobile east across the desert to Mashhad and over the border into Afghanistan. It was wildly unrealistic to think we could make it all the way to Kabul and back, with time to explore, in the ten days' leave I had negotiated from the embassy, and I was never really forgiven for flying back myself and leaving the others to do the return journey by road without me. But it was one of those journeys which we would never have made had we not made it then, during the brief window of a couple of years before the Soviet invasion of 1979 when Afghanistan under President Muhammad Daoud Khan felt safe and welcoming.

Herat, capital of the Timurid dynasty in the fifteenth and early sixteenth centuries and our first stop, was still a gem. Not for the first time, I was reminded of the legacy of British occupation, and military expeditions, in countries where we had felt the defence of our national interests required firm action. In 1885, the guide books tell you, the British army demolished a number of Herat's finest buildings, including the fourteenth-century Musallah complex, in order to deny sanctuary to Russian soldiers who never actually showed up. Ironically, this was in the middle of the forty-year period between the Second and Third Afghan Wars when our relations with Afghanistan were relatively calm. Far more damage was caused by the Russians when they did come 104 years later, and then by the Taliban in the early twenty-first century, but some of the treasures of Herat, not least the beautiful shrine of the Sufi poet Khwaja Abdullah Ansari on the edge of the town, are still intact.

Herat, close to Afghanistan's western border with Iran, was for years largely unaffected by the atrocities perpetrated by the Taliban. Sunnis and Shi'a coexisted there with little trouble. But in early 2018 I heard from a local member of parliament (MP) that there were the beginnings of Sunni–Shi'a sectarian violence. My MP friend saw the hand of the Taliban in this, of course, but had also noted a growing Saudi presence in the city, spreading Wahhabist philosophy and building Sunni mosques. Inevitably, this sparked a reaction from the local Shi'a community who felt threatened.

Why did the Saudis do it? Because, to them, Herat would otherwise be part of Shi'a Iran's growing regional hegemony. Such was the extent of the rivalry that had developed between, on the one side, Iran and its allies and, on the other, Saudi Arabia and its friends that not even Afghanistan was immune. The difference between then and now is captured in a photograph I have kept of an Afghan cobbler in the Herat bazaar cheerfully making a pair of leather sandals for my wife – something he would be forbidden to do today.

During our lightning Afghan tour, we managed to get to Bamiyan, where we overnighted in a mudbrick 'hotel' and admired the monumental sixth-century Buddhas which monks once carved into the face of the cliffs towering over the village. A quarter of a century later, the Taliban blew them up as idolatrous – giving a foretaste of the destruction which Islamic State in Iraq and the Levant (ISIL), also known as

ISIS and, in the Arab world, as Da'esh, would also cause in the name of Islam to the archaeological treasures of Syria, Iraq, Egypt and Mali.

On the way back to Kabul along a dirt road prone to violent rainstorms at that time of year, we found a large American Buick half submerged in an enormous pothole. We proudly pulled it out, showing what the Land Rover could do, to be told by the French driver that, grateful as he was, it was our duty since he had stopped to help a British tourist on the Kandahar road the day before.

I had hoped to provide the FCO with a decent return on their investment in my Farsi language training by returning to Tehran later in my career. When Tony Parsons gave a farewell dinner for my wife and myself in March 1978, he generously suggested that I might one day be back in Tehran in his role. It was a thought that had never occurred to me. Years later when, as an ambassador in other countries, I bid farewell to my own talented young political officers at the end of their tours of duty and looked ahead to the fulfilment of their potential, I understood what he meant.

Political developments, and periodic closures of our embassy in Tehran during the decades of turbulence in Irano-British relations which followed the 1979 revolution, meant that I never went back for more than a couple of days. Too bad. I would have loved the chance to build on the knowledge, relationships and judgements I had formed in this fascinating, complex country which more than repaid the attention we young enthusiasts happily gave it.

3

Brussels and Paris (1978–84)

After Iran, Europe. I spent a few months in the early summer of 1978 filling a gap in the aid policy team in the FCO and watching from a distance the dramatic events unfolding in the country I had just left. Iranian friends said, only half-jokingly, that they assumed my job had been to sow the seeds of revolution and then leave before I was found out.

In September I left for a six-week stint at the École Nationale d'Administration (ENA) in Paris. Before moving to its new home in Strasbourg, ENA used to arrange exceptionally useful courses in Paris for British civil servants which both improved our French and showed us how the *Grandes Écoles* prepared the top echelons of the French civil service for their vocation of running the country; and how the presidency, prime minister, Council of Ministers, National Assembly, Senate and departmental prefects worked together on behalf of the French state. It's a model largely unchanged since Napoleon put the system in place two hundred years ago. Elitist, certainly, but an elite of which membership is more meritocratic than class- or entitlement-based; and it tends to work.

In France, the brightest students progress through the most competitive (state-financed) high schools, or lycées, before entering one of the prestigious *Grandes Écoles* like ENA, the École Polytechnique, the École des Mines or the École des ponts et chaussées (now known as the École des Mines Paris Tech), all formed in Napoleonic times. They then join one of the even more selective Grands Corps like the Conseil d'État, the Cour des Comptes, the Inspection des Finances, the Corps des Mines or – towards the bottom of the list – the Corps diplomatique. Money and an appropriate social background are not essential, except to the extent that many of the best schools tend to be located in more affluent districts. Ability and hard work are key, which means that those who emerge at the top have good reason to believe that they are indeed the best and brightest.

I enjoyed the course and learnt a lot – incidentally, spending my time on the Paris Metro trying (and failing) to persuade left-wing Iranian students on their way to pay homage to Ayatollah Khomeini, who moved to Neauphle-le-Château in the Paris suburbs in October that year, that the ayatollah was the answer to other people's prayers, not theirs. All supported Khomeini as a means of getting rid of the shah and SAVAK. None was advocating the installation of a theocratic Islamic republic. And all of course dismissed my warnings as the views of a reactionary supporter of the status quo. Many of them will have been devoured by the revolution they helped deliver less than six months later.

The differences between the British and French administrative systems are immense. For a country with layers of regional government, and local elections of far greater political significance than those held in most of the UK, the French system was, and still is, highly centralized. Even today, almost none of the delayering of central government that was supposed to accompany the sweeping programme of decentralization introduced by Pierre Mauroy's Socialist government in 1982 has actually happened.

All roads really do lead to Paris. The country displays a remarkable ability to drive through major projects like high-speed railways and nuclear power with minimal delay, but also a remarkable inability for a country that is so centralized, and in which the parliament has so much less power over the executive presidency than its British counterpart, to deliver change in areas such as pension reform and trade union entitlement.

Understanding these and other basic realities, and which levers to pull when you need to get things done, was almost as important as having good enough French for your hosts not to regard it as an unpleasant necessity to spend time with you. ENA did a great job of getting me started.

One evening the political counsellor at the British Embassy gave a reception for our group and our French hosts, with the aim of encouraging ENA to keep the programme going and Her Majesty's Government (HMG) to send good people on the courses. Helping make the ENA course happen, he said in his welcoming remarks, was the single most important thing the embassy did. That struck me at the time as an exaggeration. Years later, I found myself understanding, and pretty much agreeing with, that remark. Our courses didn't long survive ENA's move to Strasbourg, and I found myself regretting, when I became ambassador in

Paris nearly thirty years later, the lack of understanding in Whitehall of how the French system worked.

Equipped with the knowledge imparted by ENA, my family and I set off for Brussels at the end of 1978 for a two-year stint at the European Commission where I was to be a *fonctionnaire en échange* – part of an exchange programme for officials from newly joined EEC member states (the UK had joined five years earlier, in 1973) designed to develop a first-hand understanding of how the EEC's institutions worked. I had said when leaving Tehran that I wasn't keen on an EEC job but was told by the human resources (HR) people that my request made little sense: that was where the future lay. For a while, it did.

I feared that I would find Brussels boring and bureaucratic. Already, I was more interested in bilateral diplomacy – understanding, and representing my country in, foreign countries – than in multilateral organizations. I never applied for a job at either the UN or NATO. Some years later I turned down a job at the Cabinet Office because I didn't want to spend my life drafting assessments, discussing them at meetings of experts and then sending amended versions into the ether or a Whitehall machine which might or might not act on the laboriously agreed conclusions. Not quite the attitude expected of an aspirational civil servant, but that was how I felt.

With hindsight, going to the Berlaymont, the Commission headquarters in the rue de la Loi in Brussels, was a valuable experience. But it took me a while to settle. Assigned to the Directorate-General for International Development, known as DG VIII, I had little idea what value I could add. After a few weeks, one of my colleagues told me kindly that I shouldn't feel obliged to speak and write in French since English was also an official language of the European Communities. But the fact that he had to spell it out says something about the culture of the place – and perhaps about my own desire to fit in.

My first impression of the Commission was one of amazement at how little work seemed to get done, at least at my level: long lunch breaks and early departures at the end of the day. 'How many people work in the Commission?' I asked a fellow Brit not long after arriving. 'About 20 per cent,' he replied, replaying an old Brussels joke.

It was an attractive place to work for the permanent staff. Income tax was applied at a discounted level, and Commission and Council staff had access to a duty-free shop. Among the allowances paid on top of salaries, and the generous pension scheme, was a supplement paid to officials who had extended family members dependent on them for financial support: 72 per cent of the total paid under this budget went to Italian staff.

With the exception of a few Germans and Italians, and despite there being at the time nine member states, DG VIII felt very French. After a few months I found myself writing a paper for the FCO explaining how the French had the whole place sewn up with French officials in the key positions which determined how DG VIII's (very large) budget was spent in developing countries, on the basis of bidding and qualification procedures which British firms found opaque to the point of barely bothering to apply. My colleagues across the road at the British permanent representation didn't appreciate the implication that there was more they should be doing to help British business, and to get good people into key positions, but the study went down well at more senior levels in London.

As in many French government departments, much of the most interesting – and demanding – work was done in the Commission *cabinets*, an expanded version of what Whitehall knows as ministerial private offices staffed with high-fliers who were personally attached to their commissioner. I wasn't part of that seventh-floor inner circle, but my life started to look up when after a few months my commissioner, the future French foreign minister Claude Cheysson, began to include me in some of his delegations visiting developing countries around the Mediterranean with which the EU had 'cooperation' programmes.

He spoke perfect English, but rarely used it. He did however take to the habit I developed – which struck him as an interesting innovation – of writing notes of his more interesting conversations. I was glad to be there when, as often happened in Arab capitals, the conversation turned to the still-recent Iranian Revolution, and what it could mean for the rest of the Muslim world.

Cheysson could be a tough boss. Later, when he was foreign minister, there was a famous occasion when he read a lengthy cable from the French ambassador to Indonesia telling him little he didn't know already. The tradition in those days, in Paris as in London, was for staff to draft a polite reply with just enough substance to make His Excellency feel his efforts had been appreciated. Cheysson drafted his own reply – '*En effet*' ('Indeed'). That was all. I never heard how it went down in Jakarta.

Cheysson had first-rate people in his *cabinet*, including his *directeur de cabinet*, Danièle Josselin, with whom I managed to get myself arrested by the occupying Syrian army while we took an innocent, but perhaps ill-advised, walk to the *place des Canons* during a working visit to Beirut towards the end of 1979. (I became a little concerned when we were taken into a bomb-damaged building on the edge of the square for interrogation, but we managed to talk ourselves out of trouble, and regained our freedom before our colleagues became seriously alarmed at our disappearance.)

After fifteen months, just as I began to feel I was making a useful contribution, London decided that leaving me in Brussels was a luxury which, in 'workforce planning' terms, the FCO could ill afford. A vacancy had come up at short notice in the First Secretary, Economic slot in Paris. HR didn't want to move me early but perhaps I'd like to take up this remarkable opportunity? Friends I consulted in the Paris embassy weren't sure this was the job for me, and Angie and I were about to have our third child. So I said thanks, but no thanks: I had been sent to Brussels for two years, felt I was finally managing to do something useful there and would like to complete the task. Well, if I didn't want to go to Paris, said HR, there was an interesting job for me in French-speaking sub-Saharan Africa instead. One way or another, I was on the move.

It didn't take long to reconsider so we set off down the autoroute to Paris after all, and rented a pleasant, roomy family home in the (then) very unfashionable district of Levallois-Perret just outside the *boulevard périphérique* to the north-west of the city. It was no hardship – and in practice a wonderful opportunity – to be back in Paris so soon. But I had a sense of leaving a job unfinished in the Commission.

In Brussels we had made some good friends and the family had begun to enjoy a settled existence.

I was also very aware that Britain, and British interests, were under-represented in terms of key positions and overall Commission staff numbers. Thirty-five years later, that was still the case since so few talented British officials had the language and other specialist skills needed to pass the 'concours' entrance exam or the desire to make a career out of working in Brussels.

I was beginning too to form some impressions of the culture which, over time, caused British public opinion to turn against Brussels and its ways of doing business. A small example: I once questioned the use of Commission funds for an expedition that I felt was hard to justify, and said I didn't think taxpayers would think it was a good use of their money. 'It isn't their money, it's ours,' came the reply, based on the legal reality that customs duties levied on imports into the EEC from non-member states were deemed to be the Commission's 'own resources'.

The UK, in my view, was – at least until the election of December 2019 – the European country with the most vibrant sense of everyday accountability of elected representatives for their actions and use of public funds. Over the years, public opinion has consequently found it difficult to live with the sense that EU officialdom doesn't seem to be accountable to anyone – a sentiment fuelled by the fact that every year from 1995, when it started looking at the books, until 2016, the EU's Court of Auditors filed an adverse opinion on the Commission's accounts.

In Paris, the job itself, as I had been warned, lacked the profile and the excitement of other first secretary positions which followed French internal politics and foreign policy. But it offered the potential to get out and about in areas of trade, energy and industrial policy which I found fascinating, especially as France was – and remains – a country in which the state has major industrial holdings; and the government, not least the Élysée Palace, took a close interest in all significant appointments, mergers and public contracts. It is no accident that most of the CEOs of France's most prominent CAC40 companies (roughly equivalent to the FTSE 100) are graduates of the same *Grandes Écoles* as the *hauts fonctionnaires*, or senior officials, who occupy the commanding heights of the French administration.

I rapidly learned that friends in ministerial *cabinets* one day could turn up the next in a senior position in an energy company, bank or national airline. Part of the fun of returning to Paris as ambassador more than twenty years later was discovering old friends in key positions: in France, the best and the brightest never retire and move seamlessly between the public and private sectors.

Many of the talented young members of the French civil service, including at the Ministry of Foreign Affairs, were politically aligned with one or other of the main political parties – François Mitterrand's Socialists or President Valéry Giscard d'Estaing's Rassemblement pour la République. And there were presidential elections due to be held in May 1981, a little over a year after my arrival. So, although it wasn't part of my job, I found myself joining some of my friends as they moonlighted in the months before the elections sticking up posters and going to lively weekend house parties where they discussed how best to get their man elected. It gave me a degree of childish pleasure – after the event, at least – to have predicted, contrary to the embassy's perceived wisdom, that Mitterrand was going to win.

A month later, the Socialists also won a big victory in the legislative elections, signalling all change – and a period in which President Mitterrand and Prime Minister Pierre Mauroy proceeded with a programme of nationalizing major banks and industries, which of course gave the state control of an even larger share of the economy. It also allowed the shareholders of some shaky big-name businesses to get out on far more attractive terms than if they had sold their holdings on the open market.

Just when, across the Channel, Margaret Thatcher was beginning to do battle with trade unions and embark on an equally ambitious programme of privatization, France was moving in the opposite direction. In his second term, Mitterrand came to regard the nationalizations as a mistake, and began to reverse course. But at the time the idea of getting the state to take over ownership and control of industries of national importance did not strike most French people as strange. Mitterrand had, of course, promised it in his manifesto. But in France the state was perceived – not without reason, when one looked at the relative performance of the railways, airlines, energy and water companies – to be far more successful at running businesses than civil servants in the UK.

Precisely because the French state was so involved in industrial policy, my job had some fascinating angles. On one occasion Margaret Thatcher came over for one of the annual Franco-British summits with an unusually large number of cabinet ministers and permanent secretaries. Before the formal meetings began, she liked to talk through the main issues – or the ones she wasn't clear about – over a whisky the night before. We sat down as soon as the delegation arrived and the prime minister was soon asking why the relationship between a British car parts firm, Lucas, and a French competitor and potential partner, Valeo, was on the agenda.

After a pause, when it was clear that no one else knew the answer to this very technical question, I piped up from the floor where, as the most junior person in the room, I was squatting since there weren't enough chairs to go round, and gave her a summary of what was at stake. Another pause. Then the prime minister went round the room, wagging her finger and counting the number of cabinet ministers and permanent secretaries she had brought with her who had been so unable to answer her questions that she had had to get the answers from the first secretary kneeling at her feet.

Lest the episode went to my head, her private secretary, Charles Powell, took me aside to say well done, but do bear in mind that this piece of theatre was laid on to remind her team who was boss and that she expected people to earn their passage on government trips abroad.

It would have been a terrible waste to spend four years in France and not develop some appreciation of its wonderful wines. By chance, I inherited from a friend the responsibility for running a small wine-buying syndicate for members of the embassy. My role was to collate bids for fine French wines being sold at auction in London but which were lying in France. Not many people in London could be bothered with arranging for the transportation and payment of duty, which wasn't a problem for diplomats living in France and exempt from paying the duty. We picked up some remarkable bargains.

Unfortunately, the sellers began to realize this was not a good deal for them and stopped selling wine at London auctions that wasn't already in the UK. But the buying had brought me into contact with a few Bordeaux producers, and thanks to some friends with contacts in the Loire region I became a regular customer of some lovely vineyards at Chinon and St Nicolas de Bourgueil. I was thus able to keep the sideline going and to develop a hobby of buying decent wines at sensible prices.

When I proudly shipped my modest cellar back to the UK at the end of our four years at the embassy, I found a number of my 'specials' on offer in supermarkets at no more than the price I had paid. I consoled myself with the thought that at least the professionals had made the same selections as I had.

4

Working with ministers (1984–7)

Returning to the UK from Paris in the spring of 1984, I was put straight into one of the FCO's European Community departments which dealt with the internal affairs of the EEC (which did not become the European Union until 1993). My brief was agriculture and the budget, plus a bit of public diplomacy. Not my choice, and not areas of policy where I felt I was likely to be able to make much of a difference, given that these were areas where the Ministry of Agriculture and the Treasury were respectively in the lead. But both were hugely important to UK interests.

At this time, the FCO was an important part of the policy-making machine as well as being responsible for delivery. It was our job to issue instructions and prepare briefings for the foreign secretary and prime minister in advance of meetings of European foreign ministers and heads of government, and to send instructions to our delegation in Brussels. But it was the Cabinet Office's job to coordinate those positions, and to reconcile – with FCO help – the views of different departments: the Ministry of Agriculture on the Common Agricultural Policy (CAP), the Treasury on budget and the prime minister's rebate negotiations, the Department of Trade and Industry (DTI) on trade and industrial policy.

Human nature being what it is, civil servants in other departments were often reluctant to share either the authority or the information we needed to make a difference. This could make EEC policy work unrewarding at desk level, even if the FCO's European affairs director a couple of levels above me was a highly effective Whitehall operator. As part of learning my CAP brief, I took myself off to a disused car plant outside Swindon, an hour west of London, which was being used to store grain at EEC expense. My jaw dropped at the size of the grain mountain I found there, all part of the accumulation of surpluses across Europe – of wine, butter and olive oil as well as grain – as a result of the incentives given to farmers to grow as much as they could, irrespective of demand.

The conversion of the car plant into a grain store was also a sign of how far Britain's motor industry had declined. Most of it remained in the doldrums until the creation of the single market – a largely British initiative – encouraged manufacturers and entrepreneurs from other countries to invest afresh, and very successfully, in British industry.

A few months into the job I decided the time had come to try and broaden my experience and develop some new skills by applying to run a ministerial private office.

By the summer of 1984 I had joined Richard Luce, minister of state responsible for the Middle East, arms control, China/Hong Kong and South East Asia as his private secretary. As a commander in the Royal Navy in the 1950s, my father had worked as an assistant to Richard's uncle, Admiral David Luce, who would later resign as First Sea Lord in 1966 over the then Labour government's decision to cancel plans to build a new generation of aircraft carriers. Richard Luce and I had never met but there seemed to be something appropriate about the appointment. Richard himself had recently re-joined the government after resigning in solidarity with Lord Carrington, then foreign secretary, over the FCO's failure to foresee and then deter the Argentine invasion of South Georgia and the Falkland Islands in 1982.

We had just over a year together until Margaret Thatcher promoted Luce to be minister for the arts and the civil service in September 1985, replacing him with Tim Renton. 'Prime Minister, I know nothing about the arts,' Luce had protested – quite truthfully. 'That's precisely why I want you in the job,' Thatcher replied, so she could have a minister capable of providing a detached view without any risk of being taken hostage by the arts community.

The role of private secretary was, and still is, an invaluable training experience. You learn to manage a heavy workload; to draft accurately and at speed; to deal with seniors who hold you responsible – sometimes with good reason – for the failure of their policy advice, or written work, to find ministerial favour; to balance political and administrative work; and to manage bosses who are in high-stress and often highly exposed political positions.

I also learned a lot about policy, not least in the area of arms control, about negotiating with the Chinese (and the Hong Kong media, who were both highly knowledgeable

and deeply suspicious of how we were handling the negotiations with China over the future of their territory),
and various intractable elements of Middle East policy. I
learned how to handle a boss with a variety of sometimes
conflicting obligations: UK government ministers are always
either elected members of the House of Commons or
appointed (occasionally hereditary) members of the House
of Lords. Most fall into the first category, which involves
balancing their ministerial duties with a duty of care to their
constituencies – especially those which are not safe seats.

In the United States, members of the House of Representatives are up for election every two years and are advised
by their party managers to spend half their time talking to
donors and fund-raisers. The British system is mercifully
different. MPs are elected for five-year terms – unless Parliament decides otherwise or the government of the day loses
two successive votes of confidence – and our electoral laws
place far greater constraints on the ability of special interest
groups and individuals to influence either candidate selection
or election outcomes.

But in practice, MPs who are also ministers – 20–25 per
cent of the total when a government has a normal working
majority – have to spend every Friday and the weekend in their
constituencies and often have weekday evening events of a
political rather than departmental nature. With the growing
polarization of politics we have witnessed in recent years,
some also now have to cope with the risk of deselection. At
the end of 2019, it was striking that twenty-one of the more
talented and distinguished members of the Conservative
Party – including a number of former ministers – were either
deselected by their local constituencies or expelled by Prime

Minister Boris Johnson because they were not prepared to support the idea of the UK leaving the EU with no deal.

Part of the fun of the job was helping ministers balance their ministerial and constituency duties and supporting them in the political as well as departmental role, without ever forgetting the non-partisan role of the civil servant. Once a month there are FCO Questions in Parliament when the foreign secretary and his three or four junior ministers have to field questions put to them by members of the House of Commons. We also had to deal with Early Day Motions – short notice debates – and Private Member's Questions which needed answering in hours rather than days. It was our role, along with that of the parliamentary private secretary (an MP of the same party), to ensure that the minister had the material he needed and as much background as possible about the personal interest of the MP putting the question (or leading the attack).

While we were not political staff, we worked with the whips and with politicians of all persuasions, a number of whom became lifelong friends. And we sat in the officials' box from where we could pass briefing notes to ministers when necessary.

Accompanying and supporting Luce and Renton, I saw parts of the world I had never visited, and would never see again, since a key role of junior ministers is to travel to places which rarely receive visits by the prime minister or foreign secretary.

But my career as private secretary was nearly stillborn. Before starting with Richard Luce, I was tried out for the role of private secretary for European affairs in the office of Secretary of State Sir Geoffrey Howe. This involved, among other things, going with him to an informal meeting of foreign ministers in southern France in June 1984. Ministers were supposed to attend these meetings unaccompanied except by a single senior official and an interpreter. So someone hit on the bright idea of me going along in that role, so I could be auditioned for the private secretary position and make a note afterwards of what had been said. I had told Geoffrey Howe's team that while my French was adequate, my German was worse than rusty. Not to worry, I was told, the other ministers took along real interpreters so I wouldn't be found out. All would be fine.

A government pool car came to collect me from our home in Tunbridge Wells, Kent, leaving two and a half hours to get to RAF Northolt on the other side of London. The driver took us through central London, against my advice, where we got so stuck that I missed the plane taking the official party to France (with a first stop in Paris). I diverted the driver to Heathrow in the hope of finding a commercial flight which would allow me to join Geoffrey Howe and the rest of the party in Paris, where the secretary of state had a speaking engagement.

At Heathrow, I first had to explain that my passport was with the official party en route from Northolt but I would meet up with it again when and if I could get to France. Then I had to find a seat – the flight to Paris was full. Throwing myself on the mercy of the check-in supervisor, I talked my way onto the flight and got the folding seat at the back of the plane normally reserved for the crew. And I agreed to assume the risk of not being admitted to France and having to pay the fare if I was sent back on the next plane for not having a passport.

Arriving at Charles de Gaulle, there was another difficult conversation with a French immigration official as I explained the passport problem. But I got through, jumped in a cab, set off for the Grand Hotel and took my seat at the lunch which Geoffrey Howe was addressing, hot and breathless but only ten minutes after he had started delivering the speech I'd largely written for him.

After lunch, the convoy set off for the military airfield at Villacoublay from where we flew in the official HS 125 to south-western France for the main event. At the remote but enchanting country retreat, the arrival dinner was arranged around two tables, one for foreign ministers and their wives and the other for the strictly limited number of senior officials allowed to be present. I went smartly to the second table, only to find that there was no place for me. 'Monsieur, you are at the high table with your foreign minister for whom you are going to interpret.'

I was indeed seated next to Geoffrey Howe. On his other side was the delightful but entirely German-speaking wife of the German foreign minister. After a few minutes, Howe turned to me: 'My neighbour is explaining the financial background of the corruption trial currently taking place in Bonn. I can follow her general drift but please can you fill in the details?' She began to speak quickly. I missed the opening sentences. She continued. I missed the next section. She ended. I'd missed the lot. I had no idea what she had said.

Howe, and his neighbour, looked at me expectantly. Being a bad liar and an even worse actor, I decided to confess rather than fall off my chair or pretend to be taken ill. 'I'm sorry, Minister, but I didn't entirely understand what your neighbour said to you,' and we all got on with our respective conversations. A little later, three ministers actually laughed at a joke I told. The clouds seemed to be lifting.

After dinner, we caught up with Howe's actual private secretary. 'Well,' said the foreign secretary, beaming, 'our horse fell spectacularly at the first fence.' I felt wonderful. Coffee and liqueurs followed. Later, as everyone prepared to retire, we met up with another FCO official. Still enjoying himself, Geoffrey Howe again explained, 'our friend fell at the first hurdle'. If it gives him pleasure to tell the story, I tried telling myself, perhaps I have served some purpose.

We adjourned to our respective hotels. My driver got lost but I eventually found my way to bed. I fell asleep ploughing through a German dictionary, wondering how I was going to get through the next day. Fortunately, consecutive interpretation was provided by professionals in the plenary meetings and I was spared further humiliation. Strangely, I was not invited to become Geoffrey Howe's private secretary for European affairs. But we remained in touch over the years, including after he had retired from politics. Neither of us ever forgot the episode.

With Richard Luce there were plenty of adventures but no trips quite as stressful as that two-day outing to France. We went to the Gulf states; to China and Hong Kong at difficult points in the negotiations over the future of the colony; to Egypt and Sudan; to Washington, Paris and Brussels. With his successor, Tim Renton, I went back to the Gulf; to China, Hong Kong and Thailand; to Israel and the Occupied Palestinian Territories; to the United States; to the Philippines, Singapore and Indonesia.

Our visit to the Philippines at the end of June 1986 was organized around a major ASEAN conference in Manila six months after Cory Aquino and 'People Power' had swept the corrupt regime of Ferdinand Marcos from power. The star of the show, who spent a full five days in the Philippines showing US support for the new president, was US Secretary of State George Shultz. He even produced a $200 million cheque as 'rent' for the military bases which the US maintained in the Philippines. The conference itself was less memorable than our meetings in the margin with the remarkable Cardinal Sin, archbishop of Manila, one of the heroes of the revolution, and the president herself.

Alas, one of my other abiding memories is of the numbers of US secret service personnel pouring down the grand staircase of the conference hotel and offending everyone with their loud instruction to all the other delegates to clear space for the arrival of the secretary of state. Time and again over the years I noticed how the tactlessness – and sometimes inappropriate behaviour – of their secret service undid so much of the goodwill that the United States was seeking to create.

Such pettiness was soon forgotten the next day when we visited Sarawak in northern Borneo, one of the states of the Malaysian federation, where we met the inhabitants of one of the famed longhouses and spent the night overlooking the South China Sea from the luxury of the new Damai Beach Sheraton hotel before flying on to Kuala Lumpur and Singapore for political and business calls.

Renton and I saw Shultz again in Brussels in October for a special debrief to NATO allies by the secretary of state following the historic Reagan–Gorbachev Reykjavik summit a couple of days earlier – the occasion when, to the horror of arms control experts, the two presidents almost agreed to abolish nuclear weapons.

Shultz, not a man normally given to hyperbole, spoke without notes for seventy-five minutes. He commented at the end that he had never been so proud of his president as he had been at Reykjavik. Interestingly, there was virtually no criticism from other members of the NATO Council of the position taken by Reagan, which clearly had implications for the defence of the entire Western alliance.

Straight after the meeting, Renton and I flew to New York where, the following morning, he delivered a speech on disarmament to the UN's First Committee and had a series of meetings with officials. In the evening, we took the shuttle to Washington – in the days before 9/11 and intrusive airport security, the plane was still preferable to the train as a means of making that short journey. A working dinner, an overnight, and a series of meetings on arms control and the Middle East took up most of Wednesday before we took an overnight flight back to Heathrow.

We were back in the office for the first of the day's meetings at 10 a.m. My notes of the trip record that I 'sloped off early' at 6.30 p.m. to be met at Tunbridge Wells train station by my wife with the news that our dog Monty had been killed by a car the night I had left Brussels. There weren't any mobile phones in those days, so it was much harder for families to stay in touch, with good and bad news, than it is now.

We also visited Russia in January 1987 when Renton became the first foreign official to be interviewed live on a current affairs television programme. I was bowled over by an evening at the Bolshoi where we were treated to a superb performance of Shostakovich's ballet *The Golden Age*. Also etched in my memory is a visit to the memorial to the 872-day siege of Leningrad, as St Petersburg then was, by the Wehrmacht between 1941 and 1944. I will never forget watching the −25°C frost on the marble melt in small circles round each of the candles lit to commemorate the 800,000 civilians who lost their lives during the siege.

Our travels also included the first visit to Gaza by a British government minister since Winston Churchill in 1921. Gaza then, as now, was a humanitarian horror story. Gaza City felt like one large public sewer, and the Israeli army was everywhere. As we visited one Palestinian leader in his home, I noticed an Israeli army jeep bristling with aerials parked in the driveway next to the room where we were talking.

Returning to London, Renton was invited by a number of Jewish organizations to speak of his impressions. He was a founder member of Conservative Friends of Israel and was married to a descendant of the British politician who gave his name to the Balfour Declaration of 1917 which called for the creation of a national home for the Jewish people. He thus caused some surprise by speaking out against the conditions in which Israel, as the occupying power, was governing – or failing to govern – Gaza. On one occasion he had to leave for a vote in the House of Commons immediately after his prepared remarks, leaving the Director for the Middle East, Sir David Miers, and me to deal with the less-than-straightforward question and answer session that followed.

There were other memorable moments in London during my time as private secretary to the minister of state responsible for the Middle East. On Friday, 24 October 1986, I saw for myself an interesting example of the interplay between foreign and domestic policy. That morning, a Syrian national, Nezar al-Hindawi, was convicted of attempting to blow up an El Al Boeing 747 by placing a bomb in the hand luggage of his pregnant Irish girlfriend as she boarded a flight to Tel Aviv from Heathrow airport. He was sentenced to forty-five years of imprisonment – the longest sentence ever handed down by a British judge.

Before the jury reached its verdict, which took some twenty-four hours, no one had any confidence as to how the trial would end. As good officials, we in the FCO prepared alternative strategies and parliamentary statements. As soon as the sentence was pronounced, we sprang into action. The Syrian ambassador was called in by the PUS and told that Britain was breaking diplomatic relations and he had fourteen days to leave. Ten minutes later, our ambassador in Damascus gave the same message to his hosts. The foreign secretary made a statement to Parliament, allies were informed, and the Syrians suspended overflights by all UK airlines and told the British Embassy that its staff had just seven days to leave Damascus.

Some in the FCO had hoped that, in the event of Hindawi being convicted, we could limit the damage to the expulsion of the ambassador, a reduced visa service and new constraints on the Syrian national airline, on the basis that the evidence against the Syrian government itself was not conclusive. But the jury's finding and the evidence of the Syrian embassy's complicity was too compelling for anything less than the strongest possible diplomatic response.

There were also other pressures in play. During his visit to New York and Washington ten days earlier, Tim Renton had been pushed hard on the response the Americans could expect if Hindawi was convicted. The day before the verdict, and the meeting chaired by Prime Minister Margaret Thatcher which determined our response, her press secretary, Bernard Ingham, had lunch with the editor of the *Sun* newspaper. Next morning, the paper ran an editorial explaining how monstrous it would be if all contacts with the Syrian regime were not severed in the event of Hindawi being found guilty. The prime minister chaired her ministerial meeting with the editorial on the table in front of her.

Later the same day, I found myself reflecting on a party political broadcast by the Conservatives carried on television the night before. Most senior members of the cabinet were given a slot to spell out their ideas – on health, transport, social services, the economy and education. The foreign secretary didn't feature. There was no mention of foreign affairs, and no discussion of Britain's place in the world. Nor was there in the new version of Party talking points issued afterwards for use by Conservative MPs.

Unusually, that evening I jotted down some notes of the day's extraordinary events. I noted – clearly with some bitterness – that there didn't seem to be any votes in foreign policy; and that, with the encouragement of the Downing Street political machine, the inheritors of what had once been a proud empire were now just a nation of offshore islanders.

Three years was about par for the job of private secretary, so in early 1987 I began to consider my options. Going back to a desk with minimal policy responsibility would have been a let-down after those stimulating years running a ministerial office. A move abroad seemed to make sense – for financial as well as professional reasons. In those days, the most interesting positions abroad at my level of first secretary tended to be as head of chancery – a role that no longer exists, but which was then an interesting combination of head of political section, head of HR and chief of staff to the ambassador.

The trouble was that, since so much of the interesting work went to the person doing that job, there wasn't much left for the nominally senior deputy head of mission to do beyond standing in for the ambassador as chargé d'affaires when he was away and enjoying being driven round town in his flag car. Largely for this reason, the role of head of chancery was soon rolled into that of deputy head of mission. But back then, it was still very much in existence. The position of head of chancery in the embassy in Ankara, Turkey, was coming up that summer and appealed to me for a number of reasons, which I explain in the next chapter. I put my hat in the ring and heard quite quickly that my application had been successful.

Before leaving Tim Renton's private office, I helped him with the process of choosing my successor. From a strong field, Renton chose Kim Darroch – who, nearly thirty years later, was to succeed me as ambassador in Washington. Then off I went to try and learn a bit of Turkish.

5

Back east – to Turkey (1987–90)

I t was while driving back to Iran overland in the summer of 1976 that I first felt that Turkey too was a country of remarkable beauty and history which merited further attention. We took a ferry from Venice and landed at Izmir – Smyrna of old – on the west coast. We stopped at Ephesus, one of the best-known and best-restored Graeco-Roman sites in all of Turkey, which is still producing remarkable discoveries as excavations of the town houses built around the old city reveal superb frescoes and mosaics.

On our way east we stopped off at Pamukkale, or 'cotton castle', which was then a site of extraordinary natural beauty. Over the edge of a plateau 200 metres high, limestone-bearing thermal springs had flowed for thousands of years, creating a dazzling array of brilliant white stalactites and shallow, terraced basins of mineral-rich water known as travertines, which reflect the clear blue sky above. Just yards away lay the remarkable ruins of the ancient Hellenistic city of Hierapolis (which was designated a World Heritage site by UNESCO twelve years later in 1988).

In the 1990s the natural wonders of Pamukkale were ruined as illegally built luxury hotels (now demolished) and local villagers diverted the thermal waters, causing the once-brilliant white stalactites to deteriorate into shabby grey and the shimmering travertines to become dried-up repositories for tourist waste. Attempts are now being made to repair the damage, but with artificial travertines and inadequate supplies of water. Even in the late 1980s, when I used to take the family back for weekend trips, visiting was still a breathtaking experience.

The rest of our journey back to Iran was less beautiful and more hazardous. At that time eastern Turkey was poor and dangerous, and local Kurdish villagers had become adept at stopping and robbing the growing number of up-scale European vehicles being driven out to oil-rich Iran as the shah invested in what he called the Great Civilisation (*tamaddon-e bozorg*). Those who didn't follow experienced travellers' advice never to drive at night east of Ankara sometimes didn't make it at all. We did, and got through unscathed but not without blowing two tyres on the appalling roads (the Turkish authorities were in dispute with Iran over freight transit rates and had stopped repairing the damage caused by the harsh Anatolian winters and heavy trucks heading east).

The only remarkable part of our brief overnight stay in Ankara as we headed towards Iran was my disturbance of a couple of thieves rummaging through the luggage in our hotel room while they thought we were asleep. Checking the damage afterwards, I discovered that they had got away with nothing more than a bag of nappies freshly soiled by my six-month-old son Oliver.

In the summer of 1987, nine years after the end of our tour of duty in Iran, my family and I found ourselves back in Turkey's capital for the first time since that memorable journey. We didn't get off to the best start. Shortly before we were due to leave London, the FCO's medical adviser decided we couldn't take our youngest child, Rupert, then aged 7, with us because he had had a serious respiratory disease in his infancy and Ankara was then vying with Mexico City for the title of the world's most polluted capital city – especially in the cold winter months when most buildings were still heated with lignite. He'd have to be left behind. To lessen the shock, I asked to delay our journey out to Ankara for a month, from June to July, so all three children could drive out with us for the summer holidays at the end of the school term.

My request was turned down. I was told I had to be there in June to begin meeting important people before they left town for the summer holidays (which, on the whole, they didn't – or at least not on the French scale). I learned after we arrived that the same line manager, when previously asked by one of his staff for a week off to go skiing, had offered Monday, Wednesday and Friday.

These days, people would either ignore the medical advice or cancel their posting: the office is far more family friendly than it used to be. But in 1987 things were different; or I was just more timid. The result was that all three children, then aged 7, 9 and 11, stayed behind in boarding school, with Rupert in particular hardly aware of what was happening. Windlesham House, near Worthing in Sussex, was a delightful, family-run co-educational prep school which took good care of them all. But it wasn't easy for any of us, especially Angie.

Had I thought I might return to Turkey later in my career, I like to think I would have made a better fist of learning Turkish before taking up the appointment. At the time, nothing could have been further from my mind: the Ankara job was a means of learning new skills as – I hoped – I made my way up the FCO ladder. In any case, there was a limit to how much Turkish I could learn from travelling out to my teacher in Mile End in East London, two hours' journey time from our home in Kent, three times a week, while preparing the family to head overseas again after three years in the UK. I learned enough to get by, but that was all.

At the time, Turkey was beginning the process of change and modernization that it desperately needed if it was going to fulfil its potential as the only Western-leaning secular democracy in the Muslim Middle East, with a high-quality civil service and a powerful and well-equipped military. It had the advantages of a young, increasingly well-educated population with a strong sense of national pride in the nation state of Turkey – all that remained of the Ottoman Empire once the treaties of Sèvres and Lausanne had broken it up at the end of the First World War.

Soon after arriving in Ankara, I wrote a paper asking whether an Iran-style revolution could happen in Turkey. My conclusion was that it couldn't, because the army wouldn't let it happen, because Atatürkist secularism and democracy had taken root, and because the traditions of Sunni Islam in Turkey – where even the imams were civil servants – were very different from those of Shi'a Iran, where the religion was more hierarchical and the ayatollahs enjoyed much greater authority.

Unfortunately, Turkey's experiment with modernization didn't last long. In 1989 the reformist, if controversial, prime minister Turgut Özal moved upstairs after six years in the job to the less powerful but more prestigious position of president of the republic. He died in office soon afterwards. His successors allowed Turkey to drift back to the days of weak coalition government and institutionalized corruption, culminating in financial and banking crises at the turn of the century and a humiliating defeat of all the coalition parties at the hands of the new Islamist Truth and Justice Party, or AKP, in the general election of 3 November 2002, ten months after I had returned to Turkey as ambassador – of which more in Chapter 8.

But the late 1980s were times when Turkey was open for tourism and people could travel freely and safely almost anywhere, inconvenienced only by the occasional road block in the Kurdish south-east where the military and the gendarmerie kept a close eye on the activities of the separatist PKK (still, alas, in business as a terrorist organization as I write in 2020). Around the shores of the turquoise-blue Lake Van, with the tenth-century Armenian Church of the Holy Cross with its exquisite carvings clearly visible on Akdamar Island, we would come across numerous foreigners, including intrepid Germans in 'Das Rollende Hotel' buses towing their accommodation behind them.

Turkish hospitality and helpfulness were legendary. On one trip, as we navigated the steep and very narrow road that was then the only way to travel the length of the Datça Peninsula in the south-west, the brakes on my old Range

Rover failed. I told the children I was going to drive down from the top of the switchback road using just the gears, and we made it down safely. In the first village we came to – on a Sunday afternoon when everything was closed – I found a mechanic drinking tea and playing backgammon under a tree with some friends. He rose to the challenge. Of course, he didn't have the spare parts, but he couldn't leave us stranded. So with a bit of ingenuity and a pair of pliers, he fixed us up – and suggested I had the car properly serviced next time so that at least one of the dual brake cylinders was working before we embarked on our next adventure. He refused any payment – it was Sunday, his garage was closed and he was glad to help.

During our time in Turkey, we made a point of taking the children on trips during the school holidays to the Turkish coast, to the sublime valleys, 'fairy chimneys' and tenth-century rock churches of Cappadocia, and to some of the country's other unforgettable archaeological sites. Two of my three children later chose to get married in Turkey. To this day, all three love going back to the sites they remember from childhood.

The transformation of Turkish society and institutions remained patchy. One day our Ankara landlord declared that some of his wife's jewellery had gone missing and Ali, our doorman – the ubiquitous *kapıcı* – must be responsible. Ali was taken off to the police station where he was kept for the next couple of days before eventually being released. When he came home and I asked how he had been treated, he showed me the signs of the beatings he had received at the police station. He had been released because he clearly couldn't say where the jewellery was since he hadn't taken it. The missing piece turned up soon afterwards where the owner's wife had mislaid it in her flat.

Having found out that Police Station No. 9 was well known for this kind of thing, I told the story to a friend in the Turkish prime minister's office as an example of what had to change if we were to make anything of Turkey's desire to be accepted as a candidate for membership of the then EEC. Rather than promise to do something about it, protecting Ali in the process, he simply urged me – especially if I knew what was good for me – not to report the episode back to London. I did, of course, but it bothered me that even one of the more enlightened, liberal-minded members of the civil service should react so defensively. Years later, I enjoyed working with the same friend – by then in a higher position – to boost Turkey's prospects of joining the EU. Neither of us ever mentioned Ali's story again.

There is a telling passage in Stephen Kinzer's perceptive book *Crescent and Star* (2001) where he relates asking a Turk who had been treated in similar fashion why he wouldn't lodge a formal complaint. His friend said he had been beaten by his father, he had been beaten at school, he had been beaten doing his national service and he expected to be beaten in police stations, so what was the point?

We all have skeletons, whether in English boarding schools, the Roman Catholic Church, military or fraternity hazing, or simply everyday harassment in the workplace. Realizing that life doesn't have to be like this, and that those in authority have a duty to do something about abuse, is an essential first step towards making things better. That is one of many reasons why I became convinced that Turkey needed to believe it could one day be a member of the EU, and why, eleven years later, I decided to ask the British government to send me back as ambassador. But before I returned to Ankara in 2002, my career would take me in two different, contrasting but equally stimulating and challenging directions.

6

The Palace (1990–93)

There is, rightly, a code of confidentiality and trust which applies to anyone taking up a position in the Royal household. I have no desire, or intention, to break that code. But I think that giving an idea of what the work involved may help people appreciate the extraordinarily wide range of activities with which senior members of the Royal family are involved, and how much we owe them.

In the autumn of 1989, as I began to think what I wanted to do after Ankara, I was asked if I would like my name to be put forward to St James's Palace for the position of deputy private secretary to His Royal Highness The Prince of Wales – the title which Prince Charles had assumed at the age of ten. I would be responsible for his (and his wife Diana, Princess of Wales's) overseas visits and contacts, and a number of other, unrelated policy issues. We had hosted a few Royal and other high-level visits during my time in Turkey, including one by The Prince of Wales, and I had enjoyed helping look after such guests. My amusingly caustic ambassador,

Timothy Daunt,* warned that I might find myself 'little more than a glorified travel agent'. But I was tempted and said I'd be happy to throw my hat into the ring.

My interview took place at the office in St James's Palace of the principal private secretary, the late Sir John Riddell, a witty, talented baronet who had trained as an accountant in London but whose roots were firmly in Northumberland. Far from examining my suitability for the job, he wanted to be sure that I knew what I was letting myself in for. Life at the palace, he said, would be very different. Things said and done by a member of the Royal family, he explained, had far more impact than the same things said or done by other human beings, including politicians.

John always made me laugh. Behind his laconic humour lay a profound understanding of the convening power of the Royal family; and a great gift – which I soon discovered we needed – of remaining amused, detached and unflappable regardless of the number of crises we were trying to manage at any one time.

Somehow, I got the job. I started the new role in February 1990, just in time to join a reconnaissance visit (known as a 'recce') in advance of an official trip to Hungary by the Prince and Princess, to see how it was done. Over the next three years, in addition to supporting Their Royal Highnesses (or TRH as they were called in-house) in a range of ways far removed from conventional diplomacy, I organized visits abroad for and with them to Hungary, Poland and the Czech

---

* Future governor of the Isle of Man and father of James Daunt, who hatched the idea of opening a bookshop – the brilliantly successful Daunt Books for Travellers – round the Ankara residence dining table.

Republic; Germany and Spain; France and Italy, several times; Japan, India and Nepal; Canada and Jamaica; the United States, Mexico and Brazil; South Korea and Hong Kong.

It wasn't at all like being private secretary to a politician. A government minister does his departmental job four days a week, and is then usually in his or her constituency on a Friday and for the weekends. For the private secretary there is a clear distinction between Westminster and constituency life, and almost no involvement in the minister's personal and family affairs. Except at times of crisis, you knew clearly when you were on and when you were off duty.

With royalty, the role was twenty-four hours a day, seven days a week, because for the media there was no distinction between the public and private life of TRH. The phone would ring at any time of day or night, any day of the week. My appointment was for two years and, invited by His Royal Highness (HRH) to do so, I stayed on for a third. During that time there was barely a day when even the broadsheets, let alone the red-top newspapers, did not have a 'Charles and Diana' story on page one. It was brutal and it was stressful – for the principals of course, but also for their staff. For royal-watchers in the media, we were as much fair game as our employers – but of course stories about us sold fewer copies.

Towards the end of my time at the palace, it fell to me to organize the first-ever Royal visit to the Republic of Korea. As always with official visits overseas, we went at the request of the FCO in pursuit of British interests. The business case was very strong, as Korean industries built up their investments in the UK. So too were the political arguments, with Korea a fully functioning democracy in a dangerous part of the world, in which over a thousand British servicemen had died in the bloody Korean War of 1950–53 helping South Korea defend itself against an invading force from the north supported by China and the Soviet Union.

But the visit, in early November 1992, took place at a time when there was increasing speculation about the relationship between my two principals. The accompanying press party were on the scent, and relentless in the negativity of the reporting they sent back to the UK of what was, in every other respect, a highly successful visit. At one point, at the Hyundai shipyard at Ulsan, I had a quiet word with James Whitaker of the *Daily Mirror*, one of the royal correspondents I had got to know quite well. I said I thought it was wrong for the British media to focus only on whether or not the Prince and Princess appeared to be enjoying each other's company – how could they expect broad smiles when wreaths were being laid at the memorial to the huge numbers of British and Commonwealth servicemen who had lost their lives defending Korea against communism forty years earlier? They were carrying out a very successful, first-ever Royal visit to Korea and it would be nice to see its significance recognized.

Whitaker said he understood, but surely I wasn't trying to argue that the Waleses had a marriage made in heaven? I replied that I wasn't saying that; I was saying that the media coverage of the Royal couple was unfair and exaggerated that there was so much more to the visit than what was being reported back home.

Shortly after leaving the shipyard, we left Korea for Hong Kong, where I was due to accompany the Prince on a visit to the still-British sovereign territory. The Princess was to leave us there and fly home separately.

By the time we arrived in Hong Kong, I found myself at the centre of a media firestorm. Whitaker had briefed other journalists on our conversation. Some, notably the Sky News correspondent, considered that what I had said privately to Whitaker amounted to the first declaration by a palace official that the Royal marriage was 'on the rocks' and his editors back home decided to run it as Breaking News. Other media outlets followed suit, and it wasn't long before I was identified as the source.

The Prince of Wales had gone to bed as soon as we arrived at Government House in Hong Kong. The next morning, I asked the butler if I could usurp his role and take in the breakfast tray. I told the Prince what had happened, and apologized for having made things worse. HRH could not have been more gracious – far more concerned for the pickle I found myself in than annoyed by the naiveté I had displayed.

Later in the day, I received a personal letter from Whitaker explaining that he had felt an obligation to share the gist of our conversation with his fellow journalists but pointing out the bits of the story which had been exaggerated. He had been mortified to discover that I had been named as his source, and that he was 'terribly, terribly sorry' for what had happened after he had briefed his colleagues.

It was a kind gesture from a decent man who sometimes drove us wild at the palace and is, sadly, no longer with us. But of course by then the damage had been done. I blamed myself for answering a leading question which I should have ignored, but remain unconvinced that James had been under any obligation to share the details of our conversation with less scrupulous colleagues.

I realized that I ought to leave press work to the professionals at the palace. But I never gave up trying to maintain decent, working relationships with journalists. Later, as ambassador in Turkey, France and the United States, I saw getting on the airwaves as an important part of the job of projecting the UK in the best possible light, and explaining our side of the story whenever there were crises which needed a response. Particularly in countries where foreign correspondents didn't have good local access, I also tried to provide local British journalists with off-the-record briefings of what was going on inside the corridors of power. Too often, otherwise, the British media were reduced to recycling – a day late – stories which had appeared in the local media. I like to think it helped them do their job. I like to think it also meant that their instinct was to seek our side of the story before going into print with something likely to cause embarrassment or difficulty.

Most, but not all, of the time I was fortunate enough to avoid being the subject of the wrong kind of media story. I learned the hard way that you always have to be on your guard. Years later, when I was ambassador in Washington, I was interviewed by the American television station MSNBC in July 2014 about Russian behaviour in Ukraine and the shooting down of Malaysian Airlines flight MH17 over Ukrainian airspace by a Russian Buk ground-to-air missile.

At the time, the Russians were still fabricating evidence to suggest that it was not, after all, one of their missiles that had destroyed the Malaysian aircraft. At the end of the interview, I was asked to sum up in three words what I thought of President Putin's behaviour in Ukraine. 'Thuggish, dishonest and reckless,' I said. Headlines went round the world and the Russian Embassy in London lodged a formal protest. No one in London called me out on my usage of 'undiplomatic' language, and I was comfortable that what I had said was true. But I reminded myself afterwards that I had to do a better job of remaining in control of interviews.

At St James's Palace I became involved with a lot of issues which had nothing to do with foreign affairs but were an important part of the lives of TRH. I found myself supporting and advising The Prince of Wales on subjects ranging from Shakespeare, education, volunteering and the Prince's Trust's efforts to provide a future for young offenders, to sacred geometry, architecture, inner-city issues and the future of the English language. I will never forget watching the results when we once took a group of actors from the Royal Shakespeare Company to teach theatre to 4-year-old children in a school in a deprived area of Manchester. The actors were as bowled over as we were.

I was also, of course, the Prince's – and his wife's – in-house foreign affairs adviser when important things were happening in the rest of the world. In early August 1991 I rented a cottage on a farm in North Cornwall to give my family a week's break by the seaside. It had no landline and my very early model of mobile phone had only limited coverage. The cottage was at the end of a rough farm track, and I imagine it still is. I had left the farmer's number as my emergency point of contact. On the morning of 2 August, the day Saddam Hussein invaded Kuwait, there was banging on our front door. 'Sorry to bother you, sir,' said the farmer.

'I guess it's a joke but there's someone on the line who says Prince Charles wants to talk to you.' It wasn't a joke, but a call from the Buckingham Palace switchboard. HRH did indeed want to talk to me. That week I got very used to tramping up and down the lane so I could use the farmer's telephone – much to his amusement.

There were other moments too when events of global importance intruded on palace life. One of the privileges of my time as a member of the Royal household was the opportunity to spend time supporting my principals out of London at Balmoral Castle in Scotland or on the Sandringham estate in Norfolk. On the evening of 20 November 1990 we were gathered round the television at Balmoral watching the results of the first round of the contest for the leadership of the Conservative Party being given to Prime Minister Margaret Thatcher on the steps of the British ambassador's residence in Paris – my future home. She had won the first round, but not outright. Asked what it meant, I said I thought it meant her premiership was over. Two days later, after initially promising to fight on, she announced that she was standing down.

I had done plenty of rifle shooting as a member of the Combined Cadet Force at school, so I felt confident enough to accept when offered the privilege of a day's deer-stalking on the Balmoral estate. Accompanied by a 'ghillie', whose job is to choose which stags need to be culled and to help the uninitiated 'stalk' their prey, I spent a happy and reflective day on the moor, clambering up and down hills and heather and hiding patiently, out of sight, until the moment came to take aim. To my relief I managed a clean kill. A team of 'hill ghillies' arrived to carry it down the mountain to the deer larder, but not before my face had been smeared with its blood as the rite of passage marking a stalker's first success. I still have the record of my eight-pointer kill but alas his antlers didn't follow me back to London.

My time working at St James's Palace gave me a wealth of new experiences that both broadened my horizons and deepened my understanding of what mattered to members of the public, and to members of the Royal family. On trips abroad, ambassadors wanted the Prince to be given the keys of the city, attend receptions and shake lots of hands, while he – and the Princess – wanted to make a difference, engage with businesspeople and cultural leaders, promote environmental projects and conservation, or set up local versions of volunteering. My role was to try to get others to understand what TRH's agenda was, and to make my principals feel that their time was being well spent in ways which were over and above what HMG needed them to do. Plenty of scope for diplomacy – sometimes quite delicate. I learned a lot, and wouldn't have missed it for anything.

Being highly visible members of the Royal family, The Prince and Princess of Wales had extraordinary convening power. If the Prince wanted to launch a new initiative, or make a speech about something new and different, we could call upon the biggest experts in the country, if not the world, for help. An invitation to a small lunch or dinner at Highgrove, their home in Gloucestershire, with a stimulating agenda and the full attention of the heir to the throne was irresistible. I felt privileged to be with some of the extraordinarily talented and committed people from the worlds of business, architecture, education, the environment, politics, philosophy and countless other important fields who were ready to make time to support HRH – while of course making use of his interest to advance their own agenda.

All the time, though, we had to be conscious that part of that convening power lay in the additional impact made by anything members of the Royal family said or did compared to what was said or done by other people. So while the monarchy could be a remarkably effective instrument for launching a debate, or even changing public opinion, it was the job of those of us on the staff to try and prevent controversy which might cause damage to the reputation of the family, or to the government.

Organizing overseas visits was an important part of my role. Occasionally they were private trips, such as a few magical days in the spring of 1992 when I arranged a short period of walking, painting and archaeological discovery for The Prince of Wales in eastern Turkey; when I was lucky enough to accompany him on a few days of hiking in the foothills of the Himalayas in Nepal; or on the occasions I went with him to the Villa Lante in Tuscany, which the Italian government had lent his School of Architecture as a venue for students to rediscover, under expert tutelage, the principles of classical architecture and the human – as opposed to the purely functional – dimension of building.

While I was at St James's Palace we did some fascinating and, I believe, important work going to Czechoslovakia and Hungary immediately after the fall of the Berlin Wall, when tens of thousands of people would crowd town squares to welcome TRH as symbols of the freedoms they were reclaiming after the collapse of Russian-imposed communism.

The Soviet soldiers hadn't all gone home but they were on their way.

In Hungary, Interim President Árpád Göncz played host to the Prince and Princess. His wife was so nervous that the Princess took her hand, providing the iconic photograph of a memorable visit which reminded all of us of the star power, and importance to British interests and values, of the next generation of the monarchy.

In Prague, with the strong support of President Václav Havel, The Prince of Wales established a conservation fund to help raise money for the restoration of St Vitus Cathedral and of Charles Bridge – causes that had often been neglected in communist times and for which local people were immensely keen to have the patronage and support of someone who cared so deeply about conservation and beautiful buildings as The Prince of Wales. I found myself returning several times to try and give substance to the initiative, including once with HRH for a magnificent fund-raising concert held in the cathedral courtyard.

Since it is not the role of the Royal family to conduct policy, or to represent the British government's views, its members were often able to converse in much more personal terms than politicians; and foreign statesmen and -women often felt more comfortable in their company than when they were speaking to their fellow heads of government. I noticed that on the occasions when, as ambassador, I accompanied members of the Royal family to call on President Obama in the Oval Office. I noticed it during some of the talks which The Prince of Wales used to have with President Havel of

Czechoslovakia (as it still was) during the first years after the liberation of Eastern Europe from the Soviet Union. And I noticed it during HRH's visits to France and to Germany, where he was always warmly received.

At the same time, younger members of the Royal family felt able to ask advice, without inhibition, about the realities of life as a head of state, and how best they could contribute towards maintaining close links between the UK and other countries. Records of these conversations were not circulated in the same way as records of official discussions between heads of government, which also helped create an atmosphere of confidence and trust.

In March 1993, during a visit to Germany to collect an environmental prize, The Prince of Wales was invited to call on Chancellor Helmut Kohl. Officials and the ambassador were asked to leave, so there were just the principals, an interpreter and me in the room. The conversation lasted a couple of hours and covered subjects ranging from German reunification, the Balkans and Russia, to the future of Europe. It would be wrong to divulge details of what The Prince of Wales had to say but I recall in particular an exchange about British and German attitudes towards Europe.

Kohl said he fully understood why the British people needed more time to come to terms with European integration, having avoided the invasions, defeats and redrawing of national boundaries which had afflicted continental Europe so many times during the previous hundred years. But just as other Europeans needed to understand the origins of Britain's historical, cultural and political identity, so, he argued, the British needed to understand where the other Europeans were coming from, what they needed, and why.

I have often thought back to that conversation, and concluded that over the years the United Kingdom never made enough of an effort to understand what the rest of Europe had been through; what it was prepared to give up in order to render impossible the prospect of yet another European war; or how much the United Kingdom as a whole benefited, once we had joined the EEC in 1973, from membership of that community (or union, as it became twenty years later under the Treaty of Maastricht).

The five-day visit to Canada which I helped organize on TRH's behalf in 1991, with the Royal Yacht *Britannia* and Princes William and Harry present for part of the time, was something altogether different. The Queen is head of the Commonwealth, which comprises over fifty countries. But she is also head of state of eighteen of them, including Canada, Australia and New Zealand. Those countries, known as realms, jealously guard their own links to the Royal family, whose members visit them more regularly than other countries.

So it is the Canadian government, not the British High Commission in Ottawa, that organizes Royal visits to Canadian territory, decides which provinces are included in the itinerary and liaises directly with the Royal household on the details. But although the Canadians had plenty of their own ideas about what members of 'their' Royal family should do, they were also very accommodating of, for example, The Prince of Wales's wish to hold a high-level meeting of his business leaders' forum focusing on climate change and different aspects of what later became known as corporate social responsibility (CSR). The media being the media, the photograph which attracted the most attention was the image of Princess Diana holding her arms out to greet William and Harry as they ran aboard *Britannia* while the Royal yacht was berthed in Kingston, Ontario. The press were less interested in reporting the growing body of evidence that, on a series of global issues like inequality, social cohesion, CSR, the survival of endangered species and the future of our planet, The Prince of Wales was already years ahead of his time.

My three years in the Royal household were, with hindsight, an extraordinary mixture of the utterly fascinating, the deeply rewarding, the happiest and the saddest, the most invigorating and the most exhausting. On countless occasions I drove down to Highgrove and back home to Kent late at night – so exhausted that even stopping every fifteen minutes failed to prevent me nodding off at the wheel on the M4.

When I went to take my leave of The Queen, she handed me – to my great surprise – the insignia of Lieutenant of the Royal Victorian Order, or LVO. The Victorian Order relates to services specifically rendered to the Royal family, rather than to government or the public good more generally. Six years later I was awarded a Companion of the Order of St Michael and St George (CMG) for services to diplomacy before, in 2003, being upgraded to a knighthood, or KCMG, again for services to diplomacy – sadly just a few months after my father had died. This was followed, when I left Washington, by a GCMG, or Knight Grand Cross of the Order of St Michael and St George, to give the honour its full title. But even in later years I often felt it was the humblest of them all, the LVO, that I had really earned.

My stint in the Royal household had taken a great toll on my family, even if friends clearly enjoyed it when our weekend attempts at a social life were interrupted by urgent calls from the palace switchboard. And so I began to think that this was perhaps the moment not to return to the FCO mothership but to branch out down one of the other avenues of interest that my time with TRH had opened up and do something different. After all I had learned and felt about educating future generations, I even found myself thinking – unrealistically – of applying for the position of headmaster in a leading secondary school which I saw advertised in *The Economist*.

It never happened. Perhaps because I had done little to follow up these musings, I was poorly placed to resist when I got a call from the ambassador in Washington, Sir Robin Renwick, asking me to consider joining his team as one of the political counsellors. By early July of 1993 I was on my way there, returning to the world of diplomacy. But the experiences of those three years, and the relationships, stayed with me. I saw the Princess when she came to Washington over the next few years, and I stayed in touch with The Prince of Wales, sometimes helping out over staffing issues, sometimes assisting on matters relating to architecture or foreign affairs.

Nearly a quarter of century after I had left St James's Palace, I was lying in hospital in Switzerland recovering from a serious injury I had inflicted on myself while skiing on my sixty-sixth birthday, just before Christmas of 2016. From my hospital bed I wrote an article for the travel section of the

Daily Telegraph advising other skiers to make sure they had their travel insurance in order, to wear the right equipment – the day of my accident was the first time in forty years of skiing that I had worn a ski helmet, at my son's insistence – and to take particular care skiing early in the season when there was no cushion of snow to break a fall. Who should ring up from Scotland a few days later to ask how I was and spend the next twenty minutes cheering me up? My old boss, The Prince of Wales. That's the kind of person he is.

7

Washington and the wider world (1993–2001)

The FCO told me I was going to Washington as congressional counsellor, a position which at the time included the responsibilities of head of chancery, the role I had got to know and enjoy in Ankara.

However, things didn't quite work out like that, as by the time I arrived the counsellor-level head of chancery role had been assigned to someone else. It was then scrapped altogether and, as in other embassies, subsumed into the functions of the deputy head of mission. I rapidly realized that the job of congressional counsellor on its own didn't amount to much. Most important members of the House of Representatives, and senators, expected to deal with ambassadors. Where they were ready to forget about hierarchy, it was because they wanted to talk to someone who knew about the issues that interested them or their constituents: the congressional counsellor usually lacked that expertise and so found it difficult to give substance to the relationships he was tasked with building.

It was also clear that there was not enough work to go round for the number of counsellors we had on the staff. A few months after my arrival my original position of congressional counsellor was amalgamated with that of press counsellor, and immediately became more interesting.

In one particular area there was plenty going on from day one. When I arrived in Washington in the summer of 1993, Northern Ireland was already one of the more complex elements of our bilateral relationship. Early generations of Irish Americans tended to be Scots-Irish Protestants who had come to the New World voluntarily to seek their fortune and had no grievance against the old country. But those who arrived in the mid and late nineteenth century were more likely to be Roman Catholics fleeing the potato famine or – as they saw it – oppressive British rule. So throughout the Troubles in Northern Ireland, which saw the province – and much of mainland Britain – afflicted by terrorism and sectarianism for thirty years, most Americans who were conscious of their Irish roots tended to sympathize with Sinn Fein and the Republican cause, whose adherents were predominantly Catholic.

All that came to an end with the agreement signed in Belfast – known as the Good Friday Agreement – on 10 April 1998. It ended most of the violence and put in place new political arrangements between Northern Ireland and the Irish Republic; and between the British and Irish governments. Strongly supported by politicians on all sides in the US, it led to the effective disappearance of a hard border between Northern Ireland and the Republic – an issue which assumed great sensitivity in mid-2020 when the UK government was trying to unscramble the contradictory commitments it had given about Northern Ireland's trading status with the EU and with the rest of the UK when concluding its Brexit Withdrawal Agreement in January of that year. Irish American politicians, including the Democratic presidential candidate Joe Biden, gave notice that they would not look kindly on any new UK laws which risked jeopardizing the success of the Good Friday Agreement.

Our problems with Irish American Catholics went back a long way. Joe Kennedy, US ambassador to the UK at the beginning of the Second World War in 1939–40, took his dislike of Britain – and view that the Axis powers would win – so far as to advocate the US coming to terms with Hitler. President Franklin Delano Roosevelt (FDR) replaced him with the remarkable John Winant, who has rarely received the recognition he deserves for his contribution to the maintenance of British morale and to preparing US public opinion for FDR's eventual decision to bring the US into the war, after the Japanese attack on Pearl Harbor in December 1941. The next generation of Kennedys were very different – one of Joe's nine children of course became president of the United States, while another married the Marquess of Hartington, heir to Chatsworth House in Derbyshire and to the title of Duke of Devonshire. He, tragically, was killed in action in Belgium in 1944.

Part of my job as custodian of the embassy's relations with Congress, and of parliamentary links between Capitol Hill and Westminster, was to ensure that the British government's views were understood and our interests defended. That included trying to discourage those who supported the Republican cause in Northern Ireland from giving money to not-for-profit organizations like Noraid, which claimed to be raising money for the families of victims of Protestant Loyalist and British government violence but were in fact helping to finance the terrorism of the Irish Republican Army (IRA).

Early on I realized that some of the congressmen I expected to be hostile were treating me warily, and asking about my family. The penny soon dropped. A cousin, Grenadier Guardsman Captain Richard Westmacott, had been killed in Belfast back in 1980. Serving in the SAS, the British army's special forces regiment, he was shot when leading a raid on a house in the Antrim Road occupied by the IRA's M60 gang – named after the heavy machine gun it used – led by one Joseph Doherty. While awaiting trial a year later, Doherty escaped from prison in Northern Ireland and fled to the US on a fake passport. He was eventually arrested in 1983 and for years successfully resisted the British government's attempts to get him returned to the UK on the grounds that killing Richard had been 'a political act'. In January 1992 the US Supreme Court finally overturned a decision of a lower appeals court and Doherty was returned to the UK, just a few months before my arrival in the US.

Having been convicted *in absentia*, he was imprisoned once more but freed in 1998 under the terms of the Good Friday Agreement. Doherty then became a community worker helping disadvantaged young people. At its height, his case was a *cause célèbre* in the US, supported by as many as 130 members of Congress. But I got a clear sense that some of those who had most vigorously stood up for him, because of the importance of the Irish American vote (and money), were a little sheepish when they met a real live relative of Doherty's victim.

My father, having by then retired from the Royal Navy and become a clergyman, found himself marrying Richard and his German wife, Vicky, burying Richard and christening his daughter – in that order – all in the space of little more than eighteen months. The story, ironically, helped me form relationships which were helpful over the following years as we engaged, and sometimes found ourselves at loggerheads, with the Clinton administration over how best the president could use his influence to advance the peace process and persuade the IRA to lay down their guns.

The decision of President Clinton in January 1994 to grant visas, and visits to the White House, to Gerry Adams and Martin McGuinness of Sinn Fein went down very badly in 10 Downing Street – invariably shortened in the UK to 'No 10' – where Prime Minister John Major was still trying to get Irish Republicans to renounce the use of violence for political ends. Partly because he was travelling in Australasia, Major didn't return Clinton's phone calls for almost a week – almost unheard of in the history of the 'special relationship'.

When John Major next visited the US, Clinton decided to make a special effort to put things right. This included a trip to Pittsburgh in Pennsylvania, where Major's grandfather had been a steelworker in the late nineteenth century. The White House kindly invited me to join the president and his staff on Air Force One while the prime minister, his staff and Robin Renwick travelled on the ageing RAF VC10 which had brought the delegation across the Atlantic. Not for the first time, the sight of his modest aircraft parked next to the much larger and newer 747 of the president of the United States led a British prime minister to conclude that it was time to do something about the government's official fleet. Despite the best efforts of Major's successor Tony Blair, nothing changed until agreement was eventually reached some years later to make one of the RAF's new Voyager air tankers convertible into long-haul transport for royalty and ministerial delegations (but at a level of comfort some way below business class).

The trip to Pittsburgh went well, with a visit to the rejuvenated heart of the post-industrial coal and steel city followed by a ride up a funicular railway to the Tin Soldier, one of the city's best restaurants. There were just eight of us at the table and Clinton did his best to create a relaxed, enjoyable atmosphere. But it wasn't easy. Damage had been done.

My own view, by the time my stint in Washington was ending in the spring of 1997, was that the political price the White House had paid in terms of damage to the 'special relationship' made it impossible for Adams and McGuinness to go back on their undertakings to engage seriously in a peace process, since neither could afford to risk offending or embarrassing the president of the United States. They were also going to be kept up to the mark by four leading US Democratic senators – Edward Kennedy, Joe Biden, Chris Dodd and John Kerry – who had lobbied Clinton in favour of a bold gesture of this kind to kickstart a peace process.

But that wasn't how it seemed at the time to Robin Renwick, myself or First Secretary Jonathan Powell, the political officer in my team who went on to become Tony Blair's chief of staff and a key player in the negotiations leading up to the 1998 Good Friday Agreement. One member of the White House national security staff I used to see regularly,

Jane Holl, told me nearly twenty years later that the furore over Gerry Adams's visa was the one occasion when she distinctly remembered me shouting at her. I of course have no such memory but I never found Jane untruthful on any other occasion so I fear she may have been right.*

Three years later, in March 1997 when I was leaving Washington at the end of my posting, I was surprised to receive a letter from President Clinton thanking me for what I had done in terms of 'maintaining the strong and vibrant friendship' between our two countries. He went on to say 'I am particularly grateful for your wise counsel and steadfast efforts in advancing the Northern Ireland peace process', so I don't think there can have been lasting damage to relationships.

There was talk at the time that President Clinton didn't mind ticking off the British government because of a misunderstanding that had arisen when he was first running for president. Back in 1992, Republican operatives looking for material to damage Clinton's electoral chances had arranged for the UK Home Office to be asked by a journalist whether or not Clinton had enquired about obtaining British citizenship while studying at University College, Oxford as a Rhodes Scholar, in order to avoid being drafted and sent to Vietnam. The Home Office spokesman confirmed that a 'comprehensive' search of the files had been conducted – in an effort to be 'helpful' to the media – and that nothing was found. But the impression was given to some in the Clinton

---

* This difficult passage in US–UK relations is well described in Robin Renwick's *Fighting with Allies* (1998) and Conor O'Clery's *The Greening of the White House* (1996).

campaign that the Conservative government had been more helpful than necessary to those seeking to dig dirt.

Personally, I never saw any connection between the Home Office file search story and Clinton's approach to Northern Ireland, or his attitude towards the UK. In November 1996, a few months before the end of my time in Washington, I travelled to Little Rock, Arkansas, with an old friend of the president from his Oxford days to join in the celebrations in his home town on the day Clinton won his second term. I was assured that there were no hard feelings – at least on the US side. But there was no disguising the pleasure the Clinton administration derived from Tony Blair's election victory six months later. Blair's chief of staff, Jonathan Powell, had learned many useful campaign lessons, building important relationships in the process, during his time at the embassy closely covering the Clinton campaign in 1991–2.

I returned to the FCO to become Director Americas just weeks before the general election of 1 May 1997 which swept the New Labour administration to power, and gave Robin Cook the role of foreign secretary.

The political change was at times dramatic. Not long after the election, one of the new ministers of state, with whom I had got off to a good start, told me she had been warned against me by some Labour Party colleagues because I was 'a complete Thatcherite'. She said she had replied that she didn't care what my politics were – what mattered was that I should be a competent civil servant. But she thought I should be aware of the exchange.

Puzzled, I eventually worked out that I had often invited groups of visiting MPs, of all parties, to my house in Washington for start-of-visit briefing suppers when I would certainly have done my best to explain and defend the position of the government I was serving – as I subsequently did for the Blair administration. The Conservatives had been in power for seventeen years, and Labour in opposition for just as long. It took a little time for everyone to realize that the civil service really was impartial and committed to serving whatever government the British people elected.

Director Americas was not a job I had asked for, and I knew it was going to be a challenge. I knew from experience that, unlike other director positions in the FCO with geographical responsibilities, this was not one which would allow me to grip, or even coordinate, the British government's policy towards the US. There were just too many parts of the Whitehall machine, and of the FCO, which had their own interests in America – often with their own financial and human resources too. When I later became ambassador in Washington, I discovered that there were people in my embassy and under my overall command belonging to seventeen different parts of the British government.

I decided to look after the truly bilateral parts of the relationship – providing resources for the US network of embassy and consulates, high-level visits, parliamentary and congressional exchanges, scholarship schemes and university links. At the time, Britain and the US shared between them the top ten universities in the world and 80 per cent of the top twenty. This provided valuable opportunities for both countries to ensure that young talent on each side of the Atlantic could spend time in each other's centres of higher education, broadening their horizons and, hopefully, developing links which would be valuable in later life, and to both countries.

Having responsibility for the FCO's resources in the Americas proved to be much more interesting than I had expected, as management began decentralizing human and financial assets to the directorates which owned the policies and the relationships. Then as now, the FCO finds it hard to move resources around in line with the UK's strategic priorities, and where they can make most difference, with the result that spending reductions imposed by the Treasury when the deficit needs to be reduced still tend to be addressed by a set of salami-slice reductions of equal misery applied across the board.

Some things don't change. The Duke of Wellington sent a memorable message to the Foreign Office on 11 August 1812 from the outskirts of Salamanca, Spain, during the Napoleonic campaign. Having pled guilty to being unable to account for one shilling and sixpence in one battalion's petty cash, or to clarify the number of jars of raspberry jam issued to one of his cavalry regiments, Wellington concluded that he was faced with two alternatives:

1. To train an army of uniformed British clerks in Spain for the benefit of the accountants and copy boys in London; or
2. To see to it the forces of Napoleon are driven out of Spain.

He concluded: 'I shall pursue either with the best of my ability, but I cannot do both.' Conscious that the challenges of leadership and management hadn't really changed in two hundred years, I did my best to ensure that we provided the policy guidance and resources needed to keep our most important overseas relationship in good repair, and that those resources were well spent and accounted for, without seeking to micromanage those responsible for doing the job on the spot.

The role of Director Americas took in all of North, Central and South America as well as the Caribbean, so there was plenty to do beyond managing the US account. My Spanish was almost non-existent – my Portuguese completely so – and I rapidly found that I was embarrassingly unable to communicate, other than in English or French, when visiting my new parish. So, I persuaded a reluctant FCO language centre to send me off to Granada in Spain for a week's immersion training, attending a language school and living with an Andalusian family whose Spanish I found even harder to comprehend than the language I was encountering in Latin America.

It's often the way when you are trying to learn new skills. You think you are getting nowhere but then you discover that, almost despite yourself, you have made some progress. A week in Granada wasn't enough to learn much, but I had once done a term of Spanish at school, so there was something to build on. A week later, when I was in Bolivia and Peru, I was amazed to find that I could understand most of what people were saying to me and even say a few things in the local language. During the three years that I did the job, I managed to visit every country in South and Central America – some of them a few times.

There were two other, very satisfying, strands to my role. First, managing most of the UK's Dependent Territories (as they were then called, before we renamed them Overseas Territories). Second, trying to forge enough of an understanding with the Argentine government to minimize our differences over the Falkland Islands, a British territory in the South Atlantic for which Margaret Thatcher had had to go to war in 1982 after the Argentine junta invaded them and (temporarily) took possession.

Excluding Hong Kong, which was due to be handed over to China later in 1997, we had just eleven Dependent Territories left. Many were in the Caribbean, but I also had the Falkland Islands, South Georgia, Ascension, Tristan da Cunha, Diego Garcia in the Indian Ocean, the British Antarctic Survey, and the most populous (62,000) and prosperous of all, Bermuda. Pitcairn Island in the South Pacific was not on my list. Most were so small – often with a population below ten thousand – that they could never have been viable states on their own.

In several of these territories we had some real issues of governance and transparency, often in relation to financial services and 'tax havens'. But the most immediate problem related to the volcano which had erupted – and was still erupting – on the Caribbean island of Montserrat, where the Beatles and Rolling Stones had both recorded albums in Sir George Martin's AIR studio. The volcano was spewing gas and cloud up to a height of 12,000 metres, covering most of the island, including the governor's house, with a deep layer of ash.

At one point, the politics, and cost, of funding the maintenance of the island caused such frustration to the international development secretary, Clare Short, that she exclaimed in an unguarded moment that the few thousand inhabitants of Montserrat would be asking for 'golden elephants' next. Partly as a result of the political fall-out, and partly because it was time we reviewed the way we ran these territories, Robin Cook announced that we would be publishing a white paper looking again at the status of the territories. We concluded that there were improvements to be made, that the FCO had to give due priority to the needs of the inhabitants – and to the substantial liabilities they represented – and that we would rename them Overseas Territories (OTs) to show that we were serious about moving away from dependency and towards as much self-government as possible. We also upgraded almost all the governorships to reflect the very high level of responsibility each had to exercise on a daily basis, often with low-quality and even corrupt locally elected officials.

I had few difficulties with Cook on OT issues, partly because I was working under the supervision of the admirable junior ministers to whom he delegated much of the political responsibility – initially Baroness (Liz) Symons and then Baroness (Valerie) Amos followed by Baroness (Patricia) Scotland. The latter two both had Caribbean roots and went on to greater things in Tony Blair's cabinet while Liz Symons became deputy leader of the House of Lords.

But we had some tricky exchanges over how to handle the foreign policy and protocol aspects of the detention of the former president of Chile, Augusto Pinochet, during the seventeen months he was under house arrest in the UK from

October 1998 until March 2000. Pinochet was arrested in accordance with an international warrant issued by two Spanish judges who wanted him extradited to stand trial for human rights abuses committed by the military government which he headed in Chile from 1973 until 1990. We had no foreign policy interest in detaining Pinochet, and the Chilean government – though it had no brief for the former dictator – was furious that their former president, travelling on a diplomatic passport, had been arrested. During the lengthy legal debate over whether or not Pinochet was entitled to immunity – the House of Lords eventually ruled that he was not – Cook was determined not to be seen to be putting relations with Chile ahead of the ethical dimension to foreign policy which he had championed since first arriving at the FCO.

Meanwhile, Home Secretary Jack Straw was clear that he had to act in a quasi-legal capacity and that his decisions could not be influenced by considerations of foreign policy. With the two secretaries of state unable to confer on the subject, it fell to me to keep the departmental (and diplomatic) channels of communication open at a time when our unfortunate ambassador in Santiago, Glyn Evans, was under virtual siege.

A lengthy stand-off with the Chilean government and the Spanish judges was eventually resolved by Straw's decision to allow the 83-year-old former dictator to return home on grounds of ill health (he died in Chile in 2006). But the effects were far-reaching. The principle of universal jurisdiction for war crimes and crimes against humanity had been established in practice as well as in law, as had the refusal of immunity for current or former heads of state from prosecution for human rights violations.

Argentina was even more complicated. There had been back and forth over the sovereignty of the islands since Britain first laid claim to them in 1690, with France, Spain and the United States all exercising de facto control in later years. At the urging of the UN, there were attempts by the governments of the UK and Argentina between 1965 and 1981 to reach a definitive agreement on the future of the islands, including a possible transfer of sovereignty, but they all foundered on the attachment of the islanders, and the British House of Commons, to the principle of self-determination. The days were long gone when the Falkland Islands were important to the British empire and the Royal Navy as a staging post for ships rounding Cape Horn. But the two thousand inhabitants of the islands were adamant that they wished to remain British.

All hopes of a negotiated settlement were ended at the beginning of April 1982 by the decision of the military junta which was by then governing Argentina to invade South Georgia, 1,500 miles to the south-west, and the Falkland Islands themselves. By the end of the month, a British naval task force had begun operations to regain the islands, and six weeks later the Argentine forces which had temporarily occupied the Falklands surrendered. Prime Minister Margaret Thatcher's approval ratings were transformed.

Less than twenty years after a conflict which had cost more than a thousand lives, no Argentine government could simply renounce its claim to the Falkland Islands. But by 1998 relations had improved enough for the British government to feel able to invite President Carlos Menem to pay an official visit to London, complete with a service of reconciliation in St Paul's Cathedral in remembrance of those who had lost their lives, on both sides, in the war sixteen years earlier.

Before the visit, No 10 asked me – for some reason – to inform Margaret Thatcher and see if she would like to attend the service. I tracked her down in Texas. I still remember her very direct response: 'Mr Westmacott, I appreciate you letting me know but there can be no reconciliation with the leader of a country whose aggression in the Falkland Islands caused the death of 255 of our boys. Please tell the prime minister I will *not* be attending.'

Menem's visit was nevertheless a success, and the following year I found myself accompanying The Prince of Wales on a return visit to Buenos Aires. As the supporting FCO official, it was my job to ensure that all went well and controversy was avoided. At one of the receptions given in his honour, my heart sank when a beautiful girl wearing very little approached HRH and asked him to dance a tango. His heart, however, didn't miss a beat. He accepted with good grace, and provided a very good display of his dancing skills.

But I was also, of course, responsible for the politics of the visit, against a background of the media having criticized Robin Cook for what they saw as his, and the FCO's, failure to give the Royal family proper support on a number of foreign trips.

During the visit, HRH delivered a major speech which I had had more than a hand in drafting. It included a mention of the importance of democracy (after the years of military rule) to Argentina but also to the inhabitants of a small island territory some 800 miles away in the South Atlantic, by which the Prince meant the Falklands.

With presidential elections not far away, this passage was immediately criticized by opposition Argentine politicians as unwarranted interference in the most delicate issue of sovereignty – and of course the British media let rip at me and, more importantly, the foreign secretary, for allowing The Prince of Wales to be placed in an embarrassing position.

I felt I had let everyone down. In fact, we defused the row quickly – Argentine ministers made some helpfully calming statements – and it became clear that the demonstration outside the British Embassy which the BBC reported as a protest against the Prince's speech was in fact about the rights of the Brazilian trans community who felt harassed by the local authorities. The *Independent* newspaper called it 'the gaffe that never was'.

More importantly, the speech went down very well in the Falkland Islands. With the added boost of a visit from HRH immediately afterwards, it turned out to be directly instrumental in giving local representatives the confidence to accept a limited agreement between the islanders and the British and Argentine governments covering fisheries, air services and limited people-to-people contact.

There were times when Cook believed that senior members of the FCO were closet Tories and/or disloyal officials determined to cause him embarrassment. That simply wasn't the case. But, against the advice of his private office, I wrote to him apologizing unreservedly for the embarrassment I had caused. His response could not have been more gracious.

A few months later, in July, elected representatives of the British, Argentine and Falkland Islands governments came together in the prestigious Locarno Rooms of the FCO to sign the documents – the last occasion there was any direct contact between the three bodies. It was a far more modest arrangement than I at least had been hoping for. But it was better than nothing, and it at last provided the islanders with an air route to the South American mainland, via Chile, and for Argentine nationals to have the right to visit the islands.

It was in fact the result of a couple of years of quiet, discreet diplomacy in which I had been engaged since taking over as Director Americas. I had always felt that, with the return of democracy to Argentina and the improved relations made possible by the election of President Menem in 1989, there was scope for finding a way to park, if not resolve, our differences over the Falkland Islands.

Fortunately, his foreign minister, Guido di Tella, was of a similar mind. Exiled to the UK for his Peronist sympathies after the 1976 *coup d'état* in Argentina, he spent some years as a visiting fellow at St Anthony's College, Oxford, before returning to Argentine politics after Menem's victory. He spoke perfect English and believed that the relationship with the UK needed fixing.

Guido di Tella's deputy was a lawyer by the name of Andres Cisneros. He wasn't known to the British Embassy in Buenos Aires as particularly friendly or constructive. But Cisneros and I hit it off and decided that we would see how far we could go in terms of managing our two countries' differences over the Falklands and restoring a degree of normality to the relationship.

We met privately in a number of neutral cities, and occasionally in our respective capitals. On one of my more public visits to Buenos Aires, Cisneros invited me to stay with his family in their beautiful log-built ski chalet in San Martin de los Andes. A central feature of the living area, and a highly effective part of the heating system, was an old iron steam engine, complete with pistons, wheels and a brass plaque showing it had been made in Ipswich, England, 150 years earlier. It was an industrial relic salvaged from what had been left behind by the British after they had been invited to build railways across Argentina in exchange for the right to breed cattle and export beef back to the homeland.

Like most children in South America, Cisneros's boys were football mad. Their preferred colours were the white shirts emblazoned with three lions worn by the English national team. Their father explained that they all followed the fortunes of the big Premier League teams and loved English football. But they would all, he said, lay down their lives for Argentina if there was ever another Falklands war.

Cisneros and I came quite close to reaching an understanding on a high degree of normalization of relations between the UK and Argentina, and between Argentina and the Falkland Islands, in exchange for freezing the issue of sovereignty for thirty years and then considering again, without prejudice, whether the islanders were ready to look afresh at some form of compromise. But by the time we had taken our discussions as far as we reasonably could, it became clear that any arrangement which left the issue of sovereignty unresolved was politically unacceptable in London. And so we settled for the more limited agreements signed between the foreign ministers of the UK and Argentina, and two elected representatives of the Legislative Council of the Falkland Islands, in the FCO on 14 July 1999.

Unfortunately, di Tella left office when President Menem was replaced at the end of the year, and died of cancer just two years later. The Argentine politicians who followed

Menem and di Tella, particularly President Cristina Kirchner who ran the country from 2007 until 2015, were keener on using the sovereignty of the Falkland Islands as a domestic political issue than on continuing the momentum their predecessors had established. The moment had passed.

Not many FCO officials had the good fortune, as I did, to visit the Falkland Islands three times. A group of islands roughly the size of Wales with a rugged, almost Scottish landscape, the Falklands offer unrivalled fishing and extraordinarily diverse wildlife. During my visit with The Prince of Wales, the weather was kind enough to allow us to take a short helicopter flight to Sea Lion Island, half an hour south of the capital, Stanley, and inhabited by a solitary guardian/lighthouse keeper. I could have stayed for days watching the elephant seals and skuas, and the gentoo, chinstrap, Magellanic, rockhopper and king penguins. In a Sky News interview in the spring of 2020 during the Covid-19 lockdown, the anchor, Kay Burley, asked me why there were three stuffed penguins on a sofa in the back of the study from which I was speaking. I explained that penguins were my favourite animal, that the family on the sofa were my reminder of the Falklands.

During the three years that I did the job I travelled widely in both Americas. As part of the endless search for economies, I visited every one of the small Central American states to review the effectiveness and value of our diplomatic missions there. Our economic and political interests in most were limited. But I concluded that the impact our small missions made in the region, not least in conflict prevention and the preservation of human rights, meant that we were right to maintain our modest missions in Tegucigalpa, San Salvador, Guatemala City, Panama City, Managua and San José.*

A little further south, in Colombia, I visited Bogotá, Medellin and Cartagena where I was shown several high-powered 'cigar' boats and a midget submarine confiscated by the anti-narcotics police – often with highly effective help from the US and UK – as they sought to stem the flow of drugs across the Caribbean and on to the US, Africa and Europe. Despite the risks, brave prosecutors in Colombia, protected in their courtrooms by glass several inches thick, tried and convicted many of the criminals responsible for this horrifically destructive trade.

In the summer of 1999, when my marriage to my first wife, Angie, was ending, I decided to take a holiday in Peru at the end of a week of official visits to Chile, Argentina and Bolivia. When I sent a message to my children telling them of my plans, my adventurous eldest son, Oliver, immediately replied that he was coming too, please, with a group of his close friends. By chance, my youngest son, Rupert, was planning a separate trip to Bolivia and Peru at the same time.

And so, on 25 July, Oliver, seven of his friends and I found ourselves flying into Lima, from different directions, and then on to Cusco, with me responsible (with more than a little help and hospitality from the long-suffering ambassador, John Illman, and his wife, Liz) for putting together an ambitious itinerary at what – eventually – turned out to be a price acceptable to a group of more or less impoverished students.

---

* The respective capitals of Honduras, El Salvador, Guatemala, Panama, Nicaragua and Costa Rica.

The details of our expedition are of little interest outside our small band of intrepid travellers but two elements stick in my memory. First, a tip for those wanting to visit the iconic fifteenth-century Incan site of Machu Picchu but don't have the time or inclination to walk the expensive four-day Inca Trail; and prefer not to arrive by bus from the town of Aguas Calientes at the bottom of the mountain. There is a third way, which means taking the scenic train along the Sacred Valley from Cusco and getting off at Kilometer 104, some way before the end of the line. You then take a vigorous, but highly enjoyable, hike of five hours in which you climb over 600 metres, experience three different microclimates and walk through the ruins of several Incan towns before arriving from above through the Puerto del Sol and seeing the whole of Machu Picchu laid out beneath you. Arriving mid-afternoon, we had the place to ourselves except for a few llamas and sheep. You can always return by bus the next morning for sunrise, as we did, and scamper up the near-vertical stone steps of the sugar loaf mountain of Huayna Picchu just behind the main site (the young do it in twenty-five minutes – I took forty).

Second, try and fit in a visit to Chachapoyas, a remote region of northern Peru with its own culture predating the Incas by 300–400 years and an extraordinary collection of perfectly preserved mummies discovered shortly before our visit in caves 600 metres up in the cloud forest. A museum was due to be opened a year later just outside the small town of Leymebamba, but 'our' two hundred mummy bundles, still in their original, finely woven embroidered cotton wrappings, were in cardboard boxes in a temporary, but temperature-controlled, reception centre.

We were only allowed to see them after Sonia, a local anthropologist who had come with us from Lima, had solemnly asked the mummies whether they were prepared to be viewed – the answer, she said, was sometimes no. All the mummies were in the same position, sitting with their knees drawn up to their chests, hands crossed in front of their faces, and skin, teeth and even fingernails in near-perfect condition six hundred years on. We felt very privileged to be with them, and that our twelve-hour bus journey, followed by an hour in an air taxi because the scheduled flight had been cancelled, had been well worth it.

Later in 1999, I found myself cast in the unlikely role of the first senior UK government official to visit Cuba since the 1959 *coup d'état*. (A few months after that, I was in Havana again, accompanying the FCO minister of state responsible for the region, Liz Symons, for the first British ministerial visit.) Rarity has its value, and I was given a warm welcome. The foreign minister, Felipe Perez Roque, talked with me for more than two hours on my way in from the airport, and I had fascinating conversations with many other Cuban officials, including Fidel Castro's engaging younger brother.

Among my other engagements in old Havana I was asked to open the new Princess Diana Memorial Garden – testament to the impact her death two years earlier had had even in this bastion of unreformed communism. In fact, it took only hours to sense that the reason why the Castro regime, with all its repression, corruption and inefficiency, had survived so long was the continued existence of US sanctions.

They provided a tailor-made foreign bogeyman to blame for everything that didn't work or deprived ordinary Cubans – still swaying, at all hours, to the music of Old Havana – of the freedom, opportunities and prosperity they craved.

Sure enough, when President Obama was finally able in 2009 to end the travel ban and begin opening up US policy towards Cuba, things began to change. At the end of 2014, after months of secret diplomacy involving his own national security staff and the good offices of his closest ally in the Senate, Patrick Leahy of Vermont, Obama went a step further and ordered the restoration of full diplomatic relations with Cuba. Obsessed by a desire to denigrate and where possible undo the achievements of his predecessor, President Trump reimposed sanctions on Cuba after he became president in January 2017, slowing the process of change and normalization. Over the decades, Cubans had developed a survival culture of their own, as they cannibalized and celebrated their cult 1950s American cars, deprived by sanctions of spare parts and replacements. Trump may have delayed the time when the poverty, hardship, repression and corruption are swept away, but he will also have ensured that these quirky elements of Cuba's survival economy are around for a while yet.

In 2000, after three years in charge of the Americas, I was promoted to the odd-sounding position on the FCO board of Deputy Under-Secretary for the Wider World. Other members of the board tended to have functional responsibilities, covering defence and intelligence, consular affairs, economic work, the EU, or HR and finance. My job was more geographical, and included producing annual appraisals on more than twenty senior heads of mission around the world, all outside Europe. Since the foreign secretary, and the four junior ministers who supported him, tended to visit high-profile countries and/or close allies and key markets, it fell to me to visit other parts of the world which rarely received political attention. I did the job for just eighteen months, but enjoyed it immensely and learnt a lot.

One of the duties that fell to me – and one of the other deputy under-secretaries – was to stand in for the PUS, John Kerr, when he wasn't able to attend on The Queen at the ceremonies when newly arrived foreign ambassadors presented their Letters of Credence. These 'credentials' were the highlight of their time in London for ambassadors to the Court of St James since each one, accompanied only by their immediate family and senior members of their staff, is driven in a state carriage, with full livery, from their embassy to Buckingham Palace and granted a private audience with Her Majesty – or, on the rare occasions when she is not available, with other senior members of the Royal family standing in for the monarch as Counsellors of State. I do not believe any other head of state – certainly none of Her Majesty's seniority – takes such trouble to make the representatives of other countries feel so welcome.

Credentials was also one of the rare occasions when we officials dressed up in diplomatic uniform, with sword, gloves and feathered hat. Our role was to ensure that Her Majesty was briefed, answer in advance any questions she might have, and provide support as necessary during the ceremony. The Queen, of course, had visited so many countries, many of them several times, that she was extraordinarily well-informed and never at a loss for conversation, even with ambassadors stricken with stage fright.

And she always mastered her brief. I still remember Her Majesty turning to me before the new Ethiopian ambassador entered the room and asking – since, she said, the map accompanying her brief wasn't entirely clear – whether the granting of independence to Eritrea a few years earlier meant that Ethiopia was now a land-locked country. To my shame, I had no idea.

My new job involved a lot of travel. It was difficult, and unfair to the individuals concerned, to write appraisals on ambassadors whom I hadn't seen in action. So my journeys took in the Middle East, India, China, Japan and South Korea as well as Australia, New Zealand and most South East Asian countries. Since I was line manager for the more senior ambassadors in the Americas, I also made it my business to stay in touch with the bigger posts for which I had been responsible as Director Americas.

Focusing on places where there were problems which needed attention, I went to Sudan, almost always on the brink of civil war, and to Angola, where there was a long-standing conflict between two former liberation movements, MPLA and UNITA. They had been fighting it out since the country became independent, one side financed by oil revenues and the other by what were known as 'blood diamonds'. It was hard to make progress, especially when most of the oil companies operating offshore and in Angola – BP being a notable exception – were not remotely interested in replacing the traditional way of handing over the oil revenues under the counter with the kind of transparency essential to good governance and the end of conflict.

I went to Indonesia a few times since British companies

had very large investments there, particularly in mining, and ministers were rarely able to find the time to go that far and show the measure of political support those firms sometimes needed.

My responsibility for the 'wider world' brought me into close contact with other agencies of government, including the military. In early 2000 I went twice to Sierra Leone, once accompanying the chief of the defence staff, General Sir Charles Guthrie. Sierra Leone, a small West African member of the Commonwealth, had been struggling with civil war since 1991. Various UN-sponsored efforts to end the conflict had failed and rebels supported by President Charles Taylor across the border in neighbouring Liberia were again threatening the capital, Freetown. To support the government of President Ahmad Tejan Kabbah, and with a fresh UN mandate, the British army deployed eight hundred soldiers at very short notice in May of that year.

In a critical engagement on 10 September, a squadron of SAS soldiers launched a daring raid on a jungle base run by the 'West Side Boys', a local militia loyal to the revolutionary group seeking to overthrow the government, who were holding five British soldiers hostage. I happened to be on an official visit to Cambodia at the time and waited anxiously for overnight news of the success, or otherwise, of the operation. The SAS succeeded in freeing the five soldiers as well as twenty-five Sierra Leonean civilians who were also being held prisoner, for the loss of one of their number killed in the early stages of the assault. The West Side Boys sustained heavy casualties and were effectively put out of business. By the end of the month the fighting was over, and by July 2002 the last of the British troops who had stayed behind to help supervise the elections – won in a landslide by President Kabbah in May – had returned home.

It was perhaps the last occasion when a foreign military intervention on behalf of a friendly government did exactly what was intended and helped end a war. Tony Blair, the prime minister, was deeply impressed. The Sierra Leone experience was, I believe, a factor in his decision later that year to commit UK armed forces in support of the United States should it prove necessary – as he and President George W. Bush concluded it was – to take military action against Saddam Hussein in Iraq in the spring of 2003.

The year after our visit to Sierra Leone I twice travelled abroad again with Charles Guthrie, this time on visits to Pakistan to meet with President Pervez Musharraf whom Charles had known long before at the Royal Military Academy at Sandhurst. Our first visit was in the spring of 2001, before 9/11, our second a few weeks after that terrible day. Our aim on the first trip was to warn Musharraf off the continuing Islamization of Pakistan's army and political institutions, and to persuade him to stop supporting the Taliban – largely a Pakistani creation – in next-door Afghanistan. We didn't make much progress, in part because the Pakistani president denied point blank that the Pakistani military were helping the Taliban. I told him that there was photographic evidence of military convoys crossing into southern Afghanistan from Pakistan, but it made no difference.

Guthrie and I thought it worth going back after 9/11 to see whether the shock of what had happened in the United States would make the Pakistani authorities think again.

This time there was recognition that the support the Taliban 'government' of Afghanistan had provided to al-Qaeda did not reflect well on Pakistan, and a degree of commitment to work with the rest of the international community to fight back against terrorism.

Unfortunately, then, as during most of the next two decades, Pakistan's professions of support for action against terrorism were contradicted by the bizarre belief that Pakistan's need for 'strategic depth' meant that it could not live side by side with a viable, stable Afghanistan which it did not control – not because Afghanistan itself was a threat, but because it might become some kind of proxy for the neighbour Pakistan was really worried about, India. So, despite all the pressure applied by the US, UK and other countries with an interest in stabilizing Afghanistan, the Pakistani authorities – including their military intelligence agency, the ISI – continued to regard the jihadist Afghan Taliban as a useful instrument of foreign and security policy.

Twenty years later in the autumn of 2021, when the Taliban again found themselves in control of Afghanistan after the United States withdrew, a friend at the CIA remarked to me: 'The good news for the Pakistanis is that their guys have won. And the bad news for the Pakistanis is that their guys have won.' In other words, Islamabad would no longer be able to pretend that it had nothing to do with what was going on in Afghanistan, and would be judged accordingly.

Two days before 9/11, as part of the murky understanding agreed between the Taliban and al-Qaeda, Ahmad Shah Massoud, the charismatic leader of the Northern Alliance and principal opponent of the Taliban, was murdered by a suicide bomber pretending to be a journalist visiting from

North Africa. Also in the room, badly injured and in a coma for days afterwards, was his friend Massoud Khalili, an Afghan poet and diplomat.

After his recovery, Khalili was posted to Turkey as ambassador of Afghanistan, where he and I became friends. His body was still full of metal fragments, and he of course missed Ahmad Shah. But despite the pain, my Afghan colleague showed no sign of bitterness and was always serene and optimistic. Both he and Ahmad Shah had been part of the resistance to the Soviet occupation of their country from 1979 to 1989, but both had then been victims of opportunistic alliances between proxies of outside powers playing out their fantasies on Afghan territory.

Two weeks after 9/11 I found myself accompanying Robin Cook's successor, Jack Straw, to Tehran for the first visit to Iran by a British foreign secretary since the overthrow of the shah in 1979. For Straw, it was the beginning of a fascination with the country which stuck with him all through the long and tortuous negotiations about Iran's nuclear programme, begun on his watch, which culminated in the 2015 JCPOA. It led him to publish *The English Job* in 2019, a perceptive and highly readable study of the complexities and contradictions which have always afflicted relations between the UK and Iran.

President Mohammad Khatami and the other Iranian leaders we met were their usual suave selves. I dared to think we were even making some progress with our pitch for cooperation against al-Qaeda – after all, it embodied the worst form of Sunni extremism which Shi'a Iran abhorred – as Khatami reflected on the damage to society, tolerance and governance caused by religious fanatics who adopted an over-literal interpretation of the holy book. 'So what,' he asked with a twinkle, 'are we going to do about the religious extremists in America's bible belt?'

Six months earlier, I had been back in Ankara for talks on foreign policy issues with Turkish officials. The then ambassador and an old friend, Sir David Logan, with whom I had served in Washington, gave a dinner for me to meet twenty or so senior Turkish officials. Half of them turned out to be old friends from my time at the embassy, which had ended eleven years earlier. The dinner, and the meetings I had with Turkish officials, went very well. On the flight back to London the next day, I came to the conclusion that I should apply to succeed David when he retired at the end of 2001.

I could see plenty of reasons for doing so. I knew the place and quite a number of people in Ankara and Istanbul. Turkey was a key country in a volatile region. It was a secular democracy, albeit an incomplete one, and the British government supported its aspiration to join the EU. It was a member of NATO and the Council of Europe. It was key to the UK's obligation, as a guarantor power from colonial days, to try and find a solution to the Cyprus problem. It was an energy corridor. It controlled access to the straits between the Black Sea and the Mediterranean. It had a series of unresolved sovereignty and airspace disputes with Greece which needed careful management. We had important business links but needed better ones. And it was a country of extraordinary natural beauty and breathtaking archaeology. I thought I could make a difference, and enjoy doing so.

When I told Robin Cook that I wanted to return to

Ankara, he did his best to dissuade me. He would prefer me to stay in London, he said. But if I was determined to go abroad after five years at home, I could surely do better than Turkey – not his favourite country. My level of seniority, he said, meant that I could reasonably expect something bigger. But he didn't insist: it was my life and he wouldn't stand in my way. After all, he added, he could be out of a job at any time so I shouldn't worry too much about his views. Sure enough, in June 2001, before it was even confirmed that I was going back to Turkey, Cook was replaced at the FCO by Jack Straw and made leader of the House of Commons.

I had enjoyed my time working for Robin. He was a controversial foreign secretary, not least for the 'ethical dimension' to foreign policy he had sought to promote.

Office meetings with Cook were remarkable. He had the sharpest of minds. He had always done his homework. He knew what questions to ask. He listened to the answers, adding the odd witty aside (at his own expense or that of ministerial colleagues not in the room). He summed up. And we all went away quite clear as to what was expected of us.

Cook resigned as leader of the House in May 2003 in protest at Prime Minister Tony Blair's decision to commit the UK to military action in Iraq in support of the US 'without international agreement or domestic support'. His sadly premature death from a heart attack on Ben Stack in a remote corner of the Scottish Highlands in 2005 was a loss to both the country and the Labour Party of a gifted and intelligent – if complicated – politician.

8

More Turkish delight (2002–4)

As Robin Cook had implied, going back to Ankara was a minor demotion. But I had always believed in going for jobs I wanted rather than those that were the next step up the promotion ladder, on the simple grounds that people tend to make a better job of fulfilling their potential when doing something they enjoy.

I arrived back in Ankara in January 2002, after an eventful and fairly stressful last few months in London. The 9/11 attacks had taken place in my last few weeks in my old job. On Saturday, 6 October 2001, I was due to be remarried, to Susie Nemazee, an Iranian-American whom I had originally met at a dinner in Tehran a quarter of a century earlier and who had an eighteen-year old daughter, Safieh, from a previous marriage. This was just before the launch of coalition attacks against the Taliban government who had refused to hand over Osama bin Laden. Susie couldn't quite understand why I was happy to let our wedding proceed but had decided to cancel my farewell reception in the FCO three days later – by which time I knew, but couldn't say, that the air campaign against the Taliban government in Afghanistan would have begun.

I was ready for Ankara in mid-winter to be bleak and cold. But I hadn't expected to be unable to get out of the aircraft when we got there. After all the exertions of shutting up shop at home and carrying heavy suitcases to the airport, my back had given out. I was carefully driven to our new residence, and gingerly laid flat until a doctor could be found. For the next three weeks – it should have been six – I barely moved. Opinions differed as to whether I should have surgery for what turned out to be a fragmented disc, in which case it should be done right away, or adopt a more conservative approach and simply allow time to be the healer.

It took the FCO's medical adviser six weeks to give his opinion on the X-rays and medical reports which we had couriered back to London. Amazed by the lack of response, Susie activated her highly effective network of Iranian friends in the US medical sector, with immediate results. I, meanwhile, was lucky enough to be introduced to the head of Hacettepe University Hospital in Ankara, who turned out to be a back specialist. Between them, the various experts decided that since the moment when surgery was likely to have been most effective had passed, I should simply stay horizontal for a few more weeks. Not easy when you have just arrived in a new place with an important new job requiring action and visibility; but I learned to my cost there was no alternative to following doctor's orders.

Despite the unpromising start, Susie and I settled in rapidly. I felt sure the decision to return to Turkey had been the right one. Part of the key to being accepted as a diplomat overseas is to convince your hosts that you are there because you want to be; and that you believe in the future of their country. It helped that, on this occasion, both were true. In recent years the UK's diplomatic service has made a better job than most of ensuring that vacancies are filled through a bidding system, meaning that even at relatively junior levels our diplomats tend to go to places they have themselves selected.

Knowing people from my previous stint in Ankara helped. I wanted to have a go at improving my Turkish but rapidly gave up on language lessons after cancelling the first one three times. Susie was more determined, and more successful. She already had good French, Persian and Spanish and knew that learning Turkish would help her develop relationships with Turkish women. She did pretty well with the men too. It wasn't long before Recep Tayyip Erdoğan – whom we quickly got to know as leader of the AKP, a newly formed political party, and who would go on to become Turkish prime minister a little over a year after we arrived in Ankara – started asking me why my wife spoke better Turkish than I did when she hadn't had the benefit of a previous stay in his country.

It was also an advantage that Susie's parents came from next-door Iran, although she had been born in Washington. Iranians and Turks don't generally have much time for each other, as inheritors of what were for hundreds of years two rival empires, one Shi'a and the other Sunni. But visa-free travel between the two countries had led to a million Iranians living in Turkey at the time, and to the establishment of close business and energy links.

I presented my credentials to President Ahmet Necdet Sezer in February 2002 just in time to hobble to Istanbul for a conference of the foreign ministers of the EU and the

Islamic Conference held in glorious sunshine on the shores of the Bosphorus.

My next few months were focused largely on trying to persuade the Turks to assume a leadership role within NATO's International Security Assistance Force (ISAF), which the US and its allies were setting up in Afghanistan. The military campaign launched in October had met with a good deal of early success, at least against the Taliban if not in running al-Qaeda to ground as effectively as we all would have liked. With the help of a series of senior military and FCO visitors from London, we eventually persuaded the Turks to say yes.

Turkey had had a bad decade, with poor governance, more corruption, economic crises and continuing conflict in the Kurdish south-east. In 1997, for the fourth time in less than fifty years, the army had stepped in – this time without resort to force – to change the government. It did not assume power, but it did tell the Islamist prime minister Necmettin Erbakan, after an unseemly official visit to Libya at the invitation of Muammar Qadhafi, that his position had become untenable and his government had to go.

By the early summer of 2002 it was clear that the three-party coalition government led by Prime Minister Bülent Ecevit then running the country was lacking both effectiveness and credibility. The one bright spot was the way Kemal Derviş, a former World Bank economist, had answered the call from Ecevit the year before, joined the government as minister of economic affairs and almost single-handedly put the Turkish economy back on its feet. Derviş shut down insolvent banks, carried out overdue structural reforms, reasserted the independence of the Central Bank and began to stabilize the currency.

But it was too late to save the coalition. In the space of a single farcical day in July 2002, Derviş received me with a visiting British ministerial delegation, resigned as minister of finance and changed his mind later that afternoon when President Sezer begged him to reconsider. Three weeks later one of the three deputy prime ministers resigned and a second said he would not oppose the holding of an early general election.

For a brief moment, it looked as though a new party would be formed by one of the outgoing deputy prime ministers, Hüsamettin Özkan, Foreign Minister İsmail Cem, and Kemal Derviş. But Derviş decided to go with the leader of the secular opposition party, Deniz Baykal, and the new party never got off the ground. Eighteen years later I was able to play a minor part in putting Özkan and Derviş, once close friends, back in touch.

On 2 November 2002, the Justice and Development Party (AKP), created just fourteen months earlier from the ashes of the Islamist Refah ('Welfare') Party shut down by the military in 1997, swept to victory with 34.5 per cent of the vote and two-thirds of the seats in the Turkish parliament. Turkey found itself with a single-party government for the first time in fifteen years.

There was just one problem. The leader of the AKP, Recep Tayyip Erdoğan, who had made his name as mayor of Istanbul, had been imprisoned for ten months and banned from political activity for reciting a poem which described the minarets and domes of mosques as the swords and shields of those fighting for a more Islamic way of life. The ban was still in place when the AKP won its election victory. So Abdullah Gül, a former minister in the Refah-led coalition and co-founder with Erdoğan of the AKP, took over as interim prime minister.

Dramatic as its victory had been, the AKP was regarded with deep suspicion by secular Turks, including the military and most of the Westernized elite. The 15 per cent or so of the population who were not Sunni Muslim but Shi'a Alevi shared their concern. These groups feared that the hard-won reforms of Kemal Atatürk, the founder of the Turkish Republic, would be jeopardized by an Islamist administration.

Atatürk, after all, had based his vision of the successor state of the Ottoman Empire on the model of a secular, Westernized, modern nation where women would not wear headscarves and men would wear suits and ties. In addition to dropping the Arabic script of the Ottoman language in favour of Roman letters and numbers, he replaced old Ottoman words either with new confections or a phonetic version of the French equivalent (he was a great admirer of Napoleon, the French legal system and French culture).

In the new Turkish nation, there was no room for minorities other than those recognized in the 1923 Treaty of Lausanne – Armenians, Greeks and Jews. This meant that over the years there was a steady – at times dramatic and perilous – exodus of many other minorities. Thousands of Armenians and Greeks went too when their daily lives were made intolerable. The Kurds, who made up 15 per cent of the population, had a particularly difficult time – as I explain below.

Like the Welfare Party it succeeded, the AKP was Islamist in character. It owed its electoral success to the alliance it had made with the followers of the mysterious, reclusive, cult figure Fethullah Gülen, who had lived in self-imposed exile in Pennsylvania since 1999. Gülen – who was still living there in 2020 – shared much of the AKP's vision and saw the creation of the AKP as a useful means of advancing his own agenda of a slow, peaceful but irrevocable move towards the nirvana of a world united in its adherence to Islam.

Usefully for the AKP, the movement – known first as *jamiyat* ('society') and later as *hizmet* ('service') – had followers all over the world. It also had a network of schools in dozens of countries, including the United States, which generated both income and recruits. Its agents of influence were quietly infiltrating the institutions of the Turkish state but were, for now, making no trouble.

A decade later, as ambassador to the United States, I found members of the movement everywhere, actively building relationships and arranging for elected officials from states and federal bodies to make expenses-paid trips to Turkey. Back in 2002 the Gülen organization was of huge value to the AKP in getting out the vote, especially in the early days when the party was still finding its feet.

Shrewdly, the AKP did not fall into the trap of being a carbon copy of previous Islamist parties which had been closed down by the courts, or the military. Instead, it made a point of including in its membership a number of secularists, including Yaşar Yakiş, a former ambassador to Saudi Arabia who became the AKP's first foreign minister. This helped reassure those who didn't support the party, as well as the military who had a constitutional obligation to protect the territorial integrity of the republic and preserve its secular nature.

Some months before the election, I had asked Erdoğan how he would reconcile his Islamist beliefs with the secular requirements of the Turkish constitution. He had no difficulty in explaining that government was one thing and faith another: he would abide by the laws of the country if elected, and was determined to ensure that Turkey met the criteria for EU membership.

A few years later he was quoted saying that democracy was like a tram you rode until you reached your destination and then got off. By early 2016 he was saying boldly that words like democracy, human rights and the rule of law were of no relevance to the modern Turkish Republic. But in 2002 he seemed to be in a different place, and the rest of the world was unfazed by Turkey's apparently moderate Islamism. The new minister of state for religious affairs, Mehmet Aydin, had obtained his PhD in philosophy from Edinburgh University. During the first of a number of friendly conversations, he told me how, arriving in Scotland, he had explained to his future landlady, with some trepidation, that he felt he should tell her he was a Muslim. 'Oh, that's all right,' she replied. 'I feared you were going to tell me you were a Roman Catholic.'

The first big challenge the new government faced was Europe. Ten days after the AKP assumed power, Gül and Erdoğan travelled to Copenhagen for the December 2002 European Council. They were invited because the plan was for the Turkish and Greek Cypriots finally to endorse UN Secretary General Kofi Annan's plan for a comprehensive settlement of the Cyprus problem at the same time as the European Council agreed that ten new member states, including Cyprus, would join the EU in 2004.

Such an effort was long overdue. The Cyprus dispute had festered unresolved since the Turkish military invasion of 1974, following an attempted coup by the Greek Cypriots, orchestrated by the military junta in Athens. Turkey's subsequent decision in 1983 to establish a 'Turkish Republic of Northern Cyprus', still not recognized by anyone except the Turks themselves, did little to help. For a number of reasons, well described in David Hannay's book *Cyprus: The Search for a Solution*, the Copenhagen European Council decided to proceed with the accession of the A10, as they were called, while no decisions were taken on the reunification of Cyprus. Rauf Denktaş, the popular Turkish Cypriot leader, hadn't even bothered to show up.

Kofi Annan set a fresh deadline of 28 February 2003 for a 'final' attempt to reach agreement, so that a reunited Cyprus could join the other nine candidates and become a member of the EU on 1 May 2004. After a further extension of this deadline by ten days, Annan summoned the Turkish and Greek Cypriot leaders to The Hague on 10 March. That meeting, too, ended in failure, even though Denktaş at least attended, cheerfully discussing his options over the phone with the Turkish foreign minister, Yaşar Yakiş, who was having dinner with us privately in Ankara.

Disappointed, Annan had no choice but to report to the Security Council that he had failed. The Cyprus settlement process was once again put on ice. David Hannay, who had by then been the UK's special representative for Cyprus for six and a half years, decided to hang up his boots. So did his US counterpart, Tom Weston. Regular meetings with both, over a glass of whisky at the Ankara embassy, had been an enjoyable and rewarding feature of my first year in the job.

One reason why the Turks didn't do a better job in The Hague was that they had other things on their minds. Less than ten days earlier, on 1 March, the Turkish parliament had failed to vote with a big enough majority to allow coalition forces – the US 4th Infantry Division and a modest UK military contingent – to transit Turkish territory on their way to Iraq.

Almost 90 per cent of Turks were opposed to military action against Saddam Hussein. My argument – made in good faith – was that an effective military build-up, including the creation of a northern front through Turkey, was critical to putting enough pressure on Saddam for him to conclude that it would be better to *avoid* going to war and instead comply with the demands of the UN Security Council to come clean over his stocks of weapons of mass destruction.

Three months earlier, I had been invited to find a new job by some US neo-conservatives with whom I had been attending an Aspen Institute of Berlin conference in Istanbul. My crime had been to explain that the UK would need to be satisfied on both legality (on which the attorney general would have to rule) and legitimacy (meaning that the UN Security Council had to give its consent) before joining the US in any military action against Saddam Hussein.

One of the US attendees told me firmly that I was out of line since my prime minister, Tony Blair, had already told his president, George W. Bush, that the UK would be with the Americans in Iraq, come what may. The Chilcot Report into the UK's role in the Iraq war published in London in

July 2016 suggests that they did indeed have a better idea than I did of what president and prime minister had said to each other.

Our request for permission to cross Turkish territory turned out to give the Turks more difficulty than that of the Americans. One Saturday in late February, Defence Minister Vecdi Gönül called me at home. He said he had, with great difficulty, persuaded the council of ministers to treat the UK and US applications equally. But he wanted me to be aware of why this had given him real difficulty.

Soundings the governing party had taken in the southeast, he said, suggested that people could live with an American military presence if necessary but that they really didn't want the British there too. Why? Because people in that part of Turkey still held us responsible for the decision of the League of Nations in 1926 to divide (mainly Kurdish) tribal lands and give the new British protectorate of Iraq the oil and gas fields of Mosul and Kirkuk, which would otherwise have come to the new Republic of Turkey. Here was a reminder of how much baggage British diplomacy in the Middle East acquired during and after the First World War – much of which is still with us today.

The new Turkish government, with Abdullah Gül still at its head, had in fact decided that it would accede to the US and UK requests if the National Assembly (NA) was content – not least because the Americans were offering $6.5 billion of financial aid as a sweetener. The Turks were also offered a say over future developments in northern Iraq, where they feared that the success of the Kurdish autonomous region – then protected by a no-fly zone policed by US and UK military aircraft flying out of İncirlik in south-eastern Turkey

– could encourage separatists in that part of the country to push for autonomy of their own.

But it was not to be. When the vote was taken, the first message that reached me (at the time in a cinema with the US and Spanish ambassadors and their wives) was that the NA had agreed. It had indeed. But it then became clear that this particular proposal required a super-majority to pass, which wasn't there.

Bitter recriminations followed, in Turkey and abroad. In Washington, there was widespread criticism of the Turkish military for failing to support the proposal more vigorously (the general staff, always keen to remain in step with public opinion and at this time no fan of the AKP, had been happy to keep its head down).

For the next two weeks an unseemly and ultimately unsuccessful negotiation took place between the US and Turkish governments over whether or not to ask the National Assembly to think again. The law banning Erdoğan from political activity had been lifted on 3 March and, after a hastily arranged special election in the eastern city of Siirt, he replaced Abdullah Gül as prime minister on the 14th.

This helped government coordination. But in Washington, the Turks overbid. Invited to the White House to make their case, Economy Minister Ali Babacan and (outgoing, to make way for Gül) Foreign Minister Yaşar Yakiş infuriated the administration with their talk of a $92 billion likely cost to the Turkish economy of a war with Iraq. Both subsequently told me they had not asked for anything like this amount but had simply tried to give an idea of the cost of what was being asked of Turkey.

Erdoğan, badly advised by his political staff that the US couldn't go to war without Turkish support, thought he could delay taking the issue back to the NA until his new government had received a vote of confidence.

On the evening of 17 March, I decided to go and see him with details of the reassuring, Turkey-friendly elements of a declaration made by President Bush, Tony Blair and Spanish Prime Minister Jose Maria Aznar at their summit meeting in the Azores. With Turkish markets falling fast, I told him time was running out for an agreement. Later that evening, US secretary of state Colin Powell called Gül to say Washington could wait no longer.

The next day, a summit meeting chaired by President Sezer agreed that the government should take 'all measures necessary in the national interest' now that military action in Iraq seemed inevitable. But by this time operational considerations had forced the Pentagon to make other plans, and move the ships waiting outside the port of Mersin closer to the Persian Gulf. By the time a revised resolution was put to the Turkish National Assembly, the Americans only wanted overflights, and all but $1 billion of the aid was off the table.

As my US colleague Bob Pearson put it to me, the Turks had rejected the offer of a strategic partnership that would have given them a real say over the future of Iraq at a time when Ankara was terrified that fragmentation of the country after a US invasion might create a prosperous, autonomous or even independent Kurdish state on Turkey's south-eastern border.

Some months later, Pearson's successor, Eric Edelman, who was also to become a good friend, invited me to a talk at his official residence given by Walter Russell Mead, an American academic and foreign policy commentator. Part of Mead's thesis was that Saddam Hussein brought the invasion on himself because of his responsibility for 9/11. I asked him how this could be. It was perfectly clear, Mead responded. Saddam Hussein had invaded Kuwait in 1990, which had obliged the US and its allies to take military action to liberate that country and install military bases in the region to ensure there was no recurrence. Al-Qaeda, inspired by Osama bin Laden, was founded on the belief that foreign military bases in and around Saudi Arabia were unacceptable. Since al-Qaeda was the orchestrator of 9/11, it followed that Saddam Hussein was also responsible for the greatest single act of terrorism America had ever known.

Of all the different justifications I had heard for the invasion of Iraq in 2003, this was one of the most jaw-dropping.

Against this complex background the new government had to deal with Turkish Cypriot leader Rauf Denktaş, still the most popular politician in Turkey and firmly opposed to a settlement of the Cyprus problem. New to government, under huge pressure on Iraq and with Denktaş digging in, reaching agreement at The Hague on 10 March would have been an extraordinary achievement for the AKP. In the end, it was too much to ask.

The invasion of Iraq took place from the south, with no northern front formed by troops and armour crossing the Turkish border. The strategic relationship between Washington and Ankara had altered dramatically. From April until the summer, attention in the region shifted towards what was going on in Iraq, with no one paying attention to the Cyprus problem (or to Turkey, except in so far as its modest military presence in Iraqi Kurdistan helped or hindered coalition operations).

By the autumn of 2003, with the accession of ten new EU member states – including Cyprus – due on 1 May 2004, I became convinced that it was time to make one more attempt at a settlement. I wrote a non-paper, purely on my own authority, for the Turkish foreign ministry explaining why, whether or not it succeeded, the Turkish government needed to make a fresh effort to deliver what had become known as the Annan Plan. If it didn't, I argued, a divided Cyprus, with the Greek Cypriots having the only internationally recognized government, would become an EU member state.

My colleagues at the Turkish Ministry of Foreign Affairs (MFA) – Permanent Secretary Uğur Ziyal, Deputy Under-Secretary Baki İlkin and Ertuğrul Apakan, the Cyprus/Aegean director general – told me that my thinking coincided with theirs. They were ready to get stuck in, and would like to work closely with me and my new US colleague Eric Edelman in a final search for a settlement.

During the next few months, I attended numerous meetings at the MFA, often accompanied by Edelman. It was clear from the outset that, even if the diplomats were on board with a revised version of the Annan Plan, it was going to be a tough sell to other elements of the Turkish state – notably the military and the president. I found myself going through the text with senior generals at the headquarters of the Turkish General Staff, seeking to address their concerns and to explain why the UN blueprint met Turkey's essential national interests.

On one issue, I had to negotiate almost as hard with colleagues in London as with my Turkish hosts: the need for the Annan Plan to include provision for the secretary general himself to 'fill in the gaps' in the event that the Turkish and Greek Cypriot leaders were unable to reach agreement themselves. This was essential if the process was not once again going to run into the sand, because it would ensure that neither party had a veto.

The relative calm of this diplomacy was brutally interrupted, and the lives of my staff turned upside down, by a suicide bomb attack on Pera House, the magnificent British consulate general in Istanbul, on 20 November 2003. I was going into a meeting between EU ambassadors and Jalal Talabani, the Iraqi Kurdish leader, in Ankara when I received a call from my office saying there had been a bomb outside HSBC's headquarters in Istanbul. Five minutes later, my phone rang again: there had been a further bomb at the entrance of Pera House. Several people were missing, including Consul General Roger Short and his secretary, Lisa Hallworth.

I left immediately for Istanbul, along with the minister of the interior, incurring the wrath of fellow passengers on the Turkish Airlines flight, unaware of what had happened, for keeping the plane waiting. Five days earlier suicide bombers had killed more than thirty people at two synagogues in Istanbul. When the dust cleared, in addition to massive destruction, we discovered that twelve people working at the consulate general, many of whom (including Roger and Lisa) we knew well, had been killed. Three other people who had had the bad luck to be in the vicinity also died. More than a hundred construction workers were on site at the time, so we were, I suppose, fortunate that only two of them sustained serious injuries. At HSBC there were a further thirteen fatalities and many more injuries.

The news media initially reported that Britain's top diplomat in Turkey had been killed, which understandably spread a degree of panic among my family. Mobile telephone networks were down so people started calling my son Oliver – who happened to be in Diyarbakir in eastern Turkey on his twenty-eighth birthday – and my wife Susie, who had just arrived in Washington, to find out what had happened. I managed to get word through that I at least was safe, but al-Qaeda caused Oliver several hundred pounds' worth of roaming charges on his mobile phone which he could ill afford. That evening Turkish intelligence officials presented him with a birthday cake in the Caravanserai Hotel where he was staying, as a friendly gesture – and so he knew they were keeping an eye on him.

Those few days changed the lives of us all. There was of course the devastating physical impact: the suicide bomber's pick-up was said to have been carrying 2,500 kilos of explosives. One of our visa staff sitting in his office 120 metres away was hit on the back of the head by the bomber's foot. But there were also emotional and psychological scars which were still some way from being fully healed when Susie and I left Turkey almost three years later. Guilt, anger, resentment, inadequacy, entitlement and shame all played their part. There had never been such a terrorist attack on a British diplomatic mission. We were in uncharted territory.

The afternoon of the attack, I moved the consulate general staff to temporary offices in the Intercontinental Hotel, where the management couldn't have been more helpful. Foreign Secretary Jack Straw flew out from London to see the damage and offer support. At one point his media team were so keen on him giving interviews to all the journalists covering the story that I had to almost drag him out of the press room to talk to the waiting consulate staff.

Some of us were also staying at the Intercontinental, but that didn't last long. At midnight on 21 November, two counter-terrorism experts brought me a laptop with enough sensitive intelligence suggesting that a further attack was possible to leave me with no choice but to get everyone out of bed and decamp to yet another hotel – this time the Hilton. We had by then moved the office into the recently vacated US Consulate, which was nearby, while we decided what to do next. Prime Minister Erdoğan visited and spoke to me, in all the chaos, of his concern for our staff, his deep sorrow at what had happened, and his hope that we wouldn't give in to terrorism by advising travellers to keep away from the UEFA Champions League match between local side Galatasaray and Italian giants Juventus due to be played in Istanbul the following week. (We were supportive of Turkey and its efforts to counter terrorism but UEFA decided to postpone the game anyway.)

Already, our security people were advising that the US building was so overlooked, and so vulnerable from a security perspective (the reason why it had been vacated by the Americans themselves), that we shouldn't stay. So off we went again, this time setting up shop on a semi-permanent basis in the Hilton until, more than a year later, the offices of Pera House were again fit for habitation.

At the Hilton, sport did manage to provide some respite for our battered team. Saturday, 22 November, was the date of the Rugby World Cup final, played in Sydney between

England and Australia. England won, just, by 20 points to 17, thanks to a drop goal scored by Jonny Wilkinson in the final minute of extra time. Huge celebrations ensued (except among the Australians watching). But each time I had looked in at the bar where the match was being shown, Australia scored, so I was told firmly by my staff to leave and not come back until the game was over.

Susie had arrived, having flown straight back from Washington, and joined me visiting staff who were injured and talking to bereaved families. For London, tracking down and visiting any British subjects who might have been injured was the highest priority. We found one, who had been visiting the consulate to help his Turkish fiancée get a visa. She, tragically, was one of the fatalities. I found him, not too badly injured, at the American Hospital. It later dawned on us both that if the blast had taken place three days earlier, both Susie and I would probably have died since I was sitting at exactly that time with Roger in his office and she was close by waiting for us to finish our meeting.

When Susie and I returned to Ankara a week after the bombing, I asked two of my senior and most trusted colleagues – David Fitton, my deputy, and Dominic Clissold, senior management officer – to move to Istanbul to take charge of the consulate team while new, permanent staff were chosen. They stayed five months and, together with the Istanbul team, did a remarkable job of getting the place back to business in the most difficult conditions.

There were times when it seemed as though Pera House was cursed. It had been built in the 1850s following the destruction of the previous building by a fire and was itself badly damaged by another fire in 1870. The house was duly repaired and served as the British Embassy until the late 1920s when all foreign embassies had to move to Ankara following Atatürk's decision to move the capital of the new Turkish Republic there in 1926. For a few years, envoys who couldn't bear the idea of leaving the splendour of Istanbul for a small, isolated town in central Anatolia stayed on in the old Ottoman capital. But they were no longer accredited as envoys to the Sublime Porte – the clumsy English rendering of the French translation – *la Porte Sublime* – of Bab-e Ali, the original name of the Imperial Gateway into the Topkapı Palace in Istanbul, which became synonymous with the central government of the Ottoman Empire.

Physically, Pera House survived largely unscathed until May 2000, when it again suffered severe damage from a major fire, and the water used to put it out, during a lengthy period of refurbishment. The repairs were nearly complete by the time of the terrorist outrage of 20 November 2003.

That event, of course, seriously set back the process, but led to even greater determination in London to get the job done, and to show that the terrorists hadn't achieved anything. Enough progress had been made by October 2004 for The Prince of Wales to preside over the official reopening.

Throughout, there was lengthy debate about whether to restore the building to its role of consulate general with a suite of rooms for the ambassador to use for entertaining, given that Istanbul remained by far the most important city in the country, or make it into a hub for the issue of passports and visas and the coordination of our regional commercial effort. In the usual way, a compromise was reached which left the consul-general with a dedicated apartment, allowed Susie and me to continue to use the house's fine rooms for representational work, reminding the movers and shakers of Istanbul that British diplomacy was alive and well, caused a major new visa section to be built in the grounds and our commercial operation in Istanbul to become an increasingly important regional hub.

Inevitably, questions were asked about the cost. Some creative minds in the finance department back in London thought they saw an opportunity in the two magnificent chandeliers which hung in the Pera House ballroom. Why not sell them to help offset the huge repair bill? The chandeliers were indeed special. They had been on the way to the Tsar of Russia as a gift from Queen Victoria when the Crimean War broke out in 1853. Since Pera House was just being fitted out and was in need of something special in the ballroom, they were unloaded in Istanbul and installed – as if made for the purpose.

Removing them, I felt, would have been an act of vandalism. I discovered that insurers had put a value of some £750,000 on the pair but was convinced that no one would pay that much. So I asked for a market valuation, which produced an estimate of around a third of that. The finance department let the matter drop, and the chandeliers are still hanging from the ballroom ceiling, in all their glory.

At the end of May 2005, sensing that many friends around the world had heard about but knew little of Istanbul, we invited almost a hundred of them to join us for an Istanbul weekend. As part of the programme, we organized a charity ball at the newly reopened Pera House and held an auction to raise funds for a trust to enable the children of those who had lost their lives in the terrorist attack to make a study visit, when they were old enough and ready, to the UK. A Liverpool FC shirt, signed by all the members of the team who had dramatically defeated AC Milan in the final of the Champions League in Istanbul a few days earlier, went for €11,000.

Back in Ankara, life had to go on. The Annan Plan was still firmly on our agenda. With the role of the UN secretary general as filler-in of the gaps agreed, and Special Representative Alvaro de Soto briskly shuttling between Ankara, Athens and Nicosia, good progress was made – enough for it to be worth Kofi Annan's while to take all the parties off to a mountain retreat at Bürgenstock in Switzerland in March 2004 for the final stage of the negotiations. The British, Americans and European Commission all sent delegations. Remarkably, agreement was eventually reached that a final, fifth version of the Annan Plan would be put to the Greek and Turkish Cypriot communities for their approval in twin referenda.

Despite having put his name to the deal, President Tassos Papadopoulos of Cyprus began to campaign against the Bürgenstock outcome as soon as he got home. He even denied EU commissioner for enlargement, Günter Verheugen, the opportunity to appear on Cypriot television to make the case for a Yes vote. The Turks, meanwhile, supported the Annan Plan and effectively marginalized Denktaş, the president of the 'Turkish Republic of Northern Cyprus', who finally realized that, with the full apparatus of the Turkish state lined up behind a settlement, he could no longer stand in its way.

On 24 April 2004, just a week before Cyprus and the nine other accession states were due to join the EU, the two referenda took place. The Greek Cypriots voted almost three to one against the Annan Plan, and the Turkish Cypriots only a little less decisively in favour. On 26 April, the foreign ministers of the EU expressed their regret that the Annan Plan had not been approved but concluded that Cyprus would nonetheless join the EU. They promised to take measures which would end the economic isolation of the Turkish Cypriots in the north, so that they were not to be punished for the lack of a settlement.

For years previously, the Turks had asked us – as we pressed them to engage with the secretary general – what would happen if the plan was approved by the Turkish Cypriots and rejected by the Greek Cypriots. The Turkish side had been considered the foot-draggers for so long that no one had given serious thought to the possibility. So the negotiators replied that they would simply do their best to persuade the Greek Cypriots to support a settlement, and to ensure that the Turkish side did not suffer the consequences if the process failed through no fault of theirs.

We had, of course, repeatedly told the Turks that, if they left it too late, it would be impossible to deliver a settlement in time to ensure that it was a reunited Cyprus that joined the EU. But they were understandably resentful that, after they had finally done the right thing, the other side had been allowed to sabotage the process and still be rewarded with unconditional membership of the EU.

It was an outcome which ensured that the Greek Cypriots would never again feel under any real pressure to make the compromises necessary to achieve a settlement. In the following years, whenever they came under pressure to make a concession, or complained about Turkish behaviour, they were always able to appeal to the concept of member state solidarity against a third party – Turkey.

Once Cyprus was in the EU, the rules of the game as well as the politics changed. The Greek Cypriots were disinclined to do anything to help the Turkish Cypriots out of their isolation. Instead, pressure grew on the Turkish side to normalize relations with the (Greek) Republic of Cyprus, and to recognize it. Turkey was in any case required to extend the provisions of its Customs Union with the EU (something it had refused to do since the collapse of the original 1960 power-sharing agreement) to the new member states, including Cyprus.

In practice, this meant opening Turkish ports and aerospace to Greek Cypriot shipping and aircraft, which Ankara was loath to do for two reasons. First, the Greek Cypriots in the south refused to trade direct with the Turkish Cypriots in the north, except to the very limited extent provided by what was known as the Green Line Regulation. Second, the Turks worried that extending the provisions of the Customs Union to Cyprus by signing a Protocol to the 1963 Ankara Agreement creating an association between Turkey and the EU would itself amount to recognizing the legitimacy of the Greek Cypriot state.

Despite the continuing focus on Turkey's EU ambitions, and the unresolved complications of the Cyprus dispute, other international issues continued to dominate the headlines. In June 2004 it was Turkey's turn to host the regular NATO summit, which took place in Istanbul. The alliance's involvement in Afghanistan was again on the agenda. But events in Iraq became the dominant theme as the transfer of sovereignty from the occupying US-led coalition was brought forward a couple of days to the first day of the summit, in an effort to avoid further bloodshed. President George W. Bush and Tony Blair had a torrid time at the press conference they held in the margins of the summit: Adam Boulton of Sky News opened the questioning by asking Blair if he was going to resign. I told Blair afterwards that Bush had been lucky to have him on the podium next to him as explainer-in-chief. Characteristically, Blair replied 'I'm just a better bullshitter than he is.'

Events in Iraq remained a major preoccupation in Turkey as well as in London and Washington, as the Turks kept a number of small military units in the north – partly to keep an eye on moves towards Kurdish independence and partly because Turkey's indigenous Kurdish terrorist group, the PKK, had camps in the rugged, inaccessible terrain of the Qandil mountains just across the border in northern Iraq.

But Cyprus and the EU were never far from the front of our minds. Having backed the Annan Plan and done a reasonable amount of domestic reform, Turkey was hoping that the December 2004 European Council would agree on a date for the opening of its own accession negotiations. As December approached, my EU colleagues and I continued to press the Turkish authorities to maintain the momentum of reform to show that Turkey was meeting what were known as the Copenhagen political criteria. We also pressed them, again, to sign the Protocol to the 1963 Ankara Agreement.

Just a week before the European Council, I told Erdoğan that, in addition to making further progress on religious freedoms, judicial reform, and freedom of expression, he simply had to commit to signing the Ankara Protocol. Erdoğan himself was non-committal: he just complained – as he did for years afterwards – that I'd given him bad advice to back the Annan Plan. The Greek Cypriots had reneged on the deal, as he'd suspected they would, and joined the EU regardless. Why should Turkey now make the next move?

I said then, and on many later occasions, that as much as we regretted the decision of the Greek Cypriots to reject the Annan Plan, there would have been no chance of getting Turkey's membership negotiations with the EU started if it hadn't supported the Cyprus settlement. I believed it then, and I believe it now. In the background, other ministers continued to tell me that the politics wouldn't allow Erdoğan to do more on the reform front while the Europeans continued to back the Republic of Cyprus.

Given the importance of the Turkey dossier, No 10 decided I should travel to Brussels with Prime Minister Blair and his party for the European Council. Soon after we took off from London's military airfield, RAF Northolt, Blair told me he was puzzled. The Turks had won, and were going to get their date. So what was the problem?

I explained that the date was indeed the big prize. But there was a continuing problem over conditionality. The Commission's regular report of 6 October 2004 had concluded that Turkey 'sufficiently met' the political criteria for the opening of negotiations but the Turks had yet to sign the Protocol to the Ankara Agreement.

Other members of the party were relaxed, arguing that

the Turks had nowhere else to go. I warned that a firm line from the Dutch presidency of the European Council on signing the Ankara Protocol could drive Erdoğan into a corner. I reminded the prime minister of why, in my view, the collapse of negotiations between Turkey and the EU would be serious, causing damage to UK interests in the region, to stability and to the prospects for maintaining the momentum of reform and modernization in Turkey.

Arriving in Brussels on the afternoon of 17 December, we went straight to see Erdoğan. The UK was, after all, the principal advocate of getting the negotiations with Turkey started. The meeting went reasonably well. Erdoğan set out his concerns, and Blair promised to do what he could with his colleagues. In their usual way, heads of government and foreign ministers then disappeared for their respective dinners. I went to see how the Turkish delegation were getting on in their hotel, only to be told – with a great deal of emotion – that the current texts were unacceptable. I explained equally firmly why they wouldn't get any better.

The heads of government spent much of their dinner discussing enlargement of the EU in general, and the Turkish application in particular. Various formulations were tried, and the Dutch presidency eventually produced a new text in the early hours of 18 December which was presented to the Turks just before breakfast. As it stood, they replied, the language was unacceptable because they believed they were being asked, in effect, to commit to recognizing the (Greek) Republic of Cyprus even if there was no political settlement. To them, this was tantamount to rewarding the Greek Cypriots for torpedoing the Annan Plan and ensuring they would never be under any pressure to reach a solution.

Blair immediately convened with a group of five other heads of government who could make a difference, and helped the Dutch presidency present a reworked formulation to Erdoğan. But at the critical moment the Dutch foreign minister explained that the presidency would be making an additional, unilateral statement setting out a further condition which the Turkish side would have to meet in advance of accession negotiations opening the following year.

Erdoğan believed he was being deceived, and decided he'd had enough. If that was what the EU was all about, he told his close advisers, then the Europeans could keep it. And their Christian club. He was going to the airport.

Friends in the Erdoğan team alerted me by text message, and in the corridors of the Council building. (One Turkish paper ran the headline 'Come quickly, Peter' after being briefed by a member of the Erdoğan team on what had happened.) I told them it would be disastrous if Erdoğan walked out in a huff. Would it help if Blair came and talked to him? Egemen Bağis, Erdoğan's interpreter and one of his advisers, thought there was no point: his prime minister was too upset. But he would ask. Bağis returned, with the message that it was contrary to Turkish principles of hospitality not to open the door if a guest came knocking: Erdoğan would be glad to see the prime minister if he wanted to talk.

At that moment, Blair – whom I had already alerted – came along the corridor. In we went. Over the next forty-five minutes, during which Blair and Erdoğan were joined by German chancellor Gerhard Schroeder, Italian prime minister Silvio Berlusconi and eventually Bernard Bot, the Dutch foreign minister, Blair went through Erdoğan's concerns and persuaded the other heads to join him in asserting that a commitment by the Turkish government to sign the Ankara Protocol was not tantamount to recognition of the Republic of Cyprus. He then declared this in public at his press conference, as did French president Jacques Chirac and a number of others.

After a further wrangle over which member of the Turkish government should actually sign the key document – they chose Beşir Atalay, a state minister – the deed was done and the European Council agreed that formal negotiations would open during the British presidency of the Council on 3 October 2005.

The Turks didn't enjoy the experience. As we left the Council building, Ahmet Davutoğlu, Erdoğan's foreign policy adviser and later foreign and prime minister – but by 2020 one of his principal political opponents – told me we hadn't done enough to defend Turkey's interests. If this was the EU, he wasn't sure he wanted to be part of it. I replied that, if that was his government's view, I wasn't sure the British government would be inclined to continue fighting its corner.

The sad reality was that the Brussels European Council convinced a lot of people on the Turkish side that the EU would never allow Turkey in, and fuelled their resentment that Turkey and the Turkish Cypriots were being continuously punished for the decision of the Greek Cypriots to reject the Annan Plan back in the spring. We would hear more of this. On the EU side, those who had always thought letting in Turkey was a bridge too far returned home convinced they were right.

9

Turkey and Europe (2005–6)

In the early months of 2005, there were signs that Erdoğan was looking for an alternative to opening negotiations with the EU – a process in which Turkish public opinion was beginning to lose faith. His failure to appoint a chief negotiator was widely seen as a lack of interest. So was the lack of haste with which his government handled six outstanding pieces of legislation which the European Council said it had to enact if accession negotiations were to begin on 3 October.

Erdoğan showed more interest in touring the countries which had been victims of the tsunami which struck the Pacific Rim with devastating effect just after Christmas 2004, and in visiting Africa and Central Asian republics. Normal life also continued for the rest of us. The ninetieth anniversary of the ill-fated Gallipoli landings fell on 25 April 2005; that day in 1915 marked the start of an eight-month campaign during which British and Commonwealth forces failed to take control of the Dardanelles strait and eventually withdrew at a cost of half a million casualties on both sides, including an estimated 46,000 Allied and 65,000 Turkish fatalities. It was a campaign of which the mistakes, as with the Norway campaign in May 1940, could easily have destroyed the political career of its principal architect, Winston Churchill – but fortunately didn't.

Every year a series of commemorative ceremonies was held at Gallipoli on behalf of the different nations which had been engaged there. The ceremonies always began with a dawn service organized by the Australians and New Zealanders in memory of the soldiers of the Australian and New Zealand Army Corps (ANZAC) who fought so bravely and effectively during the campaign – like the soldiers of so many other countries of the then British empire, in a European war of which they knew little and for which they had no responsibility. For the ninetieth anniversary of the Gallipoli landings, the British delegation was led by The Prince of Wales. Susie and I met him before dawn, as he came ashore from a Royal Navy frigate – at Suvla Bay where General Ian Hamilton's allied forces were supposed to have landed on 6 August 1915 in a failed attempt to relieve the ANZACs. Landing in the wrong place, and equipped with the wrong maps, the allies faced steep cliffs and gullies and determined, well-dug-in Turkish defenders.

During the recce visit, the political staff of the New Zealand prime minister Helen Clark had tried to argue that any speaking role for HRH would be met by hostility from the crowd, given the abiding sense of resentment at the role of Great Britain in leading so many young ANZACs to an early death. I, of course, couldn't accept that the heir to the throne of the United Kingdom, Australia and New Zealand should be the only visiting dignitary not to take part in the ceremony. We agreed that he would speak last, after the politicians and military chiefs. In the event, his was the only reading applauded – enthusiastically – by the 25,000 young people, largely backpackers from Australia and New Zealand, who had come to Gallipoli for the occasion. The political staff had misread the public mood.

Meanwhile, with Prime Minister Erdoğan apparently disengaged, Turkish public opinion was becoming less convinced that membership of the EU was ever going to happen. On one occasion I found myself speaking to a packed auditorium at the University of Erzurum in eastern Turkey about the importance of making a success of the accession negotiations. At the end of the Q&A session, a very articulate student shouted from the back that I should stop lying about Turkey's European prospects since I must know, as she knew, that there was no chance of Turkey ever being admitted. Massive applause.

Nor were the Europeans showing much enthusiasm for giving effect to the December Council conclusions. The tide of EU enlargement – particularly in respect of Turkish accession – had begun to ebb. The referenda in the Netherlands and France in May and June 2005, respectively, were ostensibly about the new Constitutional Treaty. But the resounding rejection of it in both countries reflected growing dissatisfaction across the EU with how the union was developing, and with the domestic performance of several EU governments. (As I and others opposed to the UK leaving the EU argued during the Brexit campaign in 2016, referenda are crude political instruments which rarely address just the question on the ballot paper.)

By June, the one outstanding requirement for the Turks was to sign the Ankara Protocol. Having obtained public reassurance from several heads of government at the December Council six months earlier that signing did not amount to recognition of the Republic of Cyprus, the Turks had given an unconditional commitment to do so.

In hindsight, they should have signed immediately after the Council, while the momentum was with them and public opinion was feeling positive about the EU. During the spring of 2005, several member states – not least the UK – encouraged them to get on with it, using the cover of the assurances they had been given back in December. But MFA officials advised Turkish ministers that they should only do so if they also formally reserved their position on recognizing Cyprus. The MFA duly began work on a declaration placing the Turkish position on record.

In the meantime, the new Luxembourg presidency of the Council tried to move ahead with implementing the promise which foreign ministers had given in April 2004, just after the Greek Cypriot rejection of the Annan Plan, to agree measures ending the economic isolation of the Turkish Cypriots. These plans centred on twin regulations, one covering aid and the other trade, which would develop economic links between Northern Cyprus and the EU. The Greek Cypriots didn't want either – particularly the trade regulation, which they argued would discourage the Turkish Cypriots from working for a comprehensive settlement (a bit rich, as the Turks pointed out, given that it was the Turkish Cypriots, not the Greek Cypriots, who had voted in favour of the Annan Plan).

The Luxembourgers worked up a package including the two regulations but also the reopening of the port of Varosha

– a Greek Cypriot resort which had been a ghost town since 1974 – and placing the Turkish Cypriot port of Famagusta under international control. But the details were never properly explained to the Turkish side, and the Turks remained suspicious since the architect of the scheme appeared to be the Luxembourg ambassador to Greece. The plan quickly ran into the sand, so everyone decided to leave the knotty Cyprus issues for the UK presidency of the European Council beginning on 1 July.

Shortly after it started, we had another reminder of the terrorist threat – not just to Turkish citizens but also to foreigners holidaying in coastal areas of Turkey. On 16 July 2005, a small pipe bomb placed on a shuttle bus in the resort of Kuşadası killed five people, including a British girl, Helen Bennett, and injured a dozen more, among them five more Britons. I went straight there with my consular team to help the victims and their families. The media no doubt expected it, but one of the reasons why we have diplomats abroad is to look after British citizens in difficulty, so there was never any question in my mind that we needed to be on the spot, and quickly, when disaster struck. On this occasion the finger of suspicion pointed at the PKK, though the organization's spokesman denied responsibility.

Back on the political front, the Turkish side became increasingly determined – and publicly committed – to a national declaration to its signature of the Ankara Protocol. When Erdoğan had breakfast with Tony Blair in Downing Street on 27 July, Blair and Jack Straw urged him and Foreign Minister Gül not to allow the issue further to complicate relations with member states. It was agreed that the UK presidency and the Turkish government would work together, informally, to ensure they came up with a sensible text. The UK side warned that the wrong declaration would make it even more difficult to agree the negotiating framework (NF) – a key document which had to be agreed by all twenty-five member states – before the negotiations proper could start on 3 October.

The Turks asked me to fly back to Ankara with Erdoğan and Gül, so I abandoned my plan to spend an extra day in London and joined them on their official aircraft. Our consultations began before we had even left UK airspace, with Gül insisting – in the nicest possible way – on the key negotiating role which I, as the British government's and the EU presidency's representative in Ankara, would have to play. After three days of almost continuous consultation, the Turks signed the Ankara Protocol, in the form of an Exchange of Letters between the UK and Turkish ambassadors in Brussels, attaching to it the least damaging declaration on non-recognition of Cyprus which I had been able to get the MFA to agree.

As we had warned Ankara, the UK presidency had to issue a statement in reply on behalf of the twenty-five member states, reiterating the EU's position on the status of the Republic of Cyprus. We hoped that a quick, firm response by the presidency would diminish the pressure from other member states for a more damaging counter-declaration.

It quickly became clear that more would be needed, particularly in terms of Turkish implementation of the Ankara Protocol. We nonetheless all disappeared for our August summer holidays feeling that something useful had been achieved, and hoping that the run-up to the formal opening of Turkish accession negotiations on 3 October would not be too eventful. Turkish colleagues were warm in their messages of appreciation for the UK's efforts.

The calm didn't last long. On 2 August, in a television interview covering a range of foreign policy issues, the new French prime minister, Dominique de Villepin, declared that it would not be possible to open EU membership negotiations with a candidate country which did not recognize one of the member states.*

The Turkish reaction was restrained, and efforts were made in the following weeks to bring the French position back from this potential deal-breaker. After all, Villepin's statement was seriously at odds with the position of President Chirac, which was that the EU should honour the commitments it had given Turkey to start negotiations on 3 October.

In fact, the French position over the following weeks became a good deal more conciliatory towards Turkey. Not surprisingly, however, Villepin's statement was picked up by Greeks and Greek Cypriots, whose position on the inclusion of 'recognition' language in the EU's counter-declaration became significantly harder.

Trouble also appeared from a different direction. Despite having signed the Ankara Protocol on 29 July, and made clear that Turkey would implement its commitments, Foreign Minister Gül had begun to say that implementation of those obligations would not include opening Turkey's ports

---

* Villepin lacked neither intellect nor self-confidence. A fellow guest at the banquet which The Queen gave in honour of President Chirac in 2004 remarked to a friend afterwards: 'I have just had the honour of dining with the cleverest man in France and the country's next president.' 'Really?' came the reply. 'How do you know?' 'Because he told me.'

and airports to Greek Cypriot shipping and aircraft. This made Greeks and Greek Cypriots – supported by a number of other member states – even more determined to ensure that the EU's counter-declaration included firm language monitoring Turkey's implementation of its obligations, with warnings that failure to comply would have an effect on accession negotiations.

By the time foreign ministers gathered in early September 2005 for their traditional informal weekend – this time hosted by Jack Straw at Celtic Manor, a golfing resort near Newport in South Wales – the Turkish side was becoming distinctly edgy. As foreign minister of a candidate country, Gül was invited to Celtic Manor too. He asked me to join him on the flight from Ankara, which gave me plenty of opportunity to warn him that we were finding it difficult to hold the line on some issues of sensitivity for the Turkish side; and that the 'R' word – recognition of the Republic of Cyprus – would have to feature somewhere in the meeting's conclusions.

I also told Gül that his public remarks about refusing to open Turkish ports and airports to Greek Cypriot vessels were unhelpful, and likely to produce even tougher language from the member states on the need for Turkey to implement its Customs Union obligations in full. My strong advice was that he should say as little as possible about how he intended to 'implement', so that any subsequent complaint could be dealt with through normal dispute settlement mechanisms, and not be a barrier to the opening of accession negotiations.

Not for the first time, I also talked Gül through the need to show that Turkey was continuing with its domestic reform programme. I showed him articles from that morning's international press headlining the decision of a Turkish public prosecutor to seek the conviction of the world-renowned novelist Orhan Pamuk for having declared that a million and a half Armenians were slaughtered by the Ottomans in 1915 – without even using the term 'genocide', to which Turkey always took exception.

This was evidence, I argued, that further changes to the Turkish penal code were necessary to guarantee freedom of expression. There was an urgent need to reform the infamous Article 301, which made it a crime to denigrate Turkishness, the Turkish nation or Turkish government institutions. An early, firm commitment from Gül to do so, I argued, would help mitigate the damage to Turkey's reputation.

Gül said this was impossible. Only after the courts had completed their proceedings against Pamuk would the government be able to take a view. I said this would take months, and be hugely damaging. The case against Pamuk dragged on until early summer 2006 when he was finally acquitted; but the inadequacies of Article 301 were laid bare by the separate conviction of an Armenian writer, Hrant Dink, for saying that what had happened to the Armenians caused 'poisoned blood' to run in the veins of Turkish citizens. Dink was murdered two years later by a 17-year-old Turkish nationalist who was strongly suspected of having close links to the police and possibly the military.

Gül took my unsolicited advice in good part. He eventually made a move on Article 301, but it remains intact and still outlaws denigration of the Turkish nation, state, parliament or government.

Gül was very upset when, shortly after our arrival in South Wales, he discovered that the UK had already distributed a draft counter-declaration which was not to his liking. After I had – on instruction – confirmed that we were not giving the text to the media, the MFA's director general for Europe, Volkan Bozkır, told me the Turks had got their copy from a Turkish journalist.

Stranded, like the Turkish delegation, at a hotel 20 miles from the conference centre, I was unable to sort out the muddle directly with my presidency colleagues at Celtic Manor. But at least I had the thrill of sharing the hotel elevator with England footballers David Beckham, Wayne Rooney and Phil Neville, who were in town for a World Cup qualifier against Wales the next day.

The following morning, I advised Gül to leave his UK and other counterparts in no doubt about the real Turkish bottom lines and to find out what theirs were. Gül didn't need much convincing. Immediately before lunch, he had forty minutes with the French foreign minister, Philippe Douste-Blazy, during which he failed to obtain any explanation of why Villepin had suddenly decided, a month earlier, that Turkish recognition of the Republic of Cyprus was an issue of major national importance for France.

On his way to the dining room, I suggested to Gül that he join in the scheduled discussion of something called the Broader Middle and Near East Initiative and explain some of the valuable contributions which Turkey was making to regional understanding, for example by brokering the first-ever meeting (in Istanbul) between the foreign ministers of Israel and Pakistan.

Gül replied that he wasn't inclined to say anything: if the EU wasn't interested in Turkey's fundamental interests, why should he contribute to the collective deliberations of the twenty-five? Even Gül wasn't immune to the Turkish tendency to prioritize national dignity over the advantages of showing others how much their country had to offer.

In fact, he spoke about the Turkish attitude towards Iran's nuclear weapons programme. Some in Ankara had wanted him to withhold Turkish support for EU demands that Iran suspend its enrichment programme. Gül refused, but the under-secretary at the MFA, Ali Tuygan, told me it had been a difficult moment.

On the flight back to Ankara, I found Gül in better humour. He felt that he had had a reasonable hearing from the dozen or so foreign ministers he'd met. He also felt – rightly, as it turned out – that he had got Straw to understand the true depth of his concerns at what was being asked of Turkey.

In Brussels, however, the debate didn't get any easier. As presidency, the UK had made clear to everyone that we wanted to see all the documents relevant to the opening of negotiations with Turkey on 3 October agreed well in advance. It took seven meetings of the Committee of Permanent Representatives to finalize all the texts, including the draft of the Negotiating Framework (NF), which would serve as the roadmap for negotiations between Turkey and the EU for the next decade.

The Turkish side was comforted by our success in seeing off attempts by France and Cyprus, supported by Greece and others, to link Turkish recognition of Cyprus to the opening of accession negotiations. The Turks were also glad of the assurance that those issues which had been addressed in the counter-declaration would not be taken up again in the discussion of the NF.

From the UK's perspective, getting the NF endorsed by twenty-four of the twenty-five member states – with only Austria holding out for further changes – was something of a triumph. However, it was not enough to stop Turkish officials grumbling later about minor additional changes made to the draft before it was signed off by EU foreign ministers in New York on 21 September.

As 3 October approached, the principal difficulty revolved around how to get the Austrians back into line. They wanted language in the NF making clear that something less than full membership was one of the possible outcomes of the negotiations with Turkey; firmer references to the 'absorptive capacity' of the EU being a factor which would have to be considered before any decision was taken to admit Turkey; and equal burden-sharing language about the eventual cost of any further enlargement of the EU. All were positions which we felt at the time were unduly obstructive; but twelve years later in 2016, when EU governments were looking afresh at Turkey's membership prospects in the middle of the largest migration crisis Europe had ever known, some of the old Austrian arguments struck me as less absurd.

On Sunday, 2 October, foreign ministers gathered in Luxembourg for dinner before the next day's General Affairs Council. Turkey dominated discussion. Several foreign ministers – Straw in the lead – piled on the pressure for an agreement. The Austrians found themselves isolated, but at least went along with language reiterating that the shared objective of the negotiations was accession.

A new text reflecting discussion over dinner, and numerous bilateral meetings, was sent to me overnight in Ankara, in advance of the opening of the Council meeting at 10 a.m.

on Monday, 3 October. I went down to the foreign ministry as soon as they opened for business, and was taken straight in to see Gül by Under-Secretary Tuygan. I explained that we thought there were the makings of a deal if we could offer the Austrians something on the need for negotiations with Turkey to take account of the union's absorptive capacity. Straw wanted to discuss the latest text with Gül before resuming discussions with his fellow foreign ministers.

Gül rejected the text out of hand. In fact, the biggest obstacle for him had now become language in paragraph 5, which the Turks feared would oblige them to stop blocking Cypriot membership of international organizations, including NATO. Negotiations, he said, were over; the UK presidency should stop trying to split the difference on alternatives to full membership, absorption capacity and so on. Gül was convinced that the Turks had somehow been hoodwinked by fresh changes made to the NF (even though Turkish officials had known about them at the time).

I asked him to let me make one last try. Outside in the car park, I called Jack Straw. We agreed that it was worth another effort, but that the chances of bringing Gül back on board were slim. Straw called Gül and pressed him to show some flexibility. Gül suggested that there might possibly be a deal if the EU could move on paragraph 5. In the early afternoon I sent round a new text with improvements to the opening paragraphs which Straw had negotiated with the Austrians, and a short 'statement by the Council' qualifying the implications of the infamous paragraph 5 (now paragraph 7) language on international organizations.

Separately, I put Erdoğan and his close advisers in the picture. The prime minister and his party were travelling back to Ankara from an AKP gathering out of town – I tracked them down (one of the party told me) eating melons with some villagers on the outskirts of the spa town of Kızılcahamam.

The Turkish team asked me to take the latest language round to AKP headquarters in the early evening. Gül and Economy Minister Babacan were there, accompanied by a dozen senior MFA, prime ministry, AKP and other officials. Erdoğan, I was told, would appear shortly. I sensed we were close to agreement when the phone in my pocket rang. I left the room. John Grant, our ambassador to the EU, was on the line. The status of the language qualifying paragraph 7 had again changed: the Cypriots would not accept a 'statement by the Council' but only a Presidency Statement 'with the consent of the Council'.

I went back into the room and broke the bad news. Gül declared that the game was over. Others round the table agreed. Gül explained that highly sceptical group leaders within the AKP had been briefed about the earlier formulation: no further changes, or concessions to the Cypriots, could be contemplated.

Straw told me on the telephone that it sounded as though we really had reached the end of our rope. He could do no more for the Turks. I asked him to give me a few more minutes: I hadn't yet put the arguments directly to Erdoğan. I went back into the room, where the prime minister had just joined the party, told him how far Straw, John Grant and the rest of the UK presidency team had moved other member states in the course of the day, and that there really was no scope for further change in Luxembourg. I offered the view that the minor change in the paragraph 7 language didn't warrant throwing away everything we had worked for over the previous three years.

Erdoğan, calm and fresher than the rest of the team, was non-committal. He wanted to talk to Tony Blair. This took a while to set up. While we waited, I did my best to press the big-picture arguments to those in the room. When they spoke, Blair was able to provide the political and legal assurances Erdoğan wanted. When he offered a minor further adjustment to the text, Erdoğan decided that he would settle after all for the version that Gül, Babacan and others had told me was unacceptable.

After Gül had briefed the unconvinced leader of the opposition, Deniz Baykal, over the telephone, he and the MFA party left for the airport – three hours after I had gone round to AKP headquarters with the presidency's 'final' offer. Erdoğan suggested I join them for the trip to Luxembourg. I declined, on the grounds that I thought I would be more use in Ankara, and went home for a drink.

When Gül arrived in Luxembourg, Straw embraced him warmly, despite some reticence on Gül's part because the foreign secretary had declined to soften his opening statement in one or two ways which the Turks had suggested. By now it was after midnight. But London was an hour behind, so the UK presidency concluded that we had after all met our objective of opening accession negotiations with Turkey on 3 October 2005.

Three days later, we gave a celebratory party at the residence for Turkish ministers, officials, journalists and our EU colleagues who had lived through the drama. Since we were in the middle of Ramadan, we made the party into an *iftar* – the evening meal Muslims eat when they have been fasting all day. We laid out a large buffet with all the usual ingredients. On the other side of the house, a bar served alcohol and more secular food for those who hadn't been fasting.

It was a curious mix, but the event we were celebrating – finally, the opening of accession negotiations – was powerful enough to bring everyone together and forget, for a moment, the differences between secularists and Islamists.

A few months later, as he said goodbye to FCO staff after five years in the job, Jack Straw said getting accession negotiations with Turkey started was the proudest achievement of his time as foreign secretary. He had worked extremely hard for the outcome – not least during the thirty hours of tortuous negotiations he conducted in Luxembourg on 2 and 3 October. When he and his wife, Alice, visited Istanbul for a private weekend with us the following June, ordinary Turks would come up to him in restaurants to thank him for his efforts. I was especially pleased to be able to arrange a private, late-night visit to Aya Sofya – the magnificent basilica originally built in the sixth century as the church of Haghia Sophia. Jack had paid many official visits to Istanbul but rarely had the chance to spend time appreciating its extraordinary cultural legacy.

A week after the opening of negotiations on 3 October, the leader of the House of Commons, Geoff Hoon, visited us in Istanbul for the annual Bosphorus Conference. I took him to call on the prime minister at his office in the Dolmabahçe Palace, on the shores of the Bosphorus. Erdoğan was in great form – I always found him more relaxed in his home town than when he was immersed in the politics of Ankara. Hoon asked about the events of the previous week and how Erdoğan had finally brought himself to accept the package on offer from the EU's foreign ministers. Erdoğan said he'd known as soon as he walked into the room at AKP headquarters that the negotiations were over. My face had said it all: he knew I had done what I could for Turkey and that there was 'no more blood in the stone'. Of course, he'd had to make the call to his friend Tony, both to show others who'd been screaming that the deal was over that he'd made a final effort, and to hear from Blair himself that he could not get a better deal.

All of us – Blair, Straw, myself and many other officials – had played our part. Ultimately, the outcome had been about respect, knowledge of the subject, relationships, credibility, persistence and knowing when and how to make the critical moves. Years later I came across a letter which Blair sent me at the end of the UK's six-month presidency of the European Council in December 2005. In it he wrote of 'the historic importance' of the decision to open accession negotiations with Turkey and how the outcome was 'a shining example of the value of effective bilateral diplomacy'. It certainly felt like a high point.

During the first half of 2006, the Turks did less than they should have done to build on the momentum created by the opening of negotiations. The pace of reform slowed. Nothing happened on judicial reform, or the promised changes to Article 301. Unpleasant, sporadic outbreaks of violence against Christians in the Trabzon area of the Black Sea and elsewhere fuelled tensions.

So did a resumption of terrorist attacks, apparently carried out by the PKK, in the south-east and in coastal areas frequented by foreign tourists. A bomb attack on one of the bastions of the secular establishment in Ankara, the

Constitutional Court, caused outrage, and much of the media decided the AKP were at least indirectly responsible after criticism of one of the court's decisions by Erdoğan.

Worst of all, just a few months after the negotiations began, it looked as though relations between Turkey and the EU were heading for the buffers because of the continuing refusal of the Turkish government to open its ports and airspace to Cypriot shipping and aircraft, as required by Turkey's membership of the Customs Union and the famous Ankara Protocol. The Association Council scheduled for 12 June 2006 might not, after all, permit the opening of even one chapter of the negotiations. In the event a little more time was bought. But the issue remained unresolved.

As the year wore on, Susie's and my attention began to focus on our departure from Ankara. Initially, I'd been sent to Turkey for three years. I stayed on for a fourth, primarily to see us through the UK presidency. By the late spring of 2006, my time was formally up. But the FCO was taking its time making senior ambassadorial appointments. First up was Paris, which was on the board's agenda in July.

I put my hat in the ring, knowing the country and the language well, with the feeling that this was a job I ought to be able to do well after Ankara. Perhaps unwisely, under pressure from London to make room for my successor, I agreed to leave in October in the hope that my future would by then have been decided. Just three weeks before our departure date, but five months before a new role was found for the incumbent in Paris, I finally heard we were off to France.

By then the December European Council was approaching, with accession negotiations with Turkey once again high on the agenda because of Turkey's failure to comply with its obligations towards Cyprus. Erdoğan asked Tony Blair to leave me in Turkey a bit longer. Blair replied, with a laugh, that he was sending me to a country where I would continue to look after Turkey's interests – a line which I sometimes felt, after I got to Paris, my Turkish friends interpreted a bit too literally.

I did my best to use my farewell meetings with the prime minister, Foreign Minister Gül, and Economy Minister and EU Chief Negotiator Babacan to press the case for continuing flexibility and reform.

But there was one other message which I was keen to get across. It was becoming increasingly clear that the tensions between the AKP and secularists – even businessmen who had been ready to give them the benefit of the doubt – were becoming acute. The AKP was putting its own people into key positions, not because of their competence but because of their loyalty and their Muslim beliefs. AKP municipalities were banning alcohol in public places – and not just during Ramadan. The AKP continued to favour entry into the secular higher education system of the graduates of İmam Hatep (Islamic) high schools, which had originally been encouraged by the military as a means of countering communism in the 1980s.

Most sensitive of all, the AKP were seen to be encouraging women and girls to wear Islamic dress – principally a headscarf known as the *turban*. This both offended the secularists, who saw it as counter to the legacy of Atatürk, and encouraged the fear that Turkey under the AKP was sliding down a slippery slope towards the kind of Islamic republic which they observed with such distaste in next-door Iran.

I talked to Turkish ministers about the need to reassure secularists that the AKP did not have a hidden Islamic agenda, and was not threatening their way of life. Gül firmly disagreed. For all the inclusiveness of his personality, and his readiness to understand other people's point of view, he could not accept that the AKP was a threat to the way of life of more secular Turks. For him, it was the other way around. It was the secularists, and the laws enacted under the 1982 constitution, which prevented his wife and his daughter from going to university and pursuing normal careers because they chose to cover their heads.

I persevered, noting that the propaganda attacks and accusations against the AKP were multiplying; and that there was talk once again of the military being secularism's last line of defence against the Islamization of Atatürk's secular republic. I believed Turkey had been better governed by the AKP than by any other government in recent times. But it needed to make a better job of protecting the secular democracy guaranteed by the constitution.

I noted that, as Gül had frequently reminded me, the rest of the Sunni Muslim world was watching with fascination as Turkey sought to reconcile the tensions within its society, and to make a success of its Western vocation without alienating its own, overwhelmingly Muslim, population. The AKP was hugely popular. But it had to show that it was a government of all Turks, not just a government of those with whom it felt comfortable, who funded the party and thought like the majority of the AKP's leaders.

I didn't make much impact. Some months later, in the spring of 2007 when I was getting settled into a new life in Paris, the same issue came to a head over the selection of Abdullah Gül to be president, in succession to the ultra-secular President Sezer.

Erdoğan's personal preference had been Defence Minister Vecdi Gönül. But the influential Speaker of the National Assembly, Bülent Arınç, nominated Gül – a move which set Erdoğan thinking about the real loyalties of some of his colleagues.

The military and other secularists grumbled that it would be intolerable for secular Turkey to have as president a prac-tising Muslim whose wife wore a headscarf, as Hayrünnisa Gül did. After the Constitutional Court – in a highly political judgement – ruled that the National Assembly vote giving Gül the job was invalid, Erdoğan called the bluff of his opponents, held a general election six months early and saw the AKP returned to power with an unprecedented increase in its share of the national vote (up from 34.5 per cent in November 2002 to 47.5 per cent in July 2007). He might not have been convinced that Gül was the right man for the presidency – though public opinion seemed convinced that he was – but he was not going to be told who the AKP could and could not nominate for the most prestigious position in the land.

There was some debate as to whether it was wise, so soon after taking on and defeating the secular establishment, for Gül to remain the AKP's candidate. He rang me in the middle of the campaign (Susie and I were back in Turkey on holiday) to explain why he had decided to do so; why the AKP supporters in the country wouldn't understand if he withdrew from the contest after such a resounding public confirmation of the AKP's decision to support him in the first place; and why it would be wrong to give way to pressure from the military and other elements of the 'deep state'.

He deserved the job. But the elevation of Gül to the presidency in August 2007 – with the generals subsequently boycotting social events at the palace where Hayrünnisa would be wearing her headscarf – was one of the developments that prompted the military and other secularists to encourage the prosecutor of the Constitutional Court in early 2008 to petition for the closing down of the AKP. The court also sought the banning of seventy-one of its members from national politics, on the grounds that they were undermining Turkey's secularism.

The case paralysed Turkish politics for months, complicated relations with the EU, and caused real concern about the survival of democracy in Turkey. In the event, the decision taken on 29 July, by just one vote among the eleven members of the Constitutional Court, to fine the AKP but not close it down caused a sigh of relief that was audible across Europe – and the Atlantic.

The AKP, once again, had dodged a bullet. Gül served out his seven-year term as president and remained in office until August 2014 when Erdoğan was elected to succeed him – under new rules, for a shorter five-year term but with the possibility of re-election for a second term. With hindsight, I am now clear that it was the stand-off over the presidency in 2007–8 that triggered the dubious court cases brought over the next few years against the military and their secular supporters by the Fethullah Gülen movement. The relationship of the AKP's former ally with the governing party was to have a baleful impact on Turkish democracy in the years to come.

10

So close and yet so far
(2006–16)

The nearly five years I spent as ambassador in Turkey were not entirely consumed with politics and Turkey's relations with the EU. We also found time to explore and enjoy the country, and to delve into its history. On a regional tour of central Anatolia, Susie and I once stopped off in Amasya, a small city which occupies a strategic position just south of the Black Sea. It was the birthplace of the Greek geographer-philosopher Strabo two thousand years earlier and of at least two Ottoman sultans. The curator of the local museum told us calmly that traces of no fewer than seventeen different civilisations spread over eight thousand years had been found in his city.

Who outside Turkey – or even inside it – is aware that the country's rich cultural heritage includes two hundred different theatres and amphitheatres from Graeco-Roman times? Or that it was at the parliament of the ancient Lycian city of Patara – recently excavated from beneath the sand dunes near Kaş on the Mediterranean coast – that the nation states of the Lycian League used to come together more than two thousand years ago in the earliest examples of pooled sovereignty the world has ever known?

There was scope too for cultural diplomacy. Turkey had never been very imaginative about the social integration of people with physical disabilities, so one of the initiatives we took at the embassy, with the help of the British Council and a creative Ankara theatre, was to arrange for the London-based CanDoCo dance company to give a performance demonstrating the extraordinary beauty of disabled dance. Explaining from the stage, off the cuff, why we had done this stretched my Turkish to its absolute limits. But the effect of the CanDoCo dancers was mesmerizing and we were left with the sense that attitudes in the Turkish capital towards disability had changed overnight.

Early in 2004 I had a visit from the artistic director of the Royal Academy in London. The Academy had a slot in 2005 for a major exhibition and was thinking of doing something around the theme of Turkey. But time was short, and so was money. Could I help? It seemed to me – and to Susie, who is an art historian – that this was a remarkable opportunity for Turkey to put itself on the map. With Pera House out of service because of the terrorist attack the previous November, we arranged a dinner for the president of the Royal Academy and potential donors in a special *köşk*, or royal pavilion, in the grounds of the Topkapi Museum, which was never normally open to the public. We used a local caterer, our own staff and our best silver.

The dinner, also attended by Turkey's minister of culture, was a rare and special event. It helped raise enough money for the Royal Academy to give a green light for the exhibition

Turks: A Journey of a Thousand Years, 600–1600, which turned out to be one of their most successful ever. So, a successful exercise in cultural diplomacy.

It also gave us some private pleasure. Much of the embassy's magnificent official silver, which we brought from Ankara, had been made by Garrard and Paul Storr in the early nineteenth century and was engraved 'British Embassy to the Porte'.* As our eminent guests dined off, and admired, the embassy's silver, we realized that this would have been the only time in history when it had been inside, rather than just accredited to, the Porte.

On another occasion, when I was preparing to leave Ankara for the opening of the new Museum of Modern Art in Istanbul, I took a call from the organizer and principal sponsor, my friend Bülent Eczacıbaşı. He wanted me to know that messages were being delivered at the opening on behalf of the German chancellor and French president, and he didn't want me to be taken by surprise. As Bülent no doubt intended, I jotted down a couple of paragraphs of congratulation and sent them to No 10 for approval by the prime minister so that we would not be outdone by the French and Germans. The machine was so well oiled, and helpful, that the private office turned round my request in a couple of hours, which gave me time to have the text translated into Turkish.

The new museum was housed in a converted waterside warehouse. A couple of thousand people were present for the opening ceremony, including most of the cabinet. Chirac's message was read out, in French, by a visiting parliamentarian.

---

* This was a compression of the usual 'Sublime Porte' (see Chapter 8, p. 142).

Chancellor Schroeder's message was delivered in heavily accented English. When it was my turn, I only had to read out the first sentence of Blair's message in Turkish to bring the house down. Afterwards, Turkish ministers complained good-naturedly that my short message had got far more applause than their lengthy speeches.

The point of the story is not to showcase my Turkish – which was well below the high standards set by most of my predecessors. It is to highlight the importance, in terms of public diplomacy, of making the effort to express yourself in the local language, and in the process show respect for the culture of the country where you are Britain's representative. That's why the quality of the FCO's language training is important, and why Foreign Secretary William Hague was right to re-establish its language centre after it had been closed down as a cost-cutting measure a few years earlier.

Shortly before the end of our time in Turkey, Erdoğan said he had never accepted hospitality from foreign diplomats in Istanbul but he would be glad to come for a meal at our rebuilt consulate, Pera House, if we wished to invite him. Quite a compliment, and in any case Susie and I had built a strong relationship with the Erdoğans. The prime minister and his wife came, together with their eldest daughter. We invited a few other members of the government and of the Erdoğans' entourage – but not all the hangers-on who called on the day to say that the prime minister wouldn't understand if they weren't also at the table.

Deliberately, we served wine while knowing that the Erdoğans themselves would decline. We had a most enjoyable evening, and in the course of it I made some progress towards convincing the prime minister that there was much more that could be done – through the involvement of the private sector, and perhaps even by the creation of a Turkish equivalent of the UK's National Trust – to take advantage of Turkey's extraordinarily diverse archaeological and cultural heritage. I saw it, I explained, as a source of prosperity for remote areas and a means of generating even greater international awareness of the country's importance to the history of numerous civilisations and religions.

Some months earlier, I had arranged a visit by The Prince of Wales to the historic town of Mardin, an archaeological gem in the south-eastern corner of the country where Turks, Arabs, Kurds and Nestorian Christians* all – more or less – happily coexisted. Mardin had never seen anything like it, and for a while enjoyed a huge boost in tourism.

In the following weeks, the prime minister mentioned our conversation in some of his speeches, and I enjoyed hearing the evidence that the message had got through.

Foundations set up by wealthy philanthropists like the Koç family (in particular) have already played, and continue to play, a vital role in financing the excavation and conservation of some of Turkey's more important historical sites like Aphrodisias, Sagalassos and Hierapolis. Overall, however, there was little take-up of Erdoğan's initiative, and some suspicion of foreign archaeological teams who were prepared to come at their own expense to explore important

---

* The Nestorian church holds that the incarnate Christ has two separate natures, one human and one divine. It is named after Nestorius, patriarch of Constantinople (428–31).

sites. But the potential is still there, exemplified by the new Museum Hotel, which opened in 2019 in Antakya (Antioch in classical times) directly above a museum that displays a superb series of Roman-era ruins and mosaics discovered during the building of the hotel, delaying its completion by several years and tens of millions of dollars.

In the summer of 2006, towards the end of our time in Turkey, Susie and I decided to spend a weekend travelling round Lake Van, the second largest inland sea in the world with a circumference of almost 270 miles. We flew to the city of Van and rented the only available car – an old Ford Focus with 87,000 miles on the clock. I took Susie to the remarkable tenth-century Armenian Church of the Holy Cross on the island of Akdamar, with its sumptuous stone carvings and frescoes, which I had first visited in the late 1980s. We drove to the top of Nemrut Dağı, one of two remarkable mountains in south-eastern Turkey bearing the same name – this one with several different lakes, some with hot springs, in its vast volcanic crater, which felt like something plucked from Sir Arthur Conan Doyle's *The Lost World*. We visited the ruins of the Armenian town of Ahlat, where beautiful cemeteries alongside Seljuk shrines and abandoned houses were all that was left of what had been a thriving community until the massacres and deportations of 1915. We visited the dramatic waterfalls of Muradiye, and we climbed to the top of Van Castle, an Ottoman structure dominating the city, built on the massive stone foundations of what had been a palace in Urartian times almost three millennia earlier.

Throughout, our battered rental car was followed by a gendarmerie team instructed to look after us. Very good company they were too, especially when we invited them to join us for meals. Normal operating procedures provided for a different team of gendarmes to take over responsibility for us each time we crossed a departmental boundary. Leaving our hotel in Ahlat on the Sunday morning, we realized that our escort had doubled down. I asked the Saturday team what had happened, knowing that they had had to drive over 60 miles home after seeing us safely to our lodgings. 'Well,' said the team leader, 'we had such a good time yesterday visiting places we've never seen before that we thought we'd spend our day off joining you for today's expedition'.

Before leaving Turkey in October 2006 there was just time to fit in the marriage of my daughter Laura to her fiancé, Simon King. She chose Istanbul, and Christ Church in the district of Beyoğlu, which had been built as a memorial to those who died in the Crimean War (1853–6) in which Britain and France had joined the Ottoman Empire in confronting Imperial Russia. The church had just been lovingly restored at the initiative of the local Anglican priest, Ian Sherwood. The reception was held at Tarabya, a few miles north of Istanbul on the shores of the Bosphorus, where the British Embassy still has eleven hectares of woodland and a couple of small houses on a plot gifted in the mid-nineteenth century by Sultan Abdülmecid – as was the land on which the Crimean church was built. It rained so hard that the day went down in family folklore as the monsoon wedding. But at least, for the only time in our lives, we saw dolphins in the Bosphorus when we took the guests for a cruise just before the skies opened.

In 2008, eighteen months after I had left Turkey and just a year after Gül had become president, a series of arrests and indictments began in response to an alleged plot by the 'deep state' to overthrow the democratically elected government. As part of the investigation into the *Ergenekon* plot, named after a mythical city in Turkish folklore, the next three years saw almost three hundred people imprisoned on the basis of evidence which had always looked questionable and was eventually deemed to be unsound by the Court of Appeal in April 2016.

The bulk of this evidence had in fact been fabricated, as a number of specialists testified at the time, only to be ignored by the courts (now believed to have been infiltrated by sympathizers of Fethullah Gülen). But dozens of senior military and media figures were jailed, including Turkey's recently retired chief of the general staff, General İlker Başbuğ, who was convicted, absurdly, of 'forming and directing a terrorist organisation'. Many liberals sided with the Islamists in concluding that, whether or not the evidence was sound, the military had for years been playing too much of a role in politics and needed to be reined in.

The 'plot' was largely the work of Gülen supporters whose 'peaceful' ways of promoting Islam did not exclude fabricating evidence and sending hundreds of innocent people to jail. Erdoğan and the AKP were not themselves behind it, but were at this stage still grateful for the help of the Gülen movement in seeing off the efforts of their opponents to delegitimize their party. Largely for this reason, they did less than they might have done to ensure that justice took its course, or to get the convictions overturned before they became an embarrassment – and had ruined the lives and careers of decent people. Erdoğan commented in a speech in 2009: 'These crimes violate our constitution and laws. Let the judiciary do their job.'

In parallel with *Ergenekon*, but a few years later, another plot known as *Balyoz* ('Sledgehammer') alleged that plans had been drawn up by the military to provoke either war with Greece or a *coup d'état*, providing echoes of the occasions in 1960, 1971 and 1980 when the army temporarily took power. Again, the allegations were nonsense, and included documents offered as evidence that were said to date from 2003, but had in fact been produced using Microsoft software not available before 2007. Hundreds were imprisoned, though the great majority of those convicted in 2012 were released in 2014 pending a fresh trial. They were finally acquitted in March 2015.

The rest of the world wasn't sure what to make of all this, though the European Commission expressed concern in 2010 at the number of *Ergenekon* cases being brought before the judiciary. Overall, Turkey continued to get credit for the remarkable economic recovery begun by Kemal Derviş and continued under the AKP as it focused on making a success of its bid to join the EU. By 2010, President Barack Obama was declaring Turkey to be a 'great Muslim democracy' and a role model for other countries in the region.

But by early 2012 divisions were beginning to appear between the AKP – Prime Minister Erdoğan in particular – and the Fethullah Gülen movement. The first visible split arose when Fethullah supporters in the judiciary tried to arrest Hakan Fidan, head of the national intelligence organization and a personal appointee and confidant of Erdoğan. The prime minister immediately had the law changed to grant Fidan immunity. For good measure, he shut down a number of the Gülen schools, which in Turkey – as in many other countries – were an important source of funds for the movement.

The most dramatic indication that the mood was changing came in May 2013 when demonstrations against the government in Gezi Park in Istanbul were brutally put down by the police. Fortunately for Erdoğan, who had become less and less inclined to brook criticism, President Abdullah Gül ordered the police to back off just before, at Ankara's behest, they were about to disperse the thousands of protesters with even greater violence.

This was a moment when even the well-off middle classes took to the streets and braved the tear gas to show their displeasure. It also marked the point when the split between Gülen and Erdoğan became irreparable. Immediately after the ending of the disturbances at Gezi Park, Gülen published an op-ed in the *Financial Times* criticizing the Erdoğan government for its autocratic tendencies and suppression of freedom of speech.

None of the plots and allegations was enough to prevent Erdoğan being elected president of the republic in August 2014 when Abdullah Gül's seven-year term ended. A few days before Gül stood down, I went to see the outgoing president to try and persuade him not to leave politics. Although the AKP had brought forward the closing date for applications to succeed Erdoğan as party leader, Gül still had the option of putting his hat in the ring.

He would have none of it. For a former president to run for the more junior position of prime minister struck him as inappropriate; in any case, he did not wish to be put in a position of potential confrontation with the new president.

Early in 2015 the Güls kindly invited Susie and me to tea at their temporary home in a guest house in the presidential complex at Tarabya. Susie and Hayrünnisa had become good friends over the years, partly because they were able to converse in Turkish (although Mrs Gül's English isn't at all bad). I again came away with the impression that the former president was not going to take any initiative of his own unless there was a split in the ranks of the AKP should the June 2015 elections not go well and the party need him to restore unity and credibility.

The early phases of the Arab Spring in 2011 had allowed Turkey to appear as a beacon of change for the Sunni world, and an even more significant regional power. But it didn't last. First, Erdoğan was indignant when the Muslim Brotherhood government in Egypt, led by Muhammad Morsi, was overthrown in July 2013 after just a year in power. Second, he became embroiled in the civil war in Syria when – encouraged by some of the Gulf Arab states which were by then heavily invested in Turkey but strongly opposed to the Syrian Baathist regime – he turned against his old friend Bashar al-Assad. The Syrian president had ignored his advice to appoint members of the Muslim Brotherhood to the government and begun brutally suppressing peaceful protesters.

As Turkey and its intelligence organization, MIT, began to support whatever opposition group it thought could weaken Assad, it found itself less and less able, or willing, to control the extremist Sunni organizations which were using

Turkish territory for basing, recruitment, transit and as a source of weapons. Journalists were imprisoned for treason after they broadcast evidence that truckloads of men and weapons destined for the brutal jihadist organization ISIL were being waved across the border on the orders of MIT.

At the same time, Turkey was becoming less and less tolerant of Kurdish successes in winning back territory from ISIL and establishing their own areas of influence along Turkey's southern border.

The Kurds had long been victims of brutality, betrayal and sometimes just plain bad luck. When the Ottoman Empire collapsed at the end of the First World War, the 1920 Treaty of Sèvres promised them autonomy with the option of independence within a year. But when Turkey's new leader Kemal Atatürk, the hero of the Gallipoli campaign, rejected that treaty and it was replaced in 1923 by the Treaty of Lausanne, all mention of autonomy for the Kurds had disappeared. The Kurds were not even included in the list of minorities entitled to their own language and identity within the new republic.

By 1925 the new Turkish government was promising to 'Turkify' the whole population, by force if necessary. Over the next half-century, literally dozens of Kurdish revolts were suppressed with brutality, with the perhaps inevitable result that the Kurds developed their own armed insurgency in the form of the PKK, now regarded as a terrorist organization throughout the Western world.

In the early days of AKP government, Erdoğan was the architect of an enlightened policy of outreach towards the Kurds, allowing Kurdish language broadcasting and publications in the south-east for the first time and overturning years of Turkish government refusal to recognize the Kurdish autonomous region in northern Iraq (where Turkish companies now do very good business). The result was a dramatic reduction in the number of terrorist acts committed by the PKK.

This gave me some personal satisfaction. In Iran, back in the 1970s, I had been involved in some modest humanitarian initiatives helping Kurdish groups who were being brutally suppressed by Saddam Hussein in next-door Iraq. At the time, until he deserted them by concluding what was known as the Algiers accord with Saddam in 1975, the shah was providing the Kurds with some logistic support as well. I got to know some of the Kurds and those supporting them, helping to build relationships which again became part of my life when Kurdish leaders from the Barzani and Talabani clans used to visit Ankara for talks with the Turkish authorities in the early 2000s and drop in for a glass of Scotch before heading home.

Encouraged by some of those Kurdish friends, my son Oliver moved to Kurdish northern Iraq – now the autonomous region of Iraqi Kurdistan – in the autumn of 2003 to help with reconstruction after the overthrow of Saddam's regime by the US-led coalition earlier that year. He stayed for seven years, developing a private security business supporting multinational companies and foreign governments. The security situation, and the logistics, were so delicate that I did not feel able to visit his operation, and my Kurdish friends, in Erbil and Sulaymaniyah as long as I was ambassador across the border in Turkey.

But I went during the few months I had spare between leaving Turkey in late 2006 and taking up my next appointment as ambassador to France in March 2007. Jalal Talabani, by then president of Iraq elected under the new constitution which he had worked closely with the US and UK to put together, invited me to lunch at his palace in Sulaymaniyah, along with other members of his family and Kurdish officials. As usual, we discussed managing the complex relationship with his Turkish neighbors as well as the future of Iraq.

Mam, or 'Uncle', Jalal, as he was known, had a stroke in 2012 and died in Berlin in 2017 aged 84. For much of his life, he and his Patriotic Union of Kurdistan (PUK) had worked, together with the Barzanis' Kurdish Democratic Party (KDP), for Kurdish independence. In the process the PUK became the unofficial partner of many groups and governments seeking to curb the excesses of, and eventually overthrow, Saddam Hussein. This is the background to the problems which arose between Turkey and the US during the Syrian civil war over Washington's choice of the Kurds as preferred partners in driving ISIL out of northern Syria, and weakening Bashar al-Assad.

For the US, the Kurdish YPG were by far the most capable and reliable of the rebel groups in northern Syria. For the Turks, they were indistinguishable from the PKK, the domestic terrorist group which has been fighting the Turkish state for independence for the last thirty years. So when the YPG started occupying territory in northern Syria which was not traditionally Kurdish, Turkey responded by complaining bitterly to the US over its choice of allies and then, in October 2019, crossing the border and creating a buffer zone of its own to block Kurdish advances.

All this was boiling away when in early 2020 Oliver and I paid a private visit to Baghdad, and to Erbil and

Sulaymaniyah in the Kurdish north of Iraq. I was very touched when the president of Iraq, Barham Salih, another Kurd whom I had known for years, invited us to lunch at the presidential palace in Baghdad as 'family' – as he struggled to persuade yet another reluctant politician to accept the position of prime minister.

Unfortunately, the important progress on Kurdish issues made in the early Erdoğan years didn't last. In October 2014 the Kurds, by now serious players in the Syrian civil war, won international sympathy for their courage in holding out against the forces of ISIL in the town of Kobane in October – while the Turkish military just across the border stood by and watched. For Erdoğan, the close alliance that existed between the PYD, as the Kurdish political group in northern Syria was known, their military arm the YPG, and the PKK was too much to stomach.

Erdoğan had reckoned without a parallel rise in support inside Turkey for a Kurdish political party, HDP, with a young and charismatic leader in the person of Selahattin Demirtaş. In early 2015 Demirtaş said bluntly that if his party won the 10 per cent of the vote it needed to get into parliament in the June election, it would not support changing the constitution to give Erdoğan the executive powers he wanted. In the event, the HDP comfortably passed the 10 per cent threshold (with just over 13 per cent of the vote) and won eighty seats in the parliament, denying the AKP an outright majority and leaving Erdoğan a long way short of the supermajority he needed for constitutional change.

Prime Minister Ahmet Davutoğlu tried to form a coalition, but lacked the support of Erdoğan. Once the deadline for doing so had expired, Erdoğan exercised his constitutional right to convene fresh elections on 1 November. All that despite a well-publicized offer by Kemal Derviş, by then a respected academic at the Brookings Institution in Washington, to rejoin politics as a deputy prime minister in charge of economic policy should a coalition be formed around the leadership of the centre-left, secular opposition party, CHP, of which he had once been deputy leader.

The politics quickly began to deteriorate. On 20 July a suicide bomber killed 33 people, injuring another 100, in an attack on a group of Kurdish sympathizers at a rally in the border town of Suruç, little more than 6 miles from Kobane. ISIL claimed responsibility but the Kurdish community accused the Turkish authorities of turning a blind eye, and the PKK killed two policemen in retaliation two days later.

In response, on 24 July the Turkish military began massive airstrikes against the PKK and the YPG, but only tangentially against ISIL targets, despite agreeing the day before to allow US military aircraft the use of Turkish airbases in joint operations against ISIL.

Attacks were also carried out against offices and members of the HDP, and against newspapers sympathetic to the Kurdish cause. Erdoğan made no bones about his strategy: to wrap himself in the national flag in order to ensure that, second time around, the HDP were not able to deny him the parliamentary majority he wanted to change the constitution.

On 10 October two suicide bombings took the lives of 103 people near Ankara's main railway station, targeting a rally of Kurdish sympathizers demonstrating against the renewed conflict with the PKK. No one claimed responsibility but

Peeling potatoes at the New College chalet at Le Prarion on the lower slopes of Mont Blanc, France, summer 1971.

Below left Fording the Shahrud River on the way to the Valley of the Assassins, Iran, September 1976.

Below Team photograph of The Prince and Princess of Wales and accompanying party at the end of their visit to Czechoslovakia, May 1991.

Above left Talking to Hillary Rodham Clinton at the US Embassy in London, November 1997.

Above Visiting the penguins on Sea Lion Island, Falkland Islands, March 1999.

Left View of the devastation at the British Consulate General, Istanbul after the suicide bomb attack of 20 November 2003, looking towards where the Gatehouse used to be.

Receiving my KCMG from The Queen, November 2003.

Right The Prince of Wales at the reopening of the Consulate General, Istanbul, 25 October 2004.

Below With Prime Minister Tony Blair and Susie in the garden of the Ambassador's Residence, Ankara, May 2004.

Above The Residence in Ankara.
Left Turkish Foreign Minister Abdullah Gül attending the Queen's Birthday Party (QBP) at the Residence, Ankara, 15 June 2005.

Above Christine Lagarde, French Minister of Agriculture (later Finance), speaking at the QBP, the Ambassador's Residence, Paris, June 2007.

Right At my credentials ceremony with French President Jacques Chirac of France, Élysée Palace, March 2007.

With Prime Minister Gordon Brown, his wife Sarah and son John on his fifth birthday, and Susie, Residence, Paris, 17 October 2008.

Above With Prime Minister David Cameron at the Residence on his first foreign visit after winning the 2010 general election, Paris, 21 May 2010.

Right Checking the aroma of ageing wine at Château Mouton Rothschild, Bordeaux, France, May 2009.

Below right The Residence in Paris.

Below Guests who visited the Paris Residence on a particularly busy day, 2 September 2011.

Left With Colin Firth at a pre-launch reception for *The King's Speech*, at the Residence, Paris, 4 January 2011.

Below Office meeting at the White House, Washington, DC, March 2012.

Below The Clinton family at our farewell dinner for outgoing Secretary of State Hillary Clinton in front of a poster promoting *Downton Abbey*, her favourite TV show, at the Ambassador's Residence, Washington, January 2013.

Admiring General
Eisenhower's 1952
painting of Field Marshal
Montgomery with former
President Bill Clinton
in the library of the
Ambassador's Residence,
Washington,
2 November 2013.

With President Barack
Obama and Fionnuala
Kenny, wife of the Irish
Taoiseach, at the Speaker
of the House's St Patrick's
Day lunch, Washington,
14 March 2014.

With Boris Johnson,
Mayor of London,
looking at the area of the
Olympic Village where we
hoped the Smithsonian
Institution would be
part of the new cultural
centre, at the Residence,
Washington,
12 February 2015.

Above The Residence in Washington.

Above left With Vice President Joe Biden, Jill Biden and Susie, Washington, October 2015.

Above right The damaged ship's bell of HMS *Illustrious*, on which my father served during World War II, on display at the Residence, Washington, 7 May 2015.

Left With Secretary of State John Kerry and Susie at a farewell lunch he hosted in our honour, Washington, November 2015.

the finger of blame was pointed at ISIL and there were again accusations of security lapses – or worse – on the part of the police and the intelligence directorate, MIT.

The results of the general election held on 1 November partially vindicated Erdoğan's gamble that reviving the spectre of Kurdish terrorism and intimidating the opposition would give the AKP a better result. The AKP won 49.5 per cent of the vote and were able to form a government on their own. The majority was such that some former ministers who had reluctantly been persuaded to run again were left without jobs as Erdoğan and Davutoğlu filled the ministerial vacancies with loyalists.

But the HDP, despite being prevented from campaigning on an equal footing and deprived of publicity by the growing number of pro-AKP media outlets (the Council of Europe deemed the campaign to have been 'unfair'), again managed to creep over the 10 per cent threshold. With 10.7 per cent of the vote, they again denied the AKP the super-majority it wanted to amend the constitution and grant Erdoğan executive presidential powers.

The United States and its allies were dismayed that the Turkish priority had become the weakening of Kurdish groups rather than the defeat of ISIL, but largely ignored the deterioration in the political situation inside Turkey. The country's geostrategic importance was growing by the day as the civil war in Syria continued and millions of Syrian refugees made their way to the EU, largely via Turkey to the numerous Greek islands just a few miles off the Turkish coast.

By early 2016, the EU had struck a deal whereby Turkey would take back one Syrian refugee arriving illegally in the EU in exchange for every refugee resettled in the EU from among the hundreds of thousands housed in Turkish refugee camps. Turkey was also promised visa-free access for Turkish citizens to EU member states within the Schengen zone. But international concern about Erdoğan's growing autocratic tendencies, and the suspension of the rule of law and freedom of expression, was increasing.

Calling on Erdoğan in Istanbul in January, US Vice President Joe Biden said as much, in public and private, as did President Obama in a press conference after his bilateral with Erdoğan in the margins of the Nuclear Security Summit in Washington in April 2016. In what was a sign of the times, Davutoğlu called off a visit to Washington at the beginning of May because the White House would not promise him a meeting with the president.

When I spent a semester at Harvard's Kennedy School of Government as a fellow at the Institute of Politics in 2016 (see Chapter 14, p. 307), I was repeatedly questioned about what had gone wrong in Turkey and how the rest of the world should respond. In various interventions, including a speech at Harvard's Centre for European Studies in the late spring, I highlighted Turkey's achievements since the elections of 2002, the efforts we in the UK had put into getting Turkey on the path to EU membership, but also my disappointment that in the last few years Turkey had set aside so much of the programme of reform and democratization that had characterized the AKP's early years in power.

In June 2016, Susie and I were back in Istanbul where I had been invited to address the Global Relations Forum. The day before my address, as we dined with friends in their magnificent garden on the shores of the Bosphorus, news came through of an ISIL-organized suicide bomb attack at

Istanbul airport which killed 48 people and injured more than 200. This was the ninth major terrorist attack Turkey had suffered in little more than a year.

I was struck by how people took the outrage in their stride with calmness and resilience – so much so that we found the airport up and running almost normally the following day. But for the country as a whole it was a further warning that finally coming down unambiguously on the side of the coalition against ISIL was not going to be cost-free. Poor Turkey had become exposed to terrorist attacks from both the Kurdish PKK and the depraved jihadism of ISIL, and was at the same time under pressure to do more to help the US and its allies fight back against ISIL.

In August, Turkish tanks crossed into northern Syria for the first time since the civil war had begun five years earlier. The incursion was billed as Turkish help with the expulsion of ISIL from the border area. But the aim was at least as much to ensure that the Kurds of the YPG were not able to occupy territory along Turkey's southern border, and to remind the US that Turkey was a regional player in its own right with its own priorities.

II

The Hôtel de Charost (2007–12)

I was genuinely thrilled to return to Paris as ambassador in the spring of 2007. Part of that pleasure came from my profound conviction that doing a job of this kind was far easier and more effective if you already knew the country, spoke the language and knew local people. My experience of going back to Turkey had only reinforced that conviction. But I was also hugely attracted by the challenge of representing Britain in the foreign country to which we were geographically closer than any other, and with which we shared an extraordinary amount of history, and yet was more 'foreign' than some countries many thousands of miles away.

Jack Straw, foreign secretary at the time, told me some years later that he had a letter from me explaining that, while I was grateful for the show of confidence, I did not want to take up his suggestion that I apply for the position of PUS and head of the diplomatic service rather than seek another ambassadorial position after Ankara. I have no recollection of writing such a letter but that was certainly what I felt. I didn't think I would be very good at defending the FCO's interests on the Whitehall battlefield; I felt that my strengths – and preference – lay in representing Britain abroad.

Paris required a change of gear, and of mindset. Susie and I had to live out of suitcases for almost five months, while another job was lined up for my predecessor. But we took advantage of the wait to spend two weeks at a language school at Rennes, on the edge of Brittany. Susie had not spoken much French since learning it as a child, so focused on conversation practice. I decided to focus on activity which would help me do my next job.

I called on the Mayor of Rennes, Edmond Hervé, a Socialist politician whom I had known during my first stint in Paris in the early 1980s when he was junior minister for energy. I visited the local Peugeot factory, where I admired the robotics and chatted about market share and which models were and were not selling with the very knowledge-able production line workers. And I gave a recorded talk to the political science faculty at the University of Rennes. Afterwards, watching my grammatical mistakes and clumsy body language on screen, I felt like a footballer watching video footage of himself missing an open goal. But research does show that recording speeches, and subjecting the result to constructive criticism, invariably produces a better performance next time around.

For our dinners, we went out whenever possible with local academics, journalists and commentators to try and combine the brushing up of our language skills with developing some understanding of what was going on in western France – a luxury we knew we wouldn't have once I started at the embassy. Experience has also taught me that it is often the minor details you pick up when doing something unrelated to your main job that turn out to be key to understanding bigger truths – or at least to be useful additions to speeches requiring a bit of local colour.

Travelling back through the Loire at the end of our immersion in the region, we stopped to visit the pretty hamlet of Saint-Florent-le-Vieil, where the mayor, a former French foreign minister, Hervé de Charette, couldn't quite believe that the next British ambassador was interested in the local goings-on of the Department of Maine-et-Loire. He could not have been more welcoming, and turned out to be an expert on the history of the Vendée Wars of 1793–5, when one of his ancestors, François-Athanase Charette, had joined local peasant leaders in a Royalist and Catholic revolt against the Robespierre revolutionaries in Paris.

Alas, Charette was involved, towards the end of the war and after tens of thousands had already lost their lives, in the failed 1795 expedition to Quiberon Bay in Brittany where the rebels hoped to be relieved by a mixed bag of returning exiles and other counter-revolutionaries courtesy of the Royal Navy – in the exact spot where the navy had won one of its greatest naval victories against France during the Seven Years War in 1759. The expedition was a failure and, in March 1796, with the revolt finally over, Charette was tried and executed by firing squad in Nantes.

Today, credited with a degree of heroism but also much bloodshed, he is also famous for having coined the phrase 'you can't make an omelette without breaking eggs'. I enjoyed the idea of spending the day, two hundred years later, with one of his direct descendants who had been foreign minister of France and was now mayor of the small village where it all began.

We arrived in Paris in March 2007. I knew the house well enough from the four years I had spent at the embassy in the early 1980s. But we still felt we had won the lottery when we arrived in the great front hall of what was going to be our home for almost five years. After Napoleon's abdication in 1814 following the retreat from Moscow, and exile to the island of Elba between Corsica and the Italian mainland, Britain's most successful general, the Duke of Wellington, was nominated ambassador to France. He did not consider the existing British Embassy remotely suitable. As was the norm then, it was a rented property. Wellington felt that the British government should own its more important diplomatic premises, so he bought, as a replacement, the *hôtel de Charost* – a wonderful early eighteenth-century *hôtel particulier* on the rue du Faubourg St Honoré – from Pauline Borghese, Napoleon's sister. Protected from the noise of the street, and taking advantage of the light and air of the garden, this type of Parisian town house constructed 'between courtyard and garden' was based on a model used for more than six centuries in France.

There was no question of helping himself to the spoils of war – Wellington paid the market price and bought with it the entire contents of the house, except for the paintings of the Borghese collection, which returned to Italy. Pauline, who was not wealthy herself, had spent large amounts of her long-suffering Italian husband's money on furnishings, clocks, candelabras, lamps and many other fittings of exquisitely good, sometimes radical, taste.

Unfortunately for the duke, his stint as ambassador to

a country of which he was genuinely fond lasted only a few months. In March 1815 Napoleon escaped from Elba, reassembled an army during what became known as the Hundred Days, and once again set about trying to achieve the military domination of Europe. Wellington reverted to the role of soldier and, carefully coordinating his moves with his Prussian, Dutch and other coalition partners, led the final, definitive rout of Napoleon's forces at Waterloo in Belgium on 18 June 1815, in what he famously described as 'the nearest run thing you ever saw in your life'.

This time Napoleon was despatched to an island from which he would find it impossible to escape – St Helena, a remote British territory in the South Atlantic, where he died in 1821 at the age of 51, leaving behind him a large number of Saints, as the locals were known, with more than a passing resemblance to the former French emperor.

For Wellington, becoming ambassador in Paris was no longer an option. Before returning to Britain, where he would eventually twice serve as prime minister, he was asked to be commander of the international force which the Congress of Vienna decided to station in France for the next three years to oversee the terms of the armistice ending the Napoleonic wars. In discharging his duties the duke was often instrumental in softening the terms imposed on the defeated France, but he did insist on the return of important artefacts looted by Napoleon's armies during its conquests, including the four horses now adorning St Mark's Basilica in Venice, which had originally been removed from the Hippodrome in Constantinople in the thirteenth century.

His successors as ambassador to France owe Wellington a huge debt of gratitude for the residence he chose but was never able properly to enjoy. Somehow, the contents have survived largely unscathed from the two hundred years of service they have given, and the temptation of the FCO at times of budgetary hardship to sell off items of family silver. Like our predecessors, Susie and I did our best to put the house to good use.

Over the years many books have been written about the residence, its contents, its colorful inhabitants and its guests. During our time we oversaw (and arranged for the funding of) the production of an updated history, with modern photographs. *The British Ambassador's Residence in Paris* explains and illustrates the unique nature of the house, and how it has been the beating heart of British diplomacy in France for more than two hundred years.

After the fall of Paris on 14 June 1940, there were numerous attempts by the Nazi occupiers to commandeer the building, including one by Hermann Goering, Hitler's right hand man and designated successor. All were rebuffed by the only two members of staff who remained at the mission – William Chrystie, the porter, and Ernest Spurgeon, a messenger.

When Paris was liberated in 1945, the new ambassador was Sir Alfred Duff Cooper, a former cabinet minister to whom in 1943 Churchill had given the delicate task of being the British government's representative to Charles de Gaulle's Free French. Brilliantly supported by his beautiful socialite wife Lady Diana, he brought the house back to life. Between them, the Coopers were responsible for introducing a number of bold new features to the house, including Duff's superb Empire-revival library, which still gives enormous pleasure to his successors. Lady Diana Cooper's extravagant personality inspired *Don't Tell Alfred*, Nancy Mitford's mischievous novel about an ambassadress who wouldn't leave when her husband was reassigned.

By the time we got to Paris, the presidential elections were almost upon us. I presented my credentials to President Jacques Chirac as one of the last new heads of mission he received before leaving office, and then threw myself into following the campaign to determine his successor. There was little likelihood of campaigning candidates finding time for office calls by new ambassadors, so I tracked them down at their *meetings*, as campaign rallies were known in France, where I could form my own judgement of their campaigning skills and likelihood of winning.

On my first outing I went to watch Nicolas Sarkozy speaking in a sports hall containing ten thousand noisy supporters in the western city of Nantes. Looking back, I recall two points in particular. First, Sarkozy's skill as an orator; energy, drive, passion and conviction, which left him physically exhausted and drenched in sweat. Second, the quite unnecessary kindness of François Fillon, a future prime minister of France but at the time just a former minister, Deputy for the Sarthe and senior member of the Sarkozy campaign team. After the speech, he ushered me backstage to the green room where the future president was hoovering up a box of dark chocolates (which he later gave up for dietary reasons) and made time to welcome me to France and his campaign.

A little later, just ten days before the second round of the presidentials, I followed Ségolène Royal, the Socialist Party's candidate, to Lyon. Not at all the same. A smaller gathering, but perfectly choreographed and lit as Ségolène took the stage in an elegant cream suit. At the end of her speech she was as unruffled and perfectly turned out as at the beginning. Her audience applauded. But they didn't enthuse, and she did not engage with her supporters as Sarkozy had. I spoke to her briefly after the event, and again later in the evening when we found ourselves in the same restaurant. She was polite, happy to discuss the state of the campaign, but reserved.

The independent centre-right candidate François Bayrou was the hardest to engage with. I caught up with him at a modest rally in central France but at a time when he clearly had better things to do than shoot the breeze with a foreign ambassador who didn't have a vote. When the people of France eventually went to the polls, they turned out in remarkable numbers – 83% in the first round on 21 April, far higher than anything we ever see in the UK or US. Sarkozy came in with 31%, Royal 26%, Bayrou 18%, and the National Front's Jean-Marie Le Pen with 10% (a much lower score than the 17% which took him to the run-off with Jacques Chirac in 2002, and much worse than the National Front did in later years with Le Pen's daughter Marine at the helm). In the second round, ten days later, Sarkozy comfortably defeated his Socialist opponent, Ségolène Royal, by a margin of 53% to 47%.

Nicolas Sarkozy felt indebted to Tony Blair for the advice he gave him on how to win elections, so the atmospherics when Blair came to Paris just days after the second round to congratulate the new president were genuinely festive. Sarkozy received him on the evening of 11 May in the garden of one of the *hôtels particuliers* in the 7th Arrondissement that normally served as ministries, and sent away almost all accompanying officials. François Fillon stayed, and Blair kindly ensured that I was there too – telling Sarkozy that I was his personal choice as ambassador and asking him to make good use of me.

Later there was a celebratory dinner with Sarkozy and a group of his friends at Thiou, a trendy local fusion restaurant. To Sarkozy's great regret, Blair had already announced that he would be stepping down and handing the keys of 10 Downing Street to Gordon Brown six weeks later. But the relationship lasted, and it wasn't long before Sarkozy was inviting Blair, as former prime minister, to dinner at Le Bristol, his favorite hotel just across the street from the Élysée Palace, to show off the dynamic, new, almost self-consciously diverse ministerial team he had assembled.

Sarkozy had in any case said publicly that he intended to give more weight to relations with the UK than his pre-decessor had been inclined to do. Chirac had a famously difficult relationship with Blair, with whom he had fallen out over the invasion of Iraq in 2003 and a number of EU issues. Yet by the time I invited the former president round for a drink with the former prime minister a couple of years later, the hatchet had clearly been buried. Chirac, who I had been assured would choose beer over wine or any other form of alcohol, surprised us all by going for a gin and tonic (or two); he then spent a happy hour and a half discussing the state of the world with his old sparring partner. As he left, Chirac confided to me that although he had not always seen eye to eye with Blair, he had greatly enjoyed seeing him again.

Blair remained a regular visitor to Paris after leaving No 10. In 2008 he was asked back to address a large convention of Nicolas Sarkozy's party, the *Union pour un Mouvement Populaire* (UMP). He arrived on an overnight flight from the Middle East, suffering from an unpleasant throat infection. After putting the speech he had written on the plane into French with the help of his translator, he put on his suit, went to wash his hands in an elegant but vintage bathroom which had been left unchanged since the days of Duff and Diana Cooper in the 1940s and was promptly soaked by the overhead shower. Hairdryer to the rescue, we did our best to tidy him up and sent the former prime minister on his way with a throat so sore he was barely able to speak. None of the several thousand UMP supporters who heard him speak, powerfully and in excellent French, were any the wiser. Sarkozy was as impressed as he was grateful.

Sarkozy and Gordon Brown, Blair's successor as prime minister, had both been finance ministers and already knew each other. Contrary to expectations on both sides of the Channel, they immediately found they could work together. For the first year, there was great emphasis on taking forward defence cooperation between France and the UK, to ensure we could remain the two genuinely capable European members of NATO and do so at the lowest possible cost, working together on new equipment programmes where we could, as we had in the past on the Jaguar fighter. There was also, then and later, a huge amount of traffic between London and Paris on EU issues.

Unusually early in his tenure, The Queen invited Sarkozy to pay a state visit to the UK in March 2008. He had married his third wife, Carla Bruni, a few weeks beforehand. The visit was a great success. The president and Carla stayed at

Windsor Castle, where The Queen gave a lunch for the two delegations and a banquet in honour of President and Mrs Sarkozy. Later, Sarkozy delivered a strong, impassioned speech in the Palace of Westminster about the importance of Franco-British relations; there was an intergovernmental summit held at Arsenal Football Club's new stadium in North London, at the invitation of the (French) manager, Arsène Wenger; and the Lord Mayor gave a banquet in honour of the Sarkozys (at which the president was seated directly opposite a statue of the Duke of Wellington).

Some months later, as a lifelong Arsenal supporter, I managed to persuade Wenger to come to lunch at the Paris residence. It turned out to be one of the hottest tickets in town. I remember especially the way conversation around the table gradually fell silent as captains of industry and politicians strained to hear Wenger's masterclass on how to manage and get the best out of young, talented but often prima donna footballers. Wenger stayed at Arsenal another decade, before being pushed out after almost 22 years in the job because the team was no longer competing successfully at the highest levels. His had been an extraordinary tenure, winning numerous trophies and somehow balancing the need to pay off the cost of the new Emirates stadium with his determination that Arsenal play attractive, winning football – all without the vast treasure chest provided to some Premier League teams by Middle Eastern or Russian oligarch owners. Two years before his departure I wrote suggesting that he leave voluntarily, on his own terms and with his dignity intact, rather than hang on until he was fired. Gracious as ever, he replied politely thanking me for my views – but clearly had others of his own.

Before Sarkozy's visit, there was some nervousness about how the British media would react to the president and his beautiful new wife, of whom naked photographs from her time as a model years earlier had been reproduced on the morning of the visit by the tabloid newspapers. A few days beforehand, Susie went to see the new Mrs Sarkozy at her home in the 16th Arrondissement to see whether she could be of any help as Carla prepared for her first major appearance on the international stage. She explained that there was absolutely no expectation that Carla, as the wife of another head of state, would curtsey when she met The Queen. Carla said it was impossible not to curtsey to Her Majesty. She asked Susie – product of a Catholic school run by nuns and therefore well used to curtseying – to help her practise (a story Carla freely told to *Paris Match* some months later). When she was greeted by The Queen on arrival at Windsor, the president's new wife, dressed in a demure grey Dior outfit topped off by a matching beret, performed a perfect curtsey, to the universal approval of the watching British media. The visit was off to a great start, from which it never looked back.

For British ambassadors around the world, June is the month when we traditionally hold The Queen's Birthday Party (QBP), regarded in every embassy with a mixture of dread (because of the preparations and the agony of getting the guest list right) and excitement, because the QBP is the flagship event of our diplomatic calendar. In Turkey, where a good number of cabinet ministers and others of the great and the good could be persuaded to attend, I decided to form a partnership with the local Sheraton hotel, who helped enormously with the food, and to ship in a selection of British cheeses, which were largely unknown to that cheese-loving country. To save on the cost of bringing in bandsmen from the Royal Marines, we persuaded the Turkish Navy's amazing band to play the national anthems for us – they stayed on enthusiastically playing dance music until rain brought the party to an end.

Paris was different. The QBP was traditionally a great event for the two thousand or so guests who came, and the band of the Royal Marines always did us proud. But it was hard to get busy people who were the embassy's important contacts to show up – partly because they really didn't have the time and partly because they felt that if they came to one diplomatic mission's national day reception, they would be pressured to attend others. And it was expensive. So I decided to hold the party every other year, but to try and make the event a bit more special and break with tradition by inviting a member of the government to make a short speech as my guest of honour.

Our first year in Paris, I chose Christine Lagarde, who had just become minister of finance. She and I had first met in Istanbul airport a few years earlier when she was junior minister for foreign trade and we were both waiting for flight connections. At the QBP, she spoke briefly in English and I, equally briefly, in French. The French foreign and defence ministers kindly did us the same honour in subsequent years. With Lagarde we had the good fortune to build a friendship which continued in later years when she was appointed managing director of the International Monetary Fund in Washington in 2011 and I followed a few months later as British ambassador to the United States.

Later in 2008 the focus rapidly shifted towards the international financial crisis triggered by the collapse of Lehman Brothers with over $600 billion of assets after the US Federal Reserve refused to bail out the firm. With its business leveraged at a dangerously high level of 30:1, this meant very severe knock-on effects for other financial institutions, including in the UK where many firms had also invested in risky derivative products no one fully understood, based on sub-prime mortgages that home-owners found they couldn't continue to service when interest rates rose and house prices fell.

By early October, world financial markets were in a tailspin. On Friday, 10 October, some of Britain's biggest banks said they were running out of money. The banking system was on the verge of collapse. The chancellor of the exchequer, Alistair Darling, flew to Washington for a meeting of G7 finance ministers. Nicolas Sarkozy, who had formed a high regard for Gordon Brown's economic competence, asked the prime minister to join a Eurozone crisis meeting at the Élysée Palace to which he would not normally be invited since Britain had long since decided against adopting the euro as its currency. Sarkozy famously remarked that weekend: 'You know, Gordon, I should not like you. You are Scottish. We have nothing in common. And you are an economist. But somehow, Gordon, I love you.' On Monday morning, markets opened in the knowledge that three of the UK's biggest banks had been bailed out by the state.

For Sarkozy, Brown's simple but critical message of 'recapitalize the banks', ably supported by Darling following his lighting trip to Washington, was what saved the day. Over the next couple of months, hardly a weekend passed when Brown was not in Paris, conferring with Sarkozy (France at the time held the rotating presidency of the European Council). Before arriving in Paris I had seen very little of the then chancellor of the exchequer. But during the three years that he was prime minister and I was ambassador to France, Brown visited France eighteen times, once – to our delight – accepting our invitation to bring his wife Sarah and their two sons John and Fraser with him when he had to be in Paris for a working weekend.

Part of the ambassador's job was to accompany visiting prime ministers to their calls on the French president. For security reasons we were rarely allowed to make the short journey up the rue du Faubourg St Honoré on foot. But going by car often meant stopping outside the entrance to the Élysée Palace where we would have to wait – patiently or not, depending on the mood – until word came through to the gate guards that the president was ready for his visitors. The car would then drive us into the courtyard before turning on the gravel so the visiting VIP could alight at the bottom of the steps up to the palace. I realized early on that, in Brown's case, my job was to see who was waiting for him at the top so he knew who would be greeting him: the damage to his eyesight from a rugby accident he had sustained as a teenager, which left him blind in one eye – and which he revealed years later became worse during his time as prime minister – was such that he wasn't able to see for himself. That sometimes left those who didn't know better with the impression that he wasn't interested in meeting them. The truth was that he often couldn't see who they were.

There were many separate strands to our relations with France. Britain was adamant that the EU should not seek to establish its own defence capability, on the grounds that NATO already existed and defence was not a responsibility of the EU but of individual member states. But we remained keen on doing more together with the very small number of other EU member states which had a significant defence capability – particularly France. We both had independent nuclear deterrence through our fleet of SSBN submarines, one of which was always at sea, and clearly had an interest in examining whether we could keep down the cost of maintaining those deterrents by working together, as long as we did not jeopardize the independence of each government's action.

The need to cooperate effectively was brought home vividly by the embarrassing moment in February 2009 when two French and British nuclear-powered ballistic missile submarines bumped into each other – at very low speed, and therefore causing only slight damage – somewhere in the Atlantic Ocean. With each country only normally having one SSBN at sea at a time, this was a freak accident. But it was immediately obvious that we needed to come to some kind of arrangement to avoid it happening again, so the navies stepped up their confidential exchanges. Towards the end of my time in Paris, we also began to take modest steps towards jointly developing some of the components necessary for the renewal of our respective nuclear weapons.

Building on the important St Malo defence agreement signed by Tony Blair and President Chirac in 1998, we moved our partnership with France up a gear with the far-reaching

Lancaster House treaties that David Cameron and Nicolas Sarkozy signed in 2010, which covered both nuclear and conventional defence cooperation.

Immigration also featured prominently in the inter-governmental relationship. This was not due to UK anxiety about high levels of immigration from other EU member states seeking to enter the UK – which became one of the main features of the Leave camp's messaging during the 2016 Brexit referendum campaign. It was, rather, our concern about the large number of non-EU citizens arriving illegally in the UK via France and either claiming asylum or simply remaining in the UK undetected (since, almost alone among the major member states, people in Britain weren't required to carry ID cards).

In a remarkable agreement which had been negotiated in 2001 between Nicolas Sarkozy and David Blunkett, who were the two countries' respective interior ministers at the time, France and the UK agreed on a system of 'juxtaposed' border controls which in essence allowed British officials to conduct their immigration controls on French territory in order to minimize the number of unauthorized immigrants reaching the UK. The controls introduced at Calais and the other Channel ports, supported by a thousand UK immigration officials working on French territory, proved generally effective. But the word was out that Britain was the land of El Dorado if people could somehow get themselves across the channel and begin either working in the black economy or taking advantage of the benefits available under the UK's social security system.

So around Calais, in particular, impromptu camps of would-be immigrants sprang up as desperate individuals and families waited for an opportunity to cross the Channel illegally by train, truck, ferry, or even in a dinghy. The presence of 'Le Jungle', as it became known, became highly controversial in political, security and humanitarian terms in the Calais area. The two governments were therefore constantly looking at ways of further discouraging immigrants from trying their luck, including the construction, at UK expense, of huge security fences around the perimeter of the Eurostar and ferry terminals at Calais. In late 2020, despite – or perhaps because of – the UK leaving the EU, the problem of large numbers of migrants constantly risking their lives by trying to cross the Channel in small boats or even refrigerated containers, was still with us.

Calais and the other Channel ports also became headline news when there were strikes by French fishermen, preventing UK yachtsmen from entering or leaving the French ports which were a vital part of their holiday plans. The owners of boats large enough to cross the Channel safely were often influential in British political and business circles, and expected everything possible to be done to help them out. During my first tour of duty in Paris in the early 1980s, I had already found myself negotiating the temporary lifting of fishermen's blockades with union leaders so that British yachtsmen trapped in French *ports de plaisance* could make their escape.

In April 2010, the Channel ports were again headline news when volcanic ash from the Eyjafjallajökull eruption in Iceland caused the grounding of all flights into and out of the UK for six days. As ill luck would have it, this was peak Easter holiday season and tens of thousands of British subjects found themselves stranded with no way of getting home. Many bought or rented cars and set off from all parts of Europe for a Channel port from which they hoped to get back home. Most chose Calais, because there were both trains and boats available. But the congestion was immense. When Susie and I decided to drive to Calais with emergency supplies of snacks and drinks for families desperately trying to get onto a ferry, we had no idea how many thousands of people we would find waiting in the bitter cold, often with no money, food or drink. Nor did I expect to find the owners of the cross-Channel ferries charging peak one-way fares for everyone desperate to get home (P&O ferries eventually accepted my advice and relented, but by then it was too late to make much difference).

On our way up the autoroute to Calais, I took a call from the FCO press office saying that the Department of Transport didn't wish me to do any media work since their minister was planning to make an announcement detailing the emergency measures which the government was about to put in place. I was also told that the prime minister was ordering an aircraft carrier to Cherbourg – the one Channel port with adequate berthing arrangements for such a large ship – to pick up cars and foot passengers trying to get home through Normandy. In vain did I argue that there was no point, since no one was going to Cherbourg, hundreds of miles to the West of where the real crisis was unfolding. The aircraft carrier was coming, I was told, whether I liked it or not. (In the end, it didn't.)

As for the media, I happily ignored Whitehall's instruction. With numerous British TV crews there to witness what was happening, it would have been absurd for the British ambassador to ignore them and fail to register that he was on the spot doing what public opinion expected diplomats to do – look after UK nationals in difficulty. My experiences in France and before that in Turkey had taught me that it was essential for the senior local diplomat to be on the scene quickly and effectively. Far better to risk getting there and finding you are not needed than to be criticized for not being there when British subjects were in distress.

In France, hardly a year passes without there being some important anniversary connected with one of the two world wars – or one of the great battles fought between the English and the French in earlier times. Each year, of course, we commemorated the D-Day landings of 6 June 1944. The 65th anniversary fell in 2009 so there was a larger event than usual, with President Obama, The Prince of Wales, the British and French prime ministers and of course President Sarkozy in attendance. The French authorities sometimes liked to suggest that D-Day was largely a French event, with a bit of help from their American friends. Just as the British love to hear American politicians talk of the 'special relationship', so the French are thrilled to be called 'America's oldest ally'. I saw it as my job quietly to remind people that more British and Empire servicemen – 83,000 – came ashore on 6 June than Americans (73,000) or Free French (177). But the anniversary invariably passed off well, with valuable opportunities for the leaders of all the countries involved to spend time together, and pay moving visits to the beautifully manicured Commonwealth, American, French – and even the occasional German – military ceme-teries with their serried rows of headstones and crosses.

I also attended commemorations marking the St Nazaire raid of 28 March 1942, when a successful assault led by the Royal Navy on the heavily defended naval basin prevented top-of-the-range German battleships like *Tirpitz* from establishing the basing facilities they needed to cause the havoc Hitler intended to the Atlantic convoys keeping Britain in the war. A total of 240 commandos took part in the raid, which culminated in an ancient destroyer, HMS *Campbeltown*, steaming at high speed into the gates of the German naval base, packed with explosives. The damage rendered the St Nazaire docks unusable, and the loss of this base meant that *Tirpitz* was never able to stray beyond Norwegian waters, where she was eventually sunk.

There was also the annual commemoration in Bordeaux of Operation Frankton, a daring raid which took place in December 1942 involving ten Royal Marines in five kayaks – a sixth was damaged while being unloaded from the mother submarine – paddling their way up the Gironde river and damaging a number of German cargo ships with limpet mines. Only two of the men who took part in the raid survived – some were betrayed as they tried to escape overland into Spain. In Bordeaux there remains a fine museum and memorial to the commandos, known – by the film of that name made after the war in 1955 – as the Cockleshell Heroes.

Other anniversaries were more painful, not least the decision to hold a ceremony marking the seventieth anniversary of the sinking of HMT *Lancastria* off the coast of St Nazaire with the loss of as many as six thousand Commonwealth servicemen's lives on 17 June 1940 – the biggest single-ship loss of life in Britain's maritime history. The *Lancastria*, a requisitioned Cunard liner, was bringing home servicemen seeking to leave western France shortly after the evacuation of the British Expeditionary Force from Dunkirk ten days earlier, but was sunk as she waited for a naval escort that never materialized.

Churchill suppressed the bad news, of which he felt the British people had had enough in these early days of the war. This gave rise to conspiracy theories in later years that there was something to hide about the loss of the ship, the cargo she was carrying or the extent to which she was overloaded. The anniversary was therefore a moving mixture of remembrance for those who died, gratitude for the extraordinary courage shown by local French people who waded into the water to help survivors, and anger from – as well as divisions between – people from the different associations representing those who perished. One of the harder ceremonies I had to attend, and address.

Twenty kilometers east of St Nazaire on France's Atlantic coast lies the small fishing port – now something of a touristic centre – of Pornic. Its small but perfectly-maintained Commonwealth War Graves cemetery contains the remains of 400 servicemen, including a number of those lost on the Lancastria. Back in the 1980s during my first stint in Paris I used to rent an old house down the road for my family's summer holidays. The owners were a magnificent 'résistante' and her brother, who became dear friends. Down the back of the old armchairs in their salon we found miniature swastika flags which had been pinned on military maps when the house had been used as the local Gestapo headquarters forty years earlier. In France, history was never far away.

In 2010, I was surprised to find myself invited to the

seventieth anniversary of the attack by the Royal Navy on the French fleet at Mers el-Kebir in Algeria on 3 July 1940. This represented another delicate diplomatic mission. Following their defeat at the hands of the invading Nazi forces, the French signed an armistice with Germany and Italy on 25 June 1940, which included a commitment that they would not hand over their naval assets for use in the war against Britain. Understandably, Churchill had little faith that Adolf Hitler would abide by the terms of the armistice, or that defeated France would be able to resist if he tried to requisition the French navy. Churchill could not, at this critical moment of Britain's survival, risk having France's considerable naval strength added to the enemy forces which the country was already facing.

The French were faced with a choice: join us in continuing the war; hand over the assets to the Royal Navy; remove them from the field of combat – to the other side of the Atlantic, for example; or scuttle the ships. Many of the French naval vessels which were at the time in British ports were only handed over after a scuffle, and with some loss of life.

Very significant assets were in the port of Mers el-Kebir, which was then part of France. The French were warned that if the ships were neither handed over nor scuttled, they would be destroyed. There is some dispute over whether every part of the ultimatum – which had already been communicated to the new French government in Paris – was understood when it was conveyed by a Royal Navy captain to the commanding French admiral. But the result was that the Royal Navy undertook a heavy bombardment, severely damaging several French warships and causing the deaths of 1,297 French servicemen.

Winston Churchill described the decision to attack the fleet of a country which had until a few weeks earlier been a close ally, and the country to which he had offered union with the United Kingdom if France would stay in the war, as 'a hateful decision – the most unnatural and painful in which I have ever been involved'.

Speaking at the commemoration of such a controversial and still-painful decision without actually apologizing was always going to be a tall order. But as I read myself into the background of what had happened, I came across a statement from General Charles de Gaulle, leader of the Free French, just three days later, saying that, had he been in Churchill's shoes, he would have felt obliged to take the same painful decision. I of course included his statement in my speech, which undoubtedly helped take the edge off the occasion. In the event, the ceremony and speech passed off as well as I could have hoped and my French audience was remarkably gracious. But it was another reminder of the difficult history which the United Kingdom and France have shared over the centuries – and of the importance of doing your homework before taking the podium at an event of such sensitivity.

Not long after we arrived in Paris, I had an earlier reminder of the complexity of that relationship, so perfectly described in Isabelle and Robert Tombs's *That Sweet Enemy*, published in 2006. The head of Électricité de France, Pierre Gadonneix, was an old friend from the days when I had first been at the Paris embassy in the early 1990s and he was in charge of steel and electricity at the then-powerful Ministry of Industry. Not long after our arrival in Paris he invited Susie and me to the opera, with dinner afterwards, for one of the evenings when the corporate sponsors were able to invite outside guests. We enjoyed a marvellous evening, and, after the opera itself, settled down at our table of a dozen or so for a relaxing meal to round it off.

As often happened at Parisian dinner parties, Pierre tapped his glass after a while and moved his guests to a single conversation. 'Monsieur l'Ambassadeur, cher Peter,' he began, 'since you know both our countries so well, can you tell us why it is that the English hate us so much?' Just like that, in front of all those grand and very nice other guests.

I was taken aback since the question seemed to me based on a completely false premise. Of course, I knew people in England who thought it was funny to say that the only thing wrong with France was the French – mainly people who loved taking their holidays there and loved French wine but who had never taken the trouble to learn the language or understand the culture and history. But the idea of 'the English' collectively 'hating' the French shocked me. As did the idea that that was how an intelligent, English-speaking head of a multinational French business felt about English people. I replied that this was such an unexpected question that I didn't know what to say. I knew no one who 'hated' France or the French people and was disturbed by the fact that my host had felt the need to put the question to me.

Perhaps Pierre was just being provocative, or putting the new ambassador to the test. These things often happened, and were part of the game. But over the years I gave some thought to his question. The answer, I eventually concluded, to my discomfort, was that a lot of people in Britain really didn't like the French. They were brought up to think that the French were a dirty, unwashed people who only invented perfume to cover up their lack of personal hygiene; were duplicitous and insincere (we British tend to have trouble looking beyond the literal translation of elegant French phrases designed to convey disagreement without being rude); that Napoleon was a self-appointed emperor who wanted to rule the world at the expense of the British empire; that General Charles de Gaulle was an ungrateful, cussed French chauvinist who didn't know his place; and that the French elite, the product of the *Grandes Écoles*, were arrogant intellectuals who considered themselves superior to the Anglo-Saxons with no good reason.

French attitudes towards the British are in many ways a mirror image of these *idées fixes*, complete with plenty of references to 'perfide Albion', but without the sense of 'hatred' identified by my friend. We British have the list of past grievances I mention above. But so do the French, usually starting with the burning of Joan of Arc at the stake in Rouen in 1431 (after being found guilty of heresy by a French court, the British like to add); the way they can hardly visit London without being confronted by reminders of Trafalgar and Waterloo; our historic rivalry in Africa, exemplified by the military stand-off at Fashoda in East Africa in 1898; the sense of betrayal when in 1940 the British army deserted (as they saw it) France at Dunkirk and then attacked their fleet at Mers el-Kebir; the apparent British determination to ensure that France, despite General de Gaulle's efforts, was treated as a defeated power at the end of the Second World War; and the way, as they see it, the British have never been fully committed to the European project and only supported the enlargement of the membership of the EU in order to keep it weak and divided.

And yet, by the second decade of the twenty-first century, hundreds of thousands of young French professionals had moved to the Greater London area of the UK because they felt freer and more at home there than in their own country, and found it easier to find gainful employment. So perhaps attitudes are finally changing.

Gordon Brown seriously considered calling a general election in the UK in the autumn of 2007, during the honeymoon period after he had succeeded Tony Blair in June. The polls were good but he was not convinced he would win and so delayed until the natural end of the parliamentary term in June 2010. By then, the consequences of the global financial crisis which had begun in 2007 – and which Brown was widely credited with managing as skilfully as anyone – together with divisions within his own Labour Party meant that he went into the general election with little chance of winning.

No party won an absolute majority but Brown's Labour government was replaced just three years after he had succeeded Tony Blair by a coalition of Conservatives and Liberal Democrats led by David Cameron. In order to win the votes of Eurosceptic MPs and secure the leadership of the Conservatives back in 2005, Cameron had committed to withdrawing his party from the centre-right alliance of the European People's Party (EPP) and European Democrats (ED) within the European Parliament – a commitment he honoured when launching the Conservatives' campaign for the European Parliament elections in June 2009.

He was warned at the time that this risked marginalizing

the voice of the most important UK group in the European Parliament, not least by Chancellor Merkel and Nicolas Sarkozy, whose parties were in the same group. Cameron's first foreign visit as prime minister was to Paris. But when he opened his account with the French president, behind the smiles and broadly similar centre-right political philosophy he shared with Sarkozy was a sense in the Élysée Palace that they were dealing with a risk-taker who lacked the strategic vision either to stop people 'banging on about Europe', as Cameron later put it, or to safeguard the long-term interests of either the UK or the EU.

French doubts about Cameron's handling of EU issues grew, and were compounded by the way the prime minister prepared for and, poorly advised by the Cabinet Office's European Secretariat, misread the December 2011 European Council. This was the moment when EU leaders came together to agree a new treaty intended to strengthen budgetary and deficit discipline within the Eurozone. Setting aside advice from the embassies in Paris and Berlin, Cameron and his team saw an opportunity to get something in return for giving the Eurozone countries what they wanted. At half past two in the morning of the second day, Cameron presented the French and Germans with a long list of largely incomprehensible, wholly unexpected, conditions for UK agreement to the new arrangement.

He rapidly found he was on his own. 'David, we are not paying you to save the euro,' Sarkozy responded. Claiming credit afterwards for having vetoed a new treaty, and applauded by Boris Johnson for having 'played a blinder', the prime minister had in fact left the rest of the twenty-seven to reach agreement without the UK and begun the process of playing Britain out of mainstream EU policy-making. But his approval ratings at home rose.

By the end of 2012 the Conservatives were so concerned by the rise of the eurosceptic UK Independence Party (UKIP), and the inroads it was making among their traditional supporters, that Cameron felt he had to go even further in their direction. So he announced in a speech at the Bloomberg Centre in London on 23 January 2013 that he would hold a referendum on the UK's future membership of the EU if he won a majority in the 2015 general election. He had by then – with a lot of help at the last minute from his predecessor, Gordon Brown – won the referendum on Scottish independence which he had promised to the Scottish National Party.

The Conservative–Lib Dem coalition was in fact working quite effectively. Conservatives conceded privately that coalition realities helped knock some of the sharper corners off their policies while Lib Dems agreed that they provided a useful excuse not to proceed with some of the less realistic aspirations of their party's manifesto. So Cameron was far from convinced that he would obtain an absolute majority for the Conservatives in 2015. He also knew that, if he once again found himself governing with the Lib Dems, his coalition partners would do all they could to prevent him from delivering on his promise of an EU referendum. But the Conservatives did such a good job of targeting marginal seats held by their Lib Dem allies, and Labour did so badly in Scotland, that, to his surprise, Cameron found himself at the head of a single-party government on 8 May.

A few weeks before the Bloomberg speech, and a few months after I had moved on from Paris to Washington at the beginning of 2012, I found myself having coffee with Tony Blair in the Washington hotel where he usually stayed. As we surveyed the political scene, I mentioned that I thought David Cameron would shortly be giving a commitment to hold a referendum should he win the next election.

Blair pulled a face. It wasn't that he thought I was wrong, he said; it was that he feared I was right. He saw no prospect of the offer of a referendum buying off hard-line europhobes in the Conservative Party – it would simply encourage them to ask for more, to hold the prime minister to his commitment and then use the referendum to force the UK out of the EU. Not for Blair the breezy, Old Etonian optimism that everything would turn out all right on the night. Cameron was fond of quoting that memorable line from the hotel manager in *The Best Exotic Marigold Hotel* that 'everything will be all right in the end; and if it's not all right, then it isn't yet the end'.

For the French, the selection of a new president of the European Commission in 2014 provided further evidence of the British government's inability to handle EU issues intelligently – and of the consequences of David Cameron's decision to withdraw the Conservatives from the EPP-ED. One of the outcomes of the new Lisbon Treaty, which came into force at the end of 2009, was that heads of government would in future have to nominate candidates in the light of the latest elections to the European Parliament, which itself had to approve their choice.

With hindsight, these provisions of the Lisbon Treaty looked like a federalist ambush which none of the heads of government really wanted – and became part of the charge sheet against the European institutions that drove Brexit sentiment in the UK. After the EPP-ED – minus the UK's Conservatives – performed strongly in the European Parliament elections in May, it became worryingly clear to everyone that the former Luxembourg prime minister Jean-Claude Juncker was the candidate the federalists wanted. Sarkozy was not keen. Nor was Chancellor Merkel, but she wanted the German Social Democrat Martin Schulz even less. David Cameron was enraged at the prospect, and by the summer of 2014 was saying that he would take the UK out of the EU if Juncker got the job.

The threats backfired, the European Parliament got what it wanted and Juncker was duly appointed for a five-year term in November 2014. In the recriminations afterwards, I heard French and German politicians complain that if Cameron had not spoken out as he did, in effect publicly challenging the provisions of Lisbon, it would have been possible in private to reach a different outcome. But the prime minister had been playing two games – one, how to get the best available person at the head of the Commission; and two, how to appease the eurosceptics in his own party and show that he wouldn't be pushed around by Brussels. In Paris and other EU capitals, concern continued to grow that, if the referendum Cameron had promised was held, it would be hard to make the case for the UK to remain.

Later, as I wrestled with the outcome of the June 2016 Brexit referendum, and the reasons why millions of British people voted for an outcome which I saw as an unnecessary act of collective self-harm, I concluded that part of the explanation lay in the psyche of the offshore islander which informs so much of the national character of the English (more so than that of the Scots, Welsh or Northern

Irish): pull up the drawbridge and never trust, or even bother to understand, foreigners unless they speak English and appear to share our culture. Most people forget that almost all the kings and queens whose sovereign rule we have proudly defended for the last thousand years have been either French (Norman or Plantagenet), German (Hanoverian) or Dutch. Too many of us prefer living with a nostalgic sense of past achievements to working out a new role for ourselves and our country based on the world as it now is.

During our time in Paris, there were nevertheless plenty of moments when the relationship felt genuinely warm. Often it was about personalities, as when Blair came over to congratulate his friend Nicolas Sarkozy on his election victory in May 2007. Royal visits also brought out the most generous instincts of the French – every member of the Royal family was made welcome. During my first tour of duty in Paris, President François Mitterrand decided, apparently on the spur of the moment, to walk The Prince of Wales back along the Faubourg St Honoré to the embassy from the Élysée Palace where he had been giving him tea – something no one could remember ever having happened before.

Not long before Susie and I left Paris for Washington at the beginning of 2012, I persuaded the Élysée Palace to award a Légion d'Honneur to the embassy's long-serving chef, James Viaene. James, despite his name, was completely French and had been chef to successive British ambassadors since being hired by Sir Christopher Soames in 1971. Before that, he had been the personal chef of The Duke and Duchess of Windsor during the years they spent in Paris after the Duke had abdicated (as King Edward VIII). James had been threatening to retire for a number of years, but Susie persuaded him to stay on the understanding that we would leave the embassy together, on the same day, when my posting came to an end.

We invited all my living predecessors who had been ambassador to France, plus Mary Soames (Sir Christopher's widow and Sir Winston Churchill's daughter) and her son Nicholas, for a dinner in chef's honour. When I asked him if he would attend as our other guest of honour and present the award to James, Prime Minister François Fillon immediately accepted – despite having told me not long before that he was the most Anglophile prime minister of France (his wife, Penelope, is part-Welsh and part-English) never to have been invited to 10 Downing Street. (After a long argument with the prime minister's staff, who contended that the French president was the PM's real opposite number, I was eventually able to arrange an invitation.) Would a British prime minister attend a dinner at the French ambassador's residence in London to celebrate the award of an honour to his cook? I suspect not.

As well as being ambassador to France, I also found myself non-resident ambassador to the Principality of Monaco. Following a reset of its very close relationship with France in 2005, Monaco became entitled to full diplomatic relations with third countries, including the UK. My predecessor hadn't made it to Monte Carlo, so in 2007 I became the first British ambassador in eight hundred years to present credentials to the head of state, His Serene Highness (HSH) Prince Albert II.

And very enjoyable it was too. After the formal ceremony, conducted in French, we lapsed into conversational English (Prince Albert was educated at Amherst College,

Massachusetts, and is comfortable in English, Spanish and German as well as French). Later, HSH invited Susie and me to his lunch for guests attending the Monte Carlo Masters tennis tournament, with the world's best players performing just below us against the breathtaking backdrop of the Mediterranean. Earlier in the day I managed my own game of men's doubles on the same perfect clay courts. And because we were in Monaco, we of course had to visit the casino – from where we retired a little after midnight with net winnings from the roulette table of €140.

Foreign policy was an important part of my work with the French, not least in the context of what to do about the revolt against Colonel Muammar Qadhafi's rule which had developed in Libya towards the end of 2010 as part of the Arab Spring.

In February 2010 Susie and I had decided that we would like to find some winter sunshine to recharge our batteries. Libya seemed a good idea, since – we thought – it might not be long before the remarkable Roman sites along its northern shore became overrun with tourists as the country emerged from its self-imposed isolation. We were all the more keen when an Arabic-speaking British friend of Egyptian-Iraqi origin, Roger Bilboul, and his wife Sally said they would be glad to join us.

I telephoned Vincent Fean, the ambassador in Tripoli, whom I had known for some years. When I asked for guidance about visas and visiting, Vincent said we really didn't have a choice but to stay with him. Without his invitation, we wouldn't get a visa (we clearly didn't need to worry that the country was about to be the next Mediterranean hotspot). And if we didn't stay with him, we wouldn't get a drink.

We went for a long weekend, and took in day trips to the east of Tripoli to Leptis Magna and, to the west, to Sabratha. Both are extraordinarily well-preserved examples of the rich Roman civilisation and architecture which thrived along the southern shore of the Mediterranean two thousand years ago – and both seem to have survived the destruction of the civil war which broke out a year after our visit. In the heart of modern Tripoli, as teasers of what lies an hour's drive outside town, stand the triumphal arch of Marcus Aurelius and a remarkable, Italian-built museum containing some of the finest Roman mosaics and glass anywhere in the world, matching even those of Antioch in south-eastern Turkey.

We travelled in a brand-new Al Afriqiyah Airlines A330, complete with unsolicited upgrades, and didn't realize how fortunate we had been until one of the only two A330s the airline possessed crashed into the desert just short of the Tripoli runway a few weeks later as a result of pilot error.

By March 2011, after some weeks of inconclusive diplomacy amid a growing threat to the civilian population from the Libyan armed forces, the situation in Libya had begun to move very quickly. In the space of a week, the international community moved from deciding at a meeting of G8 foreign ministers in Paris on Monday, 14 March that there would be no foreign military intervention, to beginning hostilities – led by France, the US and the UK – just five days later on the following Saturday.

Shortly after the meeting of G8 foreign ministers, President Sarkozy pressed the visiting US secretary of state, Hillary Clinton, to agree to military action to prevent a humanitarian catastrophe. Sarkozy himself had come under pressure from the prominent French philosopher-activist Bernard-Henri Lévy, who had been in Libya the previous weekend and reported that the lives of the civilian population of Benghazi were under severe threat.

Clinton emerged from her meeting with Sarkozy convinced that he had a point, irritating though she sometimes found his way of making it. How could the United States stand by if the civilian population of Benghazi was going to be slaughtered? She in turn got in touch with two other prominent female members of the Obama administration, National Security Adviser Susan Rice and Samantha Power, the US ambassador to the UN. Meanwhile, Lévy brought his group of Libyan opposition politicians, led by Muhammad Jibril, to see me as part of his campaign to stiffen the Security Council's resolve. By the time the Lebanese circulated a draft Security Council resolution – at the request of the Arab League – two days later calling for the introduction of a no-fly zone and 'all necessary measures' to protect civilians from 'crimes against humanity', the United States was on board.

Surprisingly, the resolution, which became known as SCR 1973, was passed with ten votes in favour, five abstentions, and none against. It was later reported that Vladimir Putin, who was at the time serving as prime minister before beginning his second stint as Russian president, was furious with his protégé and stand-in, Dmitry Medvedev, for allowing the resolution to go through. Putin convinced himself that Russia had been tricked, and became implacably opposed to any further authorization by the UN Security Council of military action for humanitarian or any other reasons – despite being quite content later to send troops into Ukraine and deploy a massive Russian force in Syria when his ally Bashar al-Assad appeared to be losing the civil war he had started in 2011. The Libya vote at the UN, and the firm line she later took as secretary of state on Russia's illegal annexation of Crimea and fomenting of civil war in Ukraine, appear to have been the two major reasons why Putin did all in his power to stop Hillary Clinton winning the US presidential election in 2016.

The British media ran a series of jingoistic headlines on Sunday, 18 March, as they reported the attacks against Qadhafi's forces. President Obama was clear from the beginning that the US would take part in the initial strikes but then take a back seat as the Europeans assumed responsibility. Britain and France, supported by a number of allies, kept up the airstrikes and the pressure, and the UK provided valuable refuelling and AWACS support to the combined effort. But from the perspective of the UK's military credibility in Washington, it bothered me that of the 110 Tomahawk cruise missiles fired at Libya on the night of 19–20 March, the UK contribution was just 3. Later, when I was serving in Washington, I found senior US political and military figures sharing with me their concerns about the UK's ability to step up to the plate as and when there was again a need for military action.

The events in Libya were, of course, part of a wider protest movement which became known as the Arab Spring. Inevitably it directly affected the lives of many of my Arab colleagues. One afternoon in February I dropped round to see my Egyptian colleague, and friend, Nasser Kemal. I joined him for a while as he sat, chain-smoking, glued to the television screen watching events unfold in

Tahrir Square, Cairo, where he had friends and relatives risking their lives. Like friends in Iran in 1979, and later in Turkey in July 2016, he was torn between excitement at the prospect of a freer future for his country and concern that the events he was witnessing might deliver something different and worse.

On 1 September 2011 Paris was again the venue for a major international gathering on Libya. With Obama still insisting that the US was not the lead player in this particular drama, Sarkozy had invited David Cameron to co-chair a conference to consider how best to help post-Qadhafi Libya transition towards a peaceful, stable and eventually democratic future. Seventy-one delegations had confirmed their participation. In Paris as in London, there was a sense that things had gone well over the six months since hostilities had begun, and Sarkozy was quietly appreciative of Cameron's acceptance that he should again be hosting a big international event.

For me, it was one of those days which highlighted the value of having an extraordinary ambassadorial residence which people loved to use, where we could make everyone welcome and which was capable of genuine multitasking. My day began with a breakfast for the chief executive of a major French investor in the UK, continued with a series of quick meetings and dictation of a few operational messages to my staff, and then took me off to the military airport at Villacoublay, south-west of Paris, to meet former prime minister Tony Blair. He was coming in from Jerusalem to see David Cameron and others about his plans for avoiding a train wreck at the UN General Assembly in New York later that month over moves to give formal recognition to

a Palestinian state. Blair, at the time, was the representative
of the Quartet, a foursome comprising the UN, the EU, the
US and Russia, which had been given the role of trying to
mediate between Israel and the Palestinians.

Arriving at the house, we had time for a quick cup of
coffee in the garden before Blair had an appointment with
Hillary Clinton in the residence of the US ambassador next
door. Typically, Blair suggested that I go with him so that he
could reintroduce me to Clinton in advance of what he and
the Americans by then knew would be my next assignment –
back to Washington as ambassador three months later. Over
the years, I found Blair unfailingly aware of how he could
help officials do their job – whether by making an introduction, attending a reception or having a quiet word in a
friend's ear. Clinton couldn't have been more welcoming,
and we got off to a great start. Unfortunately, she had already
decided that she would leave the Obama administration
after the 2012 presidential elections, regardless of who won.

Back at the house, I left Blair to his other meetings, for
which Baroness Cathy Ashton, the EU's high representative
for foreign and security policy, had also come over to the
embassy, and set off back to Villacoublay to meet the current
prime minister, David Cameron. My deputy, Ajay Sharma,
went to the Gare du Nord to meet Foreign Secretary William
Hague, who was coming from London separately for the
Libya meeting.

With the residence increasingly resembling Piccadilly
Circus, Cameron managed a brief catch-up with Blair
before setting off on foot for a pre-conference bilateral with
President Sarkozy. From that discussion, and from William
Hague's separate session with his French opposite number,

Alain Juppé, it became clear that Paris was thinking that there needed to be a new Franco-British initiative to take forward the Middle East peace process in the light of the problems which Blair had described and apparent US indifference to the risk of a bust-up at the UN over recognition of a Palestinian state.

In between these various meetings, there was time for Cameron to have a brief meeting with Rory Stewart, who became a candidate for the leadership of the Conservative Party when Theresa May stood down in 2019, and then for the position of mayor of London, but was at the time an up-and-coming MP with remarkable experience of development and conflict in Iraq and Afghanistan. He was just back from Libya, where he reported that life in the capital, Tripoli, was more normal than anyone could reasonably have expected. As if that wasn't enough meetings, the Canadian prime minister, Stephen Harper, popped in for a short bilateral before the principals went off along the rue du Faubourg St Honoré to the Élysée Palace for the main Libya event.

A little over a month later, on 20 October 2011, the allied military presence made it possible for the rebels to capture and kill Qadhafi during what became known as the Battle of Sirte. But as in Afghanistan and Iraq, it turned out to be far harder than anyone anticipated to maintain and build on early military successes and transfer power to local people able to run the country. One year later, on the anniversary of the 9/11 al-Qaeda terrorist attacks on the United States, a premeditated attack on the US Consulate in Benghazi by the jihadi group Ansar al-Sharia led to the deaths of Ambassador Chris Stevens, his colleague Sean Smith and two CIA contractors.

It was a terrible moment for the US State Department and for the colleagues and relatives of those killed. It also became – quite unjustly, in my view – a defining political moment for the secretary of state, Hillary Clinton, who went on to run for the presidency four years later in 2016. Her Republican opponents conducted no less than six separate investigations into what happened, and the extent of Hillary Clinton's personal responsibility for Stevens's death, over and above the enquiries carried out by the State Department itself. None found a shred of evidence of Clinton's culpability, even though it was clear that some State Department officials had turned down requests before the attack for additional security measures.

A more serious criticism, which can be levelled at all the governments that joined the French-led military intervention in 2011, is that we allowed action originally authorized by the UN for humanitarian purposes to develop into a full-scale regime-change operation, without any clear plan for what should come after military victory. Ten years on, Libya was still a failed state with warring factions supported by outside powers unable to agree among themselves on a way forward, leaving the field clear for assorted jihadist groups, including ISIL, to wreak havoc.

France itself left us with plenty of other fascinating memories. Shortly before visiting Corsica for the first time, I told Bernard Squarcini, the head of the DST, France's internal security directorate, about our plans. Since he was Corsican, I thought he might have some tips. Not only did he provide wonderful advice as to where and how to get the best lobster and chips, but we found that the mere mention of his name gave us the finest service – and sometimes a flat refusal to let Susie and me pay for our meal.

And of course, as ever, the travel was instructive. If we hadn't gone to Corsica, would I have ever known that there was an Anglo-Corsican Kingdom between 1794 and 1796 and that Captain Horatio, later Admiral, Nelson lost his eye at the Battle of Calvi defending it? Or that driving round the perimeter of Cap Corse is one of the most breathtaking road trips in Europe?

We left Paris in January 2012, after nearly five years at the embassy. A few weeks before our departure, the new president of the Palace of Versailles and a friend from the time she had worked for Nicolas Sarkozy in the Élysée Palace generously offered to make her first official dinner in her new role a birthday celebration for Susie. It turned out to be a delightful occasion, attended by a lot of our Parisian friends. On the way to Versailles we ran into heavy traffic. As I began to worry that the guest of honour would be late, I noticed that there was an official convoy with police escort making better time. Guessing that it was François Fillon and his wife, since they were also coming to the dinner, I cheekily asked one of the police outriders if we could tag along. We made it a little late, but no later than the prime minister of the French Republic.

12

Managing the 'special relationship'
(2012–16)

Earlier in my career, and even when I was Director Americas at the FCO, it had never crossed my mind that I might become ambassador in Washington. I was quite relaxed, even enthusiastic, about leaving the diplomatic service after Paris and starting a new life.

But once it was clear that the position would be coming vacant roughly when I was due to leave France, I decided to put my hat in the ring. After all, I knew the United States well and had an American wife who was something of a political junkie; and Washington was the top job.

It took a while for the FCO to run a competition to ensure that all credible candidates could bid. For my part, I was reassured to hear that the prime minister had said he could live with that – despite his misgivings about some aspects of how the FCO made its senior appointments – as long as one of the names on the shortlist put to him was mine.

Once the decision was taken, and announced, the outgoing ambassador, Nigel Sheinwald, invited Susie and me for a short visit so that we could start getting used to the house and what was on the US/UK agenda, and meet a few interesting people. Beyond the call of duty, but kind and helpful. We did the same thing for Kim and Vanessa Darroch towards the end of 2015 when we were on our way out of Washington, and for Peter and Suzanne Ricketts when they were about to succeed us in Paris. Curiously, it was by no means standard practice but always seemed to me both a natural courtesy and operationally essential to help your successor get started, despite it being said that all ambassadors have an equally low view of their predecessor's taste and their successor's judgement.

Human nature being what it is, being selected for such a big and challenging job as ambassador to the United States sends you delving into the history books. The only other person who turned out to have been head of mission in Turkey, France and the United States – albeit not in the same order – was Viscount Lyons, who arrived in Washington in 1858 as Minister of the Legation. Back then, ambassadors were only appointed to what were considered first-level countries and the US didn't qualify until Britain became the first foreign country to upgrade its envoy to the rank of ambassador in March 1893. Other countries followed suit later in the year.

Lyons stayed for most of the civil war, which he found – not surprisingly – stressful. Even in the best of times, the climate of Washington was disagreeable for much of the year – it remained a hardship posting for British diplomats until air conditioning became widely available in the mid-twentieth century – and Lyons left Washington suffering from 'nervous exhaustion and migraines' at the end of 1864.

He was then posted to Constantinople, the capital of the Ottoman Empire, which didn't become officially known as Istanbul until 1924, a year after the founding of the Turkish

Republic. The omens were less than propitious, since Lyons was sent out to replace the wonderfully named Lord Dalling and Bulwer, who was removed after the Ottoman government bought him an island estate and several thousand pounds appeared to have gone missing from the embassy account. In the event, Lyons only stayed in Constantinople for two years, but spent twenty more as ambassador to France after being cross-posted to Paris in 1867. At the time, Washington was the most junior of the three diplomatic posts held by Lord Lyons. By the second half of the twentieth century, the order had been reversed.

We arrived in Washington in January 2012. As in Paris, and Ankara, the job of British ambassador carried with it the privilege of living in a magnificent residence originally intended to make a statement about Britain's place in the world and more recently seen, pragmatically, as an invaluable set of tools to help heads of mission do their job. When the British government decided in the 1920s that it needed a new embassy in Washington, it turned to the pre-eminent architect of the day – and master-planner of New Delhi – Sir Edwin Lutyens. It asked him to design a grand building which would be both ambassadorial residence and office suite. It turned out to be the only house he ever built in the Western hemisphere. (By 1960 the house had been supplemented by a large concrete office block next door, which even the conservative *Illustrated London News* described as Britain's revenge for the embassy the Americans had built not long before in London's Grosvenor Square.)

The house is a blend of the English country house, for which Lutyens was already renowned, and the American colonial style. Over the years it has played host to a never-ending stream of visitors, including most US presidents since Herbert Hoover and members of the Royal family. Winston Churchill was a regular visitor. Ironically, before Brexit, when European embassies opened their doors and gardens to the general public each year on Europe Day (9 May), ours was the most popular stop on the circuit with an average of ten thousand guests. French visitors were surprised to discover they were allowed to walk and sit on the grass.

Not long after our arrival, the house was also the venue for the first meeting between Prime Minister David Cameron and President François Hollande of France. Both were in town in May 2012 for a G8 summit hosted by Obama, ten days after Hollande had defeated Nicolas Sarkozy in the French presidential elections. There was some bad blood since Cameron had declined to meet Hollande as candidate and had endorsed his opponent. In diplomatic terms, it was quite a gesture on the part of Hollande – in protocol terms, as head of state, Cameron's senior – to say he knew me from our time in Paris and so was happy to come to the British residence for his first encounter with the British prime minister.

No book had ever been written on the house and the role it has played in British-American diplomacy so, as in Paris, we commissioned, and helped edit, a book written by Anthony Seldon and Daniel Collings with photographs seeking to do justice to the building, its gardens, and its place in history. It's called *The Architecture of Diplomacy: the British Ambassador's Residence in Washington*.

By the time we arrived in Washington, plans were already underway for a high-profile visit by David Cameron, who had gone out of his way to show his support for President Obama's re-election later that year. It was, to all intents and purposes, a state visit – a thank-you for the very successful state visit the Obama family had paid to Britain in May 2011. On a perfect spring day, with the magnolia trees in the White House garden in full bloom, there was a magnificent welcome ceremony of the kind normally only granted to heads of state. The atmosphere, and the speeches, were relaxed, amusing, intimate. Mimicking the kind of English associated with Cameron's social background, Obama said he was 'chuffed to bits' to welcome the British prime minister and his wife Samantha to Washington, and promised he would keep the relationship 'top-notch'.

On the second evening, the president invited more than four hundred guests to a state banquet in a large tent on the South Lawn of the White House, complete with music provided by the British folk-rock band Mumford & Sons. Beforehand, the Obamas asked Cameron and his senior team to join them in the private apartments upstairs in the White House for cocktails and the chance to look at the view across the gardens to the Washington Monument and the Capitol, the magnificent domed building at the other end of Pennsylvania Avenue housing the two chambers of Congress. The president was welcoming, charming and amusing but, in contrast to his wife, Michelle, who seemed to like nothing more than giving a big hug to everyone she met, kept his emotional distance.

I found myself talking to him about Iran, and making the point that it was an Indo-European nation that was very different from the Arab countries of the Middle East. I explained that, at the popular level, Iranians were far more interested in prosperity and progress than in the theocracy practised by the ayatollahs who hijacked the 1979 revolution.

Iranians, I noted, were possessed of a strong sense of their own history and identity, and of grievance over the way great powers had treated them over the previous hundred years.

Obama seemed interested. As his biographer David Remnick noted in a perceptive analysis of the Obama presidency in *The New Yorker* in January 2014, he was convinced that an essential part of diplomacy was the public recognition of historical facts, however uncomfortable they might be. He was as aware as any of us of the number of false starts there had been to efforts to reset relations with Iran after 1979. One of the more comic was a secret visit to Tehran by President Reagan's recently retired national security adviser Robert McFarlane in the autumn of 1986 with a bible and a cake in the shape of a key, apparently due to an over-literal translation of a private message from an Iranian intermediary to the effect that the 'key' to unlocking relations with the United States was a *shirini* – a Farsi word which can be translated as 'pastry', 'cake', or 'sweetener'. So effective was their cover, and so few Iranians knew about their visit, that the delegation were confined to their hotel room for five days and then expelled.

President Obama's view was that it would be in the interests of people throughout the Middle East, and further afield, if Sunni and Shi'a Muslims could find a way of living alongside each other. He told Remnick: 'If we were able to get Iran to operate in a responsible fashion – not funding terrorist organizations, not trying to stir up sectarian discontent in other countries, and not developing a nuclear weapon – you could see an equilibrium developing between Sunni, or predominantly Sunni, Gulf states and Iran in which there is competition, perhaps suspicion, but not active or proxy warfare.'

His measured approach was evident in the way he used the traditional Nowruz, or New Year, message to the people of Iran on 21 March 2013 to show that he understood and respected Iran's complicated history with the US. Later, in 2015, I tried with friends in the White House to go a little further and use the visit of what was known as the Cyrus Cylinder to a number of US cities to send a further message of openness to the Iranian regime in that year's Nowruz message.

The Cyrus Cylinder is a piece of baked brick around nine inches long covered in cuneiform inscriptions which was used as a kind of early printing device. It tells the story of how, on the orders of the Persian King Cyrus the Great, after he had captured Babylon in 539 BC, the peoples held captive by the Babylonian King Nebuchadnezzar – including the Jews he had deported – were allowed to return to their homelands. Often described as the first bill of human rights, it encouraged tolerance and mutual respect between peoples.

Such is its significance that a copy of the original, which is in the British Museum, is on display at the headquarters of the UN in New York. Our thought was that mention of the cylinder's visit to the United States in the president's annual message might be a useful and uncontroversial way of signalling that today's Iranians are the inheritors of a great civilisation which has in the past defended the rights of Jewish (and other) people – quite a contrast to the chants of 'death to Israel' promoted by the present Iranian government. The initiative fell foul of the delicate stage which the nuclear negotiations with Iran had reached (of which more below), but it was worth trying.

I wasn't aware at the time of my brief conversation with President Obama in March 2012 that in the autumn of 2011

Hillary Clinton, his secretary of state, had already been in touch with the Omanis about opening up a back channel to the Iranians. So had John Kerry, then chair of the Senate Foreign Relations Committee. Mid-level meetings between US and Iranian officials began in secret in the summer of 2012 and developed into higher-level exchanges – still in secret, and still facilitated by the Omanis – about nuclear issues in February 2013, immediately after Kerry succeeded Clinton as secretary of state.

As Hillary Clinton came to the end of her time at the State Department, I offered to give a dinner in her honour and to thank her for the way she had always been available to us. During my first year in Washington we had worked closely together on number of sensitive issues including China, the export of military equipment built in the UK but containing US components, and the fall-out from the fatal accident on the BP-operated *Deepwater Horizon* oil rig in the Gulf of Mexico in April 2010.

Clinton readily accepted our invitation but then had to cancel after hurting her head in a bad fall in early December. I was both surprised and delighted when she suggested reinstating the dinner on a Monday in late January 2013, which turned out to be the beginning of the week in which her successor, John Kerry, was confirmed by the Senate. So, with her British opposite number William Hague and his wife, Ffion, coming over specially, we gathered a hundred of Washington's foreign affairs A-team for a celebration of her four years in the job. During that period Hillary had, along with Christine Lagarde, managing director of the International Monetary Fund, and Chancellor Angela Merkel, become one of the most admired and recognized female figures on the world stage.

We had discovered that, while following doctor's orders and resting after her accident, Clinton had fallen for the hugely popular British TV series *Downton Abbey*. So, as part of our tribute, we persuaded the cast to put together a short video thanking her for her service and ending with the thought that 'the best is still to come'. In the end, of course, although she won the nomination of the Democratic Party in 2016, her hope of ending her career in public service with four years in the White House was dashed by Donald Trump in the election in November that year.

As I rode in from the airport with Hague, he sought assurance that I was going to push the boat out, with good food and some appropriately celebratory wines. I told him that of course I would but that, for his and my sake, I was rigorously applying my value-for-money criteria in selecting wines which were good but not extravagant. I said I was sure that within three days journalists would be using the Freedom of Information (FoI) Act to ask what menu we had served and how much I had spent on each bottle of wine. Rightly or wrongly, austerity was the watchword of the government's economic policy – which was why I kept saying no to otherwise irresistibly good offers from the local agents of Rolls-Royce and Bentley to supply me with a new official car at a special price.

I was wrong. The first FoI request arrived one day, not three days, later. Since there was no evidence of extravagance, there was no story. Thanks to the nature of the occasion, typically witty speeches from both Hague and Clinton, a touching contribution from soon-to-be secretary of state John Kerry and the extraordinary calibre and warmth of so many of the brilliant foreign policy experts who were in Washington at the time, the evening was a great success. It set us up nicely for close engagement with Kerry and his State Department team as well as the White House and several key figures on Capitol Hill.

It was a propitious start too for our cooperation over Iran with the new team at State. There had been various attempts over the years to reach an agreement with Tehran that would limit Iran's ability to develop nuclear weapons, and in the early 2000s an effort by Britain, France and Germany – known as the E3 – foundered on the Europeans', and American, refusal to allow Iran to continue with even the smallest amount of uranium enrichment. A fresh attempt to use Iran's desire to build a research reactor to come to an understanding also failed in 2009, in part because of the re-election that year of hard-line President Mahmoud Ahmadinejad and in part because of the revelation in the autumn that the Iranians had been building a secret enrichment facility at Fordow outside Qom.

US and EU sanctions followed, but the Iranian nuclear programme continued unabated. By 2012 the Israelis were beginning to urge military strikes. The Iranians did nothing to allay their concerns, which grew as they persevered not only with enrichment but also with the construction at Arak of a heavy water reactor which would give them the option of an alternative plutonium-based route to nuclear weapons. Missiles launched in test firings continued to have 'Death to Israel' written on them and Iranian support for both Hamas (in Gaza) and Hezbollah (in Lebanon) continued. The role of Israeli diplomats in Washington was to ensure that US politicians on all sides were aware of the threat that Iran posed to their country's security. Ahmadinejad made their task easy.

As my Israeli colleague commented to me, 'he's the gift that keeps on giving'.

Obama was, and remained, unconvinced by the case for military action. In the context of Iran as of Syria later in his presidency, he liked to tell his military commanders that getting in was the easy part. What was less clear was whether US military action – with the precedents of Afghanistan, Iraq and (already) Libya in his mind – would solve the problem; and how the US could get out leaving the situation better than it had found it.

The president's view was that the most effective use of American power was when fear of what it could do made bad actors act differently without the actual deployment of force. And, as he said in an interview with Jeffrey Goldberg in *The Atlantic*'s April 2016 issue: 'When we deploy troops, there's always a sense on the part of other countries that, even when it is necessary, sovereignty is being violated.'

So, in February 2013, Obama authorized the start of very closely held discussions on a possible deal with the Iranians, this time with an understanding that the US would be prepared, in the context of an umbrella agreement, to allow Iran to continue enriching a limited amount of uranium.

The secret nature of these exchanges caused some frustration for the other European players who had, a few years earlier, been at the forefront of attempts to secure a nuclear deal with Iran. They regularly came to Washington for consultations, given that sanctions had been unable to stop the Iranian nuclear programme and the risk of another Middle Eastern conflict was rising. But their US counterparts were not authorized, at that stage, to let them know what was going on.

My own private contacts with the very small number of US officials in the know meant that I had been able to keep a handful of senior British officials in the loop. We were well-placed to monitor, if not to have much influence on, what was happening. It was only towards the end of 2013 that the State Department team, led by the hugely experienced and widely respected Deputy Secretary of State Bill Burns, felt the time had come to bring in the EU's high representative for foreign affairs, Cathy Ashton, and subsequently the other permanent members of the Security Council, plus Germany.

There wasn't any alternative since the support of the other key players was going to be essential if the international community as a whole were to be got on board. The issue was simply one of timing. The P5+1, as the group became known, then began an intensive period of diplomacy which eventually evolved, in July 2015, into the nuclear deal with Iran that carried the title of Joint Comprehensive Plan of Action (JCPOA in English or BARJAM in Persian). It was finally announced, after a series of last-minute delays, in Vienna on Bastille Day, 14 July 2015. Later, when asked about the significance of the agreement, John Kerry said he believed it had stopped a war.

From the outset, the deal proved controversial. Obama's political opponents criticized it as a matter of course, but also because public opinion in the US was overwhelmingly hostile to Iran. Everyone remembered the humiliation of fifty-two American diplomats being held hostage for 444 days after the seizure of the US Embassy in Tehran by revolutionary mobs on 4 November 1979. Iran's abiding hostility towards Israel was deeply unpopular with the Jewish community and also with Christian evangelicals. So was its support for armed groups like Hezbollah and Hamas. One of the reasons why

Prime Minister Benjamin Netanyahu openly supported the Republican candidate Mitt Romney against Obama in 2012 was that he believed Washington had gone soft on Iran.

Congressional opponents – almost all Republicans but also some Democrats – tried to kill the deal. With strong support in both houses, Congress had voted earlier in the year to give itself a sixty-day period to review any nuclear deal concluded with Iran. With the Israeli prime minister calling the JCPOA 'an historic mistake' and 'one of the darkest days in our history', a resolution of disapproval was duly tabled and the administration set about trying to ensure that there were at least thirty-four votes in favour, so that after it passed – a foregone conclusion – there was not the two-thirds majority required to overturn the veto which President Obama was certain to wield.

The ambassadors of the other signatory powers became closely involved in making the case for the deal in the media and on Capitol Hill. This was partly because all our governments wanted it to succeed but also because the Obama team judged that arguments from America's close allies, as well as from China and Russia, would help show that it was not simply a flagship achievement of the Democratic president. For two months my JCPOA signatory colleagues and I engaged in debates over arcane aspects of the deal, including 'snapback' provisions, permitted enrichment levels, centrifuge categories and how much of its frozen oil revenues Iran would get back (it turned out to be entitled to around $60 billion, much of which has still not been returned).

The influential American Israel Public Affairs Committee (AIPAC) piled in heavily, spending millions of dollars on advertising, distributing talking points which rubbished the deal and flying their entire executive board to Washington to meet with (they said) four hundred different members of the House and Senate. Sixty members of Congress also visited Israel during the August recess.

We were up against some big battalions. But I was convinced from my own contacts on Capitol Hill that we could be more ambitious than just seeking to get thirty-four senators to support the deal. There were after all forty-six Democrats in the upper house. While many were fearful of opposing AIPAC and alienating big Jewish donors, most – in private at least – realized that even an imperfect agreement limiting Iran's nuclear ambitions was a lot better than no deal at all. Throughout the negotiations, the Israeli government had been warning Washington that it might have no choice but to launch military strikes against Iran's nuclear installations if there was not a comprehensive deal. Our deal had some weaknesses – what freely negotiated agreement between adversaries doesn't? – and it never claimed to address Iran's bad behaviour in the region or to stop its ballistic missile tests. But it was a lot better than the alternative of another Middle Eastern conflict.

So I told my colleagues at State Department that we should aim to get forty-one of the forty-six Democratic senators on board, not just thirty-four, since that would be enough to block the motion coming to the floor of the Senate for a vote – and was politically far better than the president having to exercise his veto. Despite State's scepticism, that was what we did, with a couple of votes in hand. Sometimes alone, sometimes with my admirable P5+1 colleagues, I talked to dozens of senators and more than a hundred members of the House of Representatives (even though we knew the big

Republican majority in the House would vote for the motion of disapproval).

As ever, foreign policy was closely linked to domestic politics and the electoral timetable. One of my friends in the US Senate was Senator Joe Manchin of West Virginia, who used to invite Susie and me to visit him and his wife Gayle on the houseboat which was their DC home not far from the Capitol building. Joe was a special case – a Democratic Senator representing a strongly Republican state. When I talked to him about Iran, Joe said to me disarmingly that he fully understood the points I was making about diplomacy being preferable to war, but I had to understand that he was the senator of a state where Obama's approval ratings were in single figures.

It wasn't often that the British, Chinese, Russian, French and German ambassadors made common cause in front of America's legislators. But on that occasion, we did, supported by the EU representative. I like to think that we prevailed because we had the relationships, a sufficient grasp of the detail and a common conviction that the deal represented the best, if not the only, way of avoiding an arms race and perhaps even war.

Not long after the key vote on Iran in the US Senate on 10 September 2015, British Foreign Secretary Philip Hammond visited Washington, in part at least to sustain the case for allowing the deal to be implemented. One of the more memorable meetings was our call on Bob Corker, the plain-speaking Republican senator from Tennessee and chair of the Senate Foreign Relations Committee whose name was on the bill providing for Congress to review the deal. Normally affable, we must have caught him in a bad mood. He launched immediately into a complaint about the UK's efforts to shore up support for the JCPOA, warning that he would consider any further interference of this kind in America's domestic politics 'a personal affront'.

I hadn't prepared Hammond for this attack, and he was initially lost for words. So I asked Corker why he considered it acceptable for the prime minister of Israel to lobby every senator personally against the US government's policy but not for the British ambassador to support it, when – unlike Israel – we had been a co-negotiator and co-signatory? Because President Obama did not treat the Israeli prime minister with the respect he deserved, Corker replied.

The next time we met, Corker could not have been more civil and was clear this exchange was water under the bridge. But it was a revealing indication of how raw the nerves had been – and would remain – on Capitol Hill in relation to everything concerning Iran and Israel.

Two years after our common, and successful, efforts to keep the JCPOA alive, and more than a year after I had left Washington, Donald Trump began moving towards dissociating the US from the deal – mainly because it was the flagship diplomatic achievement of his predecessor, Barack Obama. By then, it was no longer possible to create the same sense of common purpose among the P5+1 diplomats. An Iranian diplomatic friend told me I shouldn't be surprised: neither Russia nor China was interested any more in facilitating better relations between Iran and the United States.

President Trump's decision to tear up the deal in May 2018 was, in my view, a profound error. I believed it was at least in part the result of pressure – financial and political – from donors in America, Israel and states like Saudi Arabia and the UAE which were determined to see Iran cut down to size after events in Iraq, Syria, Lebanon and Yemen had given Tehran such significant geostrategic gains. Trump said he wanted to negotiate a better deal than the one he rejected, but some of the hawks around him in Washington clearly saw destroying the JCPOA, and the economic benefits it promised Iran, as a means of delivering regime rather than policy change.

The trouble with sanctions is that they only work if they are linked to outcomes which the party being penalized can deliver, and aren't just an expression of hostility. The reality is that the members of the regime (and the Revolutionary Guard) which the Trump administration claimed to be targeting were precisely the ones who benefited most from the black market created by the sanctions – both financially and because they can blame America for the hardship their policies, their incompetence and their corruption cause the Iranian people.

I thought then, and have often thought since, that the Iranians underestimated the damage which US sanctions could do to their economy, however unreasonable and extraterritorial the rest of us might consider them. But the Americans also underestimated the ability of even an economically wounded Iran to ensure that if they couldn't export their oil, others in the Gulf wouldn't be able to either. This was the very clear message they sent to their Arab neighbours when in 2018 and 2019 they launched deniable attacks on tankers around the Straits of Hormuz and then put half of Aramco's oil and gas production facilities in Saudi Arabia temporarily out of business with a series of surgical drone and missile strikes. Almost immediately, Saudi Arabia and the UAE began quiet overtures to Iran to see whether there were ways of lowering the threats to regional security. The answer, following the killing of General Qassem Soleimani, head of the Revolutionary Guard's Qods Force, on President Trump's orders in January 2020, seemed to be not until the November 2020 US presidential elections were out of the way.

For a British ambassador in Washington, the priority is to develop relationships with local movers and shakers, be they administration, Congressional, entrepreneurs or commentators. But diplomatic colleagues matter too. There has sometimes been a tendency on the part of British diplomats to feel that the strength of the 'special relationship' with America is such, and our interests in America so extensive, that we don't need to spend time with the representatives of other countries. A retired Iranian ambassador once told me of his farewell meeting with the shah before taking up his appointment in Washington. 'There are two foreign countries that matter in the US,' the shah told him: 'the Israelis, who are all over the city and Congress; and the British, who operate less visibly, below the surface, but even more effectively.'

That hasn't always been the case but it's nice to know when the competition rate you. In fact, links with colleagues from other countries are a valuable two-way street, as well as being part of the enjoyment of a foreign posting. I stay in touch with friends of many different nationalities who were ambassadors in each of the countries where I was posted. In Washington I had plenty to do with, among others, the Saudi ambassador Adl al-Jubair. When he was promoted to the position of foreign minister, he was replaced by a member of the ruling family who had previously spent some years in a commercial role in Jeddah. He told me he sometimes used to have difficulty explaining his full name to foreign visitors, and had once introduced himself as Abdullah bin Faisal bin Turki bin Abdullah bin here too long.

As a child he had survived being sent to a minor boarding school in England, despite once running away at the age of 14 and making it all the way back to Saudi Arabia on his own. But he bore no grudges and we had several enjoyable meals together before I left and he was replaced by the younger brother of Crown Prince Mohammad bin Sultan.

The very effective and well-connected ambassador of the UAE, Yousef Al Otaiba, also became a good friend. Not long after Trump's election victory in November 2016, Yousef and I found ourselves speaking on the same panel. I asked him what a Trump presidency looked like from an Emirati perspective. 'No lectures on human rights. No restrictions on the arms we can buy. And a US government that hates Iran,' Yousef replied. 'What's not to like?' Relations with my Russian colleague Sergiy Kislyak took a bit longer to get off the ground. In my first months in Washington I tried a couple of times to get him round for a meal, to no avail. Later, working together on the Iran nuclear deal helped us get to know each other. When he invited me to his residence for an excellent lunch and a number of rare vodkas, Sergiy said he was sorry I hadn't responded to any of his invitations to lunch when I had first arrived in the city. None had reached me, or my office, but he clearly felt that levelling the score was a useful way of making a fresh start.

There is form between British and Russian diplomats.

Back in December 1876 an important conference of the great powers opened in Istanbul to press the Ottoman government to reform following a series of massacres in Bulgaria which attracted international outrage. The British delegate was Lord Salisbury, then secretary of state for India and later a distinguished Conservative prime minister. He didn't much care for the British ambassador to the Sublime Porte, who he said had 'gone native'. But he did rate his Russian opposite number, Count Nicolai Ignatiev, who he noted 'had the reputation, in a heavily contested field, of being the most accomplished liar on the Bosphorus'.

Lord Salisbury had another good reason to stay on good terms with Ignatiev, since he often seemed to be better informed about British foreign policy then he was himself, possibly because the Russian ambassador in London was reported to be sleeping with the wife of a senior cabinet minister. Unfortunately, neither the conference nor efforts by Ottoman liberals to begin a reform process were enough to prevent an outbreak of war between Russia and Turkey a few months later, which Ignatiev used to negotiate the Treaty of San Stefano, marking a further weakening of Ottoman power in the Balkans.

While Iran was the single most specific area of policy in which foreign diplomats in Washington, like me, felt able to make a difference, there was plenty else happening on the international stage with which we were involved. In early 2012, Afghanistan was still a high priority for us all, and more or less constantly subject to strategic review. More than ten years after the atrocities of 9/11, ninety thousand US troops were still there, as were some nine thousand British service personnel. I hadn't been there since visiting as a tourist in 1977 and so I decided to make a refresher visit, including a stopover in Islamabad, Pakistan.

I went just a couple of months after taking up my appointment in Washington. Leaving the aircraft at Kabul airport, the first person I met – who had also just arrived, on a US military aircraft – was Lindsey Graham, a Republican senator from South Carolina. A long-time National Guard reservist, he was a frequent visitor and had become a great expert on Afghanistan. During my time in Washington, we often discussed Afghan problems, and much else. The senator was a great Churchill admirer, which helped our personal relationship. We had our disagreements, not least over Iran. But it never affected our friendship, which continues to this day.

I began with a series of meetings in the Afghan capital, including a talk with General John Allen, the US commander of ISAF, who also became a close friend. There was then a quick flight down to Helmand province to meet some of the British troops at Camp Bastion and Lashgar Gah, which gave me a flavour of what everyone was up against.

There were nevertheless some bright spots. Apart from the remarkable morale of our people in Helmand, the Afghan governor of the province could not have been more welcoming or appreciative of what the UK was trying to do, although there did seem to be a general sense that, once we had gone, the jungle would again take over the clearing we had made and normal life – including almost complete dependence on the narcotics trade – would take over. In Kabul itself, it was hard to escape the impression that the high security levels, which foreign diplomatic missions had no choice but to prioritize, meant that few embassies had much chance to get out and about and acquire a sense of what was happening beyond their bubble.

In Pakistan, I was put up by a friend and colleague, the high commissioner Adam Thomson. He had been keen that I renew my acquaintance with some of the influential players in the Pakistani government before I became too affected by the general despondency which tends to settle on US attitudes towards the Pakistani authorities each time a fresh initiative fails. As always, I learned a huge amount from the visit. One particular conversation sticks in the memory. Over dinner at Adam's house, I found myself discussing terrorism with a former senior military officer. Predictably, I made the case that facilitating terrorist operations in Afghanistan was both wrong and counter-productive – a variation of the argument I had tried to put to President Musharraf nearly fifteen years earlier.

In reply, my genial dinner companion argued that every country in the region used terrorist proxies in pursuit of its strategic interests. They had learned to do so from the British when we were the dominant power in the region, and I was naive if I thought they were going to give it up now.

Unlike Iraq and Afghanistan, and Libya, Syria was a country in which local developments rather than outside military intervention were the cause of the turmoil and bloodshed. There were widespread demands for the incumbent dictator, Bashar al-Assad, to go. But the slaughter and the risk of further regional contagion were such that there was more or less continuous debate within and between the major political capitals over how the international community should respond.

Demands for Assad to step down were no more effective than they had been in the early stages of the uprising in Egypt in 2011 when Washington and others were repeatedly calling for President Mubarak to leave the stage. When he finally went, the Muslim Brotherhood had developed enough support to win the subsequent elections but then proved so unfit to govern that Egypt ended up with a military coup taking its political and cultural life back to square one.

In Syria, modest 'train and equip' programmes helped rebel groups stand up to Assad's ruthless army but often got caught up in local rivalries or turned out to be helpful more to the cause of Sunni Jihadist groups than to the needs of the suffering population.

Red lines were nonetheless drawn, in particular in relation to the use of chemical weapons (CW), which Saddam had deployed to such murderous effect against Iraqi Kurds. In late August 2013 it became clear that Assad's regime had used CW against civilians on an industrial scale on the 21st of that month. The credibility of President Obama's warnings, and readiness to act, was on the line. So was that of America's Western allies.

During the following days, while many foreign political leaders were on holiday, Obama's National Security Council (NSC) held several meetings to decide what it should do. As was so often the case in Washington, the machinery of the NSC whirred away but without bringing close allies into the loop until it had reached a decision. By 24 August, Obama had decided that the time had come to launch limited military strikes against the Syrian installations responsible for the storage and launch of the barrel bombs containing CW.

As in Afghanistan in 2001, Iraq in 2003 and Libya in 2011,

the United States' preference was not to go it alone. When the call came through to the British prime minister that weekend to ask if the UK was prepared to join the US in launching strikes in just a couple of days' time, David Cameron was on holiday at Polzeath, one of North Cornwall's finest surfing beaches. Conscious of the criticisms he had sustained for not having consulted Parliament before joining in the air strikes against Libya, Cameron stalled. He would have to take professional advice, he said, and seek the approval of the House of Commons.

That took a few days to organize. Parliament was recalled from its summer recess and a vote was taken on the evening of Thursday, 29 August. I had myself been on holiday in Turkey but, after calling No 10 to check on the politics, decided to return to Washington early in case things did not go as planned. I was in the air when the vote was taken and arrived at Dulles airport a couple of hours later, to survey the damage.

Going into the vote, No 10 thought they had a deal with the Labour opposition, which meant they didn't need to worry about the thirty Tory and nine Liberal Democrat MPs who didn't support airstrikes. But the deal didn't survive the Labour Party's internal consultations or the febrile debate in the House, and the government was defeated by an embarrassing 285 votes to 272. Cabinet ministers were stunned, and began to warn that questions would now be asked about 'Britain's role in the world' (George Osborne, chancellor of the exchequer, Radio 4) and harm to the 'special relationship' (Philip Hammond, defence secretary, *Newsnight*). In case anyone had missed the point, France immediately said the vote would have no effect on its willingness to join the US in taking military action in Syria.

Others have written in detail about what happened next, as Obama first decided that he would go ahead anyway and then, after one of his habitual walks round the White House garden with his indispensable chief of staff, Denis McDonough, changed his mind. He would instead consult Congress – having been assured by the congressional leadership that the votes were there.

It rapidly became clear that they weren't. By chance, John Kerry was in London a few days later. On Monday, 9 September, the prime minister gave him breakfast at No 10. During a lull in the conversation, I asked whether the US might defer missile strikes but threaten military action if the Syrian government's stocks of chemical weapons were not destroyed or removed by a given deadline of, say, two weeks' time. Kerry replied that there had been signs from the Russians that they might be prepared to make that happen, if there was a stay of execution on the US side. The conversation then moved on.

Speaking shortly afterwards at a press conference with his UK opposite number, William Hague, Kerry announced that Assad had a week to hand over his entire stock of CW if he was to avoid military strikes. The White House was alarmed, and Kerry had to spend part of the flight back to Washington telling journalists that he had been speaking rhetorically and had no expectation that the Syrians would comply.

But the Russians moved quickly. By 12 September Kerry and Russian Foreign Minister Sergei Lavrov were together in Geneva discussing modalities and within a few months Kerry felt able to say that the diplomatic solution had probably been more effective as a means of ruling out any further Syrian use of CW than airstrikes would have been.

From my point of view, the immediate task was to set about limiting the damage inflicted by the vote in the House of Commons on the bilateral relationship and the UK's global credibility. Initially, as Obama also decided to go down the route of consulting his legislators, I felt that this could be explained as an example of how democracy now worked, and the vote of 29 August didn't need to be more than a bump in the road of our uniquely close defence partnership. I also pointed out to White House friends – who took the point – that proper consultation meant more than a phone call to the prime minister once Washington had finally reached a decision and was ready to go. But I knew, and explained to London, that we would have to ensure this didn't happen again.

In a subsequent interview with Jeff Goldberg of *The Atlantic*, Obama spoke of his pride in having resisted the automatic way in which Washington tended to respond to military challenges of this kind. He also confirmed that the vote in the House of Commons did affect his own decision to hold off from airstrikes against Syria. John Kerry said as much to me privately. Later in the campaign, because he realized that the UK could not again be found wanting by its most important ally – and that he had set a precedent by consulting Parliament in advance – David Cameron made sure that he had parliamentary approval for the deployment of UK combat aircraft over Iraq when airstrikes were needed against the most murderous of all the jihadi groups, ISIL.

The Syria vote on its own did not inflict irreparable damage on our credibility. The Americans understood as well as anyone how democratic politics worked. But over the next two years senior US cabinet secretaries, officials and generals, and the president, would tell me at regular intervals that they were worried about the UK's declining military capability as our armed forces shrank along with our ability to conduct any kind of sustained combat. Addressing this perception was a major theme of a personal note I sent the prime minister about our place in the world, and fixing the relationship with America, the day after he was re-elected on 7 May 2015.

Washington didn't always make it easy for us. The United States has a number of regulations which limit how far foreign partners can sell defence equipment to third countries – which is one reason why the French have for many years sought a high degree of autonomy for their defence industry. There are also limits on how far even America's closest allies, like the UK, are trusted with the codes to ensure that the equipment they buy from the US will perform to the same standard as the equivalent equipment supplied to the US armed forces. Not long ago, for example, the Royal Air Force took delivery of a number of Boeing Chinook helicopters which spent years in storage because they were unusable for the tasks for which the RAF had bought them.

There was a particular problem with the supply of defence equipment to countries in the Middle East. In Washington, I spent years – literally – trying to get approval from the US authorities for the export to Saudi Arabia of Paveway IV guided weapons, or smart bombs, built in the UK by the US defence contractor Raytheon. The problem was the effective veto given to the Israeli government back in the Reagan era by US laws guaranteeing Israel that no equipment made in America, or with US components, would undermine the qualitative military edge which it enjoyed over its neighbours.

The UK argument – which the US government never

directly addressed – was that it was unreasonable for the exports of military equipment made by US companies on the territory of America's closest ally to be subject to an Israeli veto – a veto which, in the view of some defence experts, was sometimes manipulated for the benefit of other US-based defence firms.

Eventually, a compromise was reached including special controls over the storing and usage of the Paveways. But it took years; and the irony was that, by then, the Saudi Air Force had begun using versions of the Paveway to attack targets in Yemen as they took sides in the civil war on behalf of the ousted former president Abdrabbuh Mansur Hadi. What the US, and the UK, should have been considering was how to ensure the weapons were not used against inappropriate civilian targets, rather than worry about Israel, with which Saudi Arabia and the UAE are now closely allied against Iran and other common enemies like the Muslim Brotherhood and ISIL.

Apart from the concerns I was hearing in 2014–15 about the declining capabilities of the British armed forces, the links between British and American armed services and commanders were always strong, and the contact frequent. We used much of the same equipment, we exchanged personnel, and of course the UK's nuclear deterrent is closely integrated with the US navy's own Trident programme.

During my time in Washington I had the chance to showcase the history of our naval links. The First Sea Lord, Admiral George Zambellas, rang me from London one day to say that he was wondering what to do with the badly damaged ship's bell of the last British aircraft carrier named HMS *Illustrious*, which had just been decommissioned. He recalled that my father had been on board the previous *Illustrious* when she had come under sustained bombardment by the Luftwaffe in January 1941 while leading a convoy to relieve the island of Malta. Would I like the bell for the rest of my time in the US?

The answer was an enthusiastic yes, since my father had both been on board the carrier throughout the worst of the bombing attacks but had also sailed with *Illustrious* afterwards to the US naval base in Norfolk, Virginia. He spent six months with her there while she was repaired before returning to active duty with the carrier later in the year. So I put the ship's bell, complete with the dramatic damage it had sustained from molten shrapnel and bomb fragments, on display on the terrace of the residence, with a short note explaining how it symbolized the way our two navies had worked together to fight against fascism, and what happens when diplomacy fails.

Just before we left Washington, Defense Secretary Ash Carter and his wife Stephanie very kindly gave a reception in Susie's and my honour in the Pentagon, complete with a military band playing some Beatles and other golden oldie British songs. HMS *Illustrious'* bell came too, and now resides on permanent loan in the office of the secretary of the US navy.

Given how closely the US and UK had worked together over the years in defence of shared values, I was often surprised by how hard it was to persuade the US to support the principle of self-determination for the Falkland Islanders, which had taken up so much of my time as the FCO's Director Americas. At the time of the 1982 war with Argentina, Margaret Thatcher had already had some difficulty in seeing off an attempt by

Secretary of State Al Haig to mediate on sovereignty. Thirty-five years later I still found it impossible to get the State Department to endorse the idea that the inhabitants of the islands had the right to decide their own future.

It was partly that Washington had an understandable reluctance to take sides against a fellow American state on any sovereignty or territorial issue. But it was also, or so US diplomats argued, related to concern that ceding the principle of self-determination for the Falkland Islanders might open up the risk of Puerto Rico deciding to secede from the United States. This was far-fetched, and still is, despite the war of words the Puerto Ricans had with President Trump over the damage caused by Hurricane Maria in 2017, since Puerto Rico is wholly dependent on the US for financial support.

Perhaps the argument provided cover for a more general reluctance, which was harder to explain to a close ally, to be seen to take sides in someone else's dispute in your own back-yard – or hemisphere. Instinctively, the United States has always been non-interventionist. Isolationists often quote these powerful lines from the Independence Day address delivered by President John Quincy Adams back on 4 July 1821: 'America does not go abroad in search of monsters to destroy. She is the well-wisher to the freedom and independence of all. She well knows that by enlisting under other banners than her own, were they even the banners of foreign independence, she would involve herself beyond the power of extrication in all the wars of interest and intrigue, of individual avarice, envy and ambition, which assume the colors and usurp the standards of freedom.'

America had been deeply reluctant to get involved in either of the two world wars, until attacks by Germany and Japan respectively changed the public mood. Given its own history with the UK, US political leaders were also reluctant – as Winston Churchill discovered during the Second World War and when he was prime minister for a second time in the 1950s – to support the UK whenever it looked as though we were seeking to hang on to the vestiges of colonialism.

In the letter I sent him on 8 May 2015, I underlined to David Cameron the importance of keeping alongside the Americans as he pursued his declared aim of using the referendum he had promised in his Bloomberg speech of 23 January 2013 to keep the UK at the heart of a reformed, better-functioning EU. The Americans knew Cameron wanted to stop his party 'banging on about Europe', and that he was worried about the rise of the United Kingdom Independence Party (UKIP), which by 2012 was running at 15 per cent in the polls and making inroads into the Conservative base. But they feared that actually holding the referendum would enthuse rather than discourage the eurosceptics who had been threatening to split the Conservative Party since the 1980s when Margaret Thatcher was in power.

The Conservatives' unexpected victory in the May 2015 general election left them with a parliamentary majority of seven. The Lib Dems lost 48 of their 56 seats, bearing out Chancellor Merkel's maxim that coalitions are always bad electorally for the junior partner, while the Scottish Nationalists added 50 seats to their 2010 tally of 6, mainly at the expense of the Labour Party whose total was down 24 at 232.

Cameron immediately realized that he would have to honour the commitment he had given to hold an in/out referendum on EU membership. After doing his best to negotiate improvements to the terms of the UK's membership in Brussels, he announced on 20 February 2016 that the referendum would be held on 23 June, and that he would campaign for the UK to remain a member of a reformed EU. There was a sense of disappointment in 10 Downing Street that the press were not kinder about the package Cameron brought back from Brussels, and unhappiness that the EU did not go further in allowing limits on the free movement of labour. Some Europeans say now that they had further concessions in their pocket that they could have given Cameron, but that he was so confident of his ability to win the argument back home that he didn't ask. If so, they might have done a better job of signalling such flexibility before it was too late.

Part of the problem on immigration and free movement was that neither Conservative nor Labour politicians were prepared then, or during the referendum campaign itself in 2016, to admit that the bulk of the immigrants Brexiteers wanted to keep out came from outside the EU, not inside; or that the UK couldn't manage without the 3 million-plus citizens from other EU countries who kept the country's financial, hospitality, agricultural and national health services functioning. An honest approach to immigration, rather than the nonsense that Boris Johnson and his fellow eurosceptics talked about the UK being invaded by 80 million Turks if we didn't leave the EU, might have produced a higher-quality debate and a better-informed outcome to the referendum itself.

From the US perspective, Brexit was a worrying prospect. The British always attached more importance to the concept and language of the 'special relationship' which Winston

Churchill had invented than the Americans did. But most presidents – including Donald Trump, who spoke of 'the greatest alliance the world has ever known' during his state visit to the UK in June 2019 – have been happy to speak of the unique nature of our bilateral links. For President Obama and many other Americans in 2016, a key element of that relationship was the influence the UK wielded inside the EU and its ability to reflect within Europe the policies and values that mattered to the US. Conversely, the significant role the UK played in EU foreign policy had much to do with the influence we enjoyed in Washington.

Americans also feared a weakening of Western security if the UK was no longer at the heart of Europe, even though there was no question of it leaving NATO. The Obama administration was unimpressed by the Brexiteer argument – since peddled enthusiastically by the Trump team – that a comprehensive free trade agreement (FTA) with the US would make up for the loss of tariff- and quota-free access to the EU's single market for the 45 per cent of Britain's exports (2019 figures) which were going to the rest of Europe.

Following the hugely successful state visit the Obamas paid to the UK in 2011, I tried but failed to arrange for The Queen to pay a return visit to the United States. I had suggested one to the White House early in my term, in the full knowledge that Her Majesty would soon be giving up long-haul travel. There was no response until, in 2015, the White House began asking me to fix a date. Sadly, despite their and my best efforts, we had missed the boat. In that case, Obama responded, I will go to London myself to say goodbye before I leave office at the end of 2016.

And so he did. When he came to London in April that

year for a lunch to celebrate The Queen's ninetieth birthday, Obama told a press conference at the FCO that the UK was going to be 'at the back of the queue' in any post-Brexit trade negotiations with the US. The referendum, after all, was just two months away. Both he and Cameron were clear that we would do far better negotiating with the US as part of the EU rather than on our own.

Speaking warmly of his admiration and affection for the Royal family, which I had observed on many occasions in the Oval Office, and of Britain more generally, Obama declined to respond to questions about an article which Boris Johnson, then mayor of London, had written saying that his 'part-Kenyan' ancestry caused him to be anti-British.

Obama may have over-spoken in his desire to debunk some of the myths which the Brexit lobby was disseminating about the opportunities of post-Brexit free trade, but there was no doubting the sincerity of his views. The subject came up during all my farewell calls in Washington at the end of 2015, when almost everyone I saw said they hoped the UK would not commit such a monumental act of self-harm as to leave the EU, damaging our shared interests in the process.

Perhaps I didn't do a good enough job of reassuring the people who mattered. I told the president that I would shortly be leaving Washington when I took Prince Harry to see him in December 2015. 'Well, Peter,' he said, 'we'll miss your wife.' This might or might not have had something to do with Susie having been born in Washington, being a lifelong supporter of the Democratic Party and having done a brilliant job of supporting me in Washington, as she had in Turkey and France.

My *amour propre* survived. Just before we finally left

Washington in January 2016, John Kerry, the secretary of state, gave a farewell party for us in the State Department. He had become a good friend over the years – we had first got know each other at a Sunday lunch given by mutual French friends during my time as ambassador in Paris. Kerry spoke of the 'special relationship' with great warmth, spoke of how we had worked together and ended with words of welcome to my successor, Kim Darroch, who, he said, would have 'the toughest act to follow since the magician Fred Kaps took the stage after the Beatles on the Ed Sullivan show in 1964'. That cheered me up.

One of the more fun and successful diplomatic parties we gave in Washington was in fact a fiftieth anniversary celebration of the Beatles' first visit to America, complete with a lookalike Beatles tribute band. Next most popular was the party we gave for the cast of *Downton Abbey* to mark the launch of the second season of the series on the PBS network.

And yet… Washington wasn't always the easiest place for British ambassadors to feel they were making a difference. The work I and my P5+1 colleagues did on Iran was a rare example of countries other than Israel and Ireland, with their powerful domestic lobbies, affecting US domestic policy. But there was always lots going on, and always an insatiable appetite back home for up-to-the-minute reports on US politics, campaign trends and debate outcomes.

Just as in France, there were painful anniversaries to be marked of moments in our shared history when the relationship had not been that special. Few people recall that it wasn't stable or warm enough after the trauma of the Revolutionary War, as Americans call it, or the War of Independence as it is known in the UK, and the later War of 1812, to permit a visit by a British monarch until King George VI's hugely successful visit in 1939.

No one on the British side wanted to pay much attention to the 200th anniversary of the War of 1812, which was the last occasion when Britain and America found themselves on opposing sides. This by-product of the Napoleonic wars, which confusingly lasted from June 1812 until January 1815, cost a total of twenty-five thousand lives and was a result of British efforts to enforce a trade blockade of France as Napoleon pursued his efforts to conquer the European continent. To make the blockade effective, Britain forced American merchant sailors to man ships of the Royal Navy, inflaming American public opinion (as did British supplies to Native Americans raiding settlements on the frontier with Canada where the Americans had territorial ambitions of their own).

In the UK few people have even heard of the conflict, except perhaps through the story of the burning of the White House by British 'Redcoats' in August 1814. For Americans, however, it's an important part of their history. They failed in their attempts to acquire chunks of Canadian territory but they effectively saw off the British expeditionary force. And so as British ambassador I found myself making speeches at numerous events ranging from the 200th anniversary of the American victory at the Battle of Baltimore in September 1814 to a ceremony honouring the sacrifice of those who lost their lives in the huge defeat suffered by the British at the Battle of New Orleans in January 1815, two weeks after the signature of the Treaty of Ghent had ended the war but news of which had yet to reach the deep south.

I was at least able to point out that had it not been for the siege of Baltimore, the flying of the garrison banner over

Fort McHenry and the presence of Francis Scott Key on a truce vessel observing the British bombardment, Key would never have written 'The Star-Spangled Banner', which later became America's national anthem.

Fortunately, there were other anniversaries that were more agreeable to commemorate. I had a wonderful visit to Fulton, Missouri, in January 2015 for the fiftieth anniversary of Winston Churchill's death in 1965. Fulton had been the venue for Churchill's famous 1946 'Iron Curtain' speech which warned of what was to come as the Soviet Union took possession of Eastern Europe, so the occasion had a special poignancy.

The great wartime leader knew a thing or two about public relations. Churchill had agreed to give the lecture at Westminster College in Fulton on condition that President Truman went with him. As a result, over forty thousand people turned out for his speech. Shortly before arriving at the venue, Churchill asked his driver to stop the car. He fished out a cigar, put it in his mouth, unlit, and asked the car to drive on. 'Never forget your trademark,' he told his travelling companion.

Stalin dismissed Churchill's warnings as 'war-mongering' and even *The Times* of London criticized him for being alarmist. But Churchill was right about the threat which the Soviet Union would pose to international security. He was also convinced about the mission of the United States to make the world a better place. In one of his most powerful radio addresses, back in 1941 before America had entered the war, Churchill declaimed: 'Believe me, for I know – the action of the United States will be dictated not by methodical calculations of profit and loss but by moral sentiment and that gleaming flash of resolve which lifts the hearts of men and nations and springs from the spiritual foundation of human life itself.' Then at least, he was also right about that.

Churchill hadn't always been so convinced of US benevolence. In June 1927, annoyed by US efforts to establish parity with the Royal Navy, Churchill wrote in a private cabinet memorandum: 'It always seems to be assumed that it is our duty to humour the United States and minister to their vanity. They do nothing for us in return but exact their last pound of flesh.'*

Ninety years later, whatever else was going on between London and Washington, recalling the role played in our shared history by the most famous Anglo-American of all invariably went down well. As ambassador, I was given a constant reminder of Churchill's importance to the relationship by the statue of him by the American sculptor William McVey erected in 1966 on Massachusetts Avenue at the edge of the embassy property, one foot on British territory, one on American, two fingers aloft in that famous Victory sign; and by his final invocation to members of his cabinet when he left office in 1955: 'Never be separated from the Americans.'

At gloomier moments, I would recall with a smile another famous Churchillism: 'You can always trust America to do the right thing – after it has exhausted all the alternatives.'

It wasn't easy to persuade US senators, or even members of the House of Representatives, to come to the house. There

---

* Churchill's memorandum was recalled in Andrew Roberts's biography *Churchill: Walking with Destiny*.

were rules about accepting hospitality from foreign governments or their representatives. But it was easier if there was a purpose, or theme, to the event. Discussing the problem once with a senator friend, I suggested a Churchill-themed dinner. That, he felt sure, would do the trick. So I got in touch with Nicholas Soames, Churchill's grandson and an old friend, and asked if he would come over and sing for his supper. Fifteen senators joined us, from both the Democratic and Republican parties, and Nicholas did us proud.

A little further up Massachusetts Avenue from the Churchill statue, and the British Embassy, stands the US Naval Observatory. Its grounds include a modest but pleasant house which has been the official home of the vice president since 1974. So, during our time at the embassy, Vice President Joe Biden was our next-door neighbour. He was a people person. Genuinely interested in other human beings, and warm to the point of being more tactile than some people found comfortable but which we found endearing, he understood that the secret to getting another person to do what you want is to gain their trust and to understand their needs as well as your own.

Biden had been a member of the US Senate since 1973 and over the years had acquired great experience and a wide range of contacts around the world. We often discussed foreign affairs, including Iraq – on which he was President Obama's point person for three years – and Turkey, in which we had a shared interest.

When he wasn't apologizing for the noisy clattering of the Marine Two helicopters which brought him in and out of the grounds, and endlessly practised doing so at weekends when he was away, Biden and his wife, Jill, were the most gracious of neighbours. Half Irish, as he liked to remind me, he also had a British great- great- great-grandfather who had been a sea captain employed by the East India Company. After retiring early, Christopher (or possibly George) Biden wrote a book about rules and discipline on board ship of which the enlightened theme was that if you treat people with respect, they will not abuse your trust.* He seemed genuinely pleased when, with the help of the FCO's Library & Records Department, I found the short book which his ancestor had written, had it bound, and presented him with a copy.

The tensions with the Irish American community over Northern Ireland, which had been a feature of my first spell in Washington in the mid-1990s, were a thing of the past by the time I arrived back in DC in 2012. The Good Friday Agreement (GFA) of 1998, and the common efforts of the UK and Irish governments to ensure its success – strongly supported by Democrats and Republicans alike in the US – had changed all that. St Patrick's Day (17 March) was still an important day in Washington's political calendar. After all, 40 million Americans claim Irish descent. The Taoiseach and his wife came over each year for the celebrations. These included a bilateral with the president, a large reception at the White House, and a lunch given by the Speaker of the House of Representatives for the visiting delegation and leading lights of the Irish American community.

Vice President Joe Biden was always involved. He had, after all, been one of the four leading Democratic senators who had urged President Clinton to take risks for peace in

---

* Further details in Professor Tim Willasey-Wilsey's August 2020 article for Gateway House entitled 'Biden's ancestral Chennai connect'.

Northern Ireland back in 1993–4; and when running for president in September 2020, he tweeted a warning to the British government not to allow the GFA to become 'a casualty of Brexit' by allowing the return of a hard border between Northern Ireland and the Republic.

Conscious that Northern Ireland was part of the United Kingdom, the Speaker – who since January 2011 had been John Boehner, a Catholic Republican from Ohio – was careful always to include senior visitors from the North and from Westminster in his St Patrick's Day lunch. Protocol dictated that the Irish and British ambassadors and their spouses joined the president, the Speaker and the Taoiseach at the top table, while the vice president and secretary of state took care of other guests. Despite their political differences, Speaker and president invariably seemed to enjoy each other's company and the annual lunch was a rare opportunity to have a good, informal conversation with Obama, and not just about Irish or European affairs.

With the rise of the conservative Tea Party wing of the Republican Party, the centrist Boehner was coming under increasing pressure. The Tea Party was firmly opposed to the kind of deal-making which once characterized the way Congress worked and criticized Boehner for supporting higher taxes on wealthy Americans. In September 2015, after refusing to go along with a budget which defunded the non-profit organization Planned Parenthood, he decided to step down and a reluctant Congressman Paul Ryan – who had been Mitt Romney's running mate in 2012 – agreed to take over.

Shortly before he left office, Susie and I went to say goodbye to Boehner in his large, invariably smoke-filled office. He had been instrumental in placing a bust of Winston Churchill in the US Capitol, at the foot of what had been known as 'the English steps' since the building had been attacked and burned by British troops during the War of 1812. He, I and members of the Churchill family spoke at the unveiling and Boehner began a tradition, continued by his successors Paul Ryan and Nancy Pelosi, of giving a small party every November to mark the great man's birthday. The least I could do was wish him well. Boehner said he had never enjoyed diplomatic courtesies – he never came to the residence while in office – but we had always got on. I treasured some of his turns of phrase. Describing his difficult last weeks with the Tea Party, he told me how he had been 'run over like a postage stamp' by 'knuckleheads'.

One of Boehner's predecessors had been the great Tom Foley, who was Speaker of the House from 1989 to 1995 and had represented Spokane in Washington State since 1965. Unusually for an Irish American Catholic and Democratic politician, he was unequivocally opposed to the campaign of violence led by the IRA during the thirty years of the Troubles and a powerful advocate for a peaceful settlement. I had got to know him quite well in the mid-1990s and so went to the memorial service held for him in the Capitol's Statuary Hall.

Among those gathered to show their respects was former president Bill Clinton, with whom Foley had worked closely as Speaker. A little surprised by my account of how much I thought the peace process in Northern Ireland owed Foley, Clinton told me his own story of how Foley had lost his seat in the 1994 elections – the first time since 1862 that a sitting Speaker had been defeated. Clinton had been pushing for a limited, ten-year ban on the manufacture of assault weapons for civilian use, after an all-too-familiar series of mass shootings across America. The gun manufacturers' lobby, the National Rifle Association, as usual opposed the ban but the law was signed into effect on 13 September 1994, less than two months before the mid-term elections.

Clinton related that Foley had told him he would vote for the ban, but wanted the president to know that it would cost him his seat. Clinton said he replied that it simply wasn't possible for such a respected Speaker as Foley to be voted out for doing the right thing. But he had been wrong, and Foley right. Foley lost his seat (Clinton subsequently sent him to Tokyo as US ambassador). The Republicans took control of both houses of Congress for the first time since 1952 – ushering in a new era of scorched earth, take-no-prisoners Republican politics led by the new House Speaker, Newt Gingrich, from which, in my view, the country has yet to recover.

The Clintons were fairly regular visitors to the residence. On one occasion, when we gave a sponsored dinner for the Clinton Foundation, we showed them round the ground floor of the house. When the former president entered the library, with its perfect proportions – almost a cube – and liquidambar wooden panels designed by Sir Edwin Lutyens, he turned to me and said 'If I had the good fortune to live in this house, I'd never leave this room'.

I particularly enjoyed showing him the portrait of Field Marshal Viscount Montgomery of Alamein, painted in 1952 by his former boss, General Dwight D. Eisenhower, a few months before the latter became president of the United States. On the back Eisenhower had written 'To my friend Monty from Ike'.

The oil painting had been bought from Montgomery by a former US ambassador to the UK, Walter Annenberg, who kindly presented it to the British government in 1970. Not only was it a fine painting, it was also a sign of the respect, perhaps even affection, which the two soldiers had for each other, despite the famously difficult relations that existed between Montgomery and his US colleagues – which eventually led even Eisenhower to describe him, in 1958, as 'egocentric' and 'a psychopath'.

There was also a personal angle. When my first wife, Angie, and I bought our house in Tunbridge Wells, Kent, in 1983, I noticed that the parquet floors of the former Victorian rectory – of which we had half – were covered with small indentations as if from golf shoes. 'Yes,' said the (elderly) former owners, 'that's because Eisenhower was billeted here for the months before D-Day and used the back lawn as a putting green but never took his golfing shoes off when he came indoors. He liaised with his military commanders in the neighbouring houses through the underground tunnels you will find still there, close to the specially built air-raid shelters.' Not even David Eisenhower, author and grandson of the president, could confirm the story when he and his wife Julie came to dinner with us in Washington – but he thought it could well be true.

On one of his visits to London, Joe Biden kindly offered me a seat on his plane for the flight back to Washington. It wasn't quite like flying on Air Force One, which President Clinton had once invited me to do when John Major was visiting the United States. But it was a privilege and an experience. Shortly before we took off, one of Biden's staff gave me a word of warning: 'Make sure you pretend to be asleep when the vice president comes by or he'll talk to you all night.' I managed a bit of sleep.

We always enjoyed going to the Bidens' Christmas parties, and they came quite often to the house. The Vice President visited the residence to sign the book of condolence when Margaret Thatcher died in April 2013 and he attended an event I hosted in honour of 'No Labels', a not-for-profit group dedicated to finding bipartisan solutions to problems of national – and international – importance.

Not long before the end of my time in Washington, I gave a lunch in honour of Michael Bloomberg, former mayor of New York City and owner of the eponymous Bloomberg global data business, at which I presented him with an honorary knighthood on behalf of The Queen. It was a very enjoyable, quite intimate occasion attended by several members of the Bloomberg family and a small number of Mike's close friends. Among them was Vice President Joe Biden. The best photographs taken that day were of Biden playing with Bloomberg's infant grandson – the formal pictures of the former mayor with the insignia of an honorary KBE generated rather less interest. But the award was richly deserved. Bloomberg had been an outstanding mayor of New York, a tireless campaigner for gun control and the environment, and a very significant contributor to the UK economy through his investments in the City of London.

Bloomberg decided not to run for president in 2016 because his (very thorough) research showed he wouldn't beat Hillary Clinton to the Democratic nomination. But I wasn't surprised when he entered the race in late 2019, driven, he told me, by an absolute determination to avoid Donald Trump winning a second term. When he dropped out, after a poor showing in the primaries, Bloomberg firmly nailed his colours to Biden's mast.

Following, and trying to make sense of, the domestic politics of the United States is one of the more fascinating aspects of being a foreign ambassador in Washington. The president may only be elected every four years, but the entire House of Representatives and a third of the US Senate are up for election every two. No sooner are members of the House elected than they are already beginning to raise funds, and political support, for their re-election campaign. And that is just at the federal level. Separately, each of the fifty states of the union elect a governor, deputy governor, attorney general and other senior officials as well as (except for Nebraska) having their own upper and lower houses. Elections are huge business: the estimated cost of all the elections which took place in the US in 2020 was $14 billion.

Given the importance of Congress in the system of checks and balances put in place by the Founding Fathers, the congressional races assume huge importance, particularly in those states and districts which are up for grabs. In 90 per cent of the congressional districts, it is known in advance whether the winner will be a Democrat or a Republican, which gives particular importance to the primary process selecting the candidate – and to the favours candidates have to promise their donors in order to win the nomination. In the Senate, in which each state has two elected representatives regardless of size or population, there is more uncertainty and therefore more excitement when each seat comes up for renewal every six years.

But the greatest interest, of course, revolves around the presidential election. The primary elections, in which each party selects its candidate, kick off in the February of election year, and the election itself is always held on the first Tuesday after 1 November. Hopefuls begin making their pitch as much as two years before the election itself. Many drop out early because they can't raise the funds necessary to stay in the race – which is often a lot. But the party challenging the incumbent president usually has a dozen candidates still running by the time the Iowa caucuses and New Hampshire primary at the beginning of election year signal the start of months of intense campaigning as each candidate seeks to win the nomination at his or her party's convention in the summer.

Susie and I had arrived in Washington in January of 2012, an election year. To no one's great surprise the Republicans chose the former governor of Massachusetts, Mitt Romney, as their candidate to run against the incumbent, Barack Obama. Attending the primaries before Romney had finally won enough delegates at the end of May, and then going to the Democratic and Republican conventions in the summer, was a vital and enjoyable part of the job of taking the pulse of American politics and making sense of it to London – and to fellow ambassadors around the world who were watching with almost as much interest.

The 2012 Democratic convention was held at the beginning of September in Charlotte, North Carolina. As usual, confirmation that the incumbent president was his party's choice for a second term was less politically exciting than a convention confirming the choice of challenger. But it was memorable for an outstanding speech by Michelle Obama on her husband's behalf and an overlong, but unmissable, address from former president Bill Clinton officially nominating Obama for re-election. Both seemed to get the audience going more than the president himself. Obama was confident enough in himself and his prospects not to worry about others stealing the show.

Perhaps too confident. Once the conventions were over, the two candidates campaigned in earnest against each other, rather than for the nomination. As part of the process, there was a series of televised debates. We went to the first, in Denver, Colorado, with the aim of feeling the pulse and judging the performance of Obama and Romney. Obama started out as the strong favourite, against the somewhat wooden Romney. Audience reactions, including applause, were not allowed but I recall turning to Susie after a few minutes and whispering that things weren't going according to script. Romney had a clear message which he was delivering with some force; Obama was playing defence, and wasn't far from coming across as entitled – a fatal impression for any candidate to give, as Hillary Clinton found to her cost four years later.

During a commercial break, I hopped up on stage and spoke to Romney. He was relaxed, chatty, confident but clearly not convinced that he was ahead. It looked as though Obama's team were having some sharper words with their man.

By the end of the debate, it was clear that Romney had won. No knock-out, but substantially more points on the board. The Obama team took much longer than usual to field their usual team in the spin room afterwards, where Romney's people were clearly enjoying themselves, and getting their story out first. I learned later that Team Obama had had some trouble persuading the president that he hadn't, after all, wiped the floor with his opponent. He did far better in the next two debates, and in the end won both the electoral college and the popular vote by a comfortable margin.

While in Charlotte for the Democratic convention, I went to call on the mayor, Anthony Foxx. We got on famously, discussing British Airways' plans to begin direct flights from the UK and British investments in and around the city. Soon afterwards, Obama appointed Foxx Secretary of Transportation in Washington where we continued to meet quite regularly. The relationship came into its own when I was asked for help in ensuring that Aston Martin were not put out of business in the US because they were unable to comply with new sidebar safety regulations applicable to their sports cars by a prescribed deadline. I called Foxx up and asked to see him. When we met, he had done his homework, immediately understood what was at stake, and granted Aston Martin an extension which gave them enough time to comply with the new regulations.

The Republican Convention had been held in Tampa, Florida, a week before the Democrats', just as Hurricane Isaac was about to hit that part of the Sunshine State. For Republicans, this was the moment when they anointed their candidate and gave him the best possible send-off for the two months of official campaigning against his Democratic opponent. Overall, Tampa lacked the star power which the Democrats later displayed. And their star turn fell flat when Clint Eastwood made an incoherent – and clearly unvetted – address to an empty chair apparently representing Barack Obama.

On 3 November, just a few days before election day, I went to West Chester, Ohio, political home of Republican House Speaker John Boehner, for one of Romney's last rallies. I was accompanied by Scott Furssedonn-Wood, head of my political team at the embassy, who had been told the rally would be indoors. It took place in an open-air fifteen-thousand-seat stadium built for the purpose where the faithful waited patiently in the freezing cold for the candidate, accompanied by his running mate Paul Ryan and most of the other Republican wannabes who had by then fallen in behind him. Luckily, we ran into Stuart Stevens, Romney's chief strategist (who in 2020 became a member of the Lincoln Project, a group of veteran Republicans determined to stop Donald Trump winning a second term). He miraculously produced two highly sought-after fleeces embossed across the back, bizarrely, with 'Romney–Ryan Real Recovery Road Rally'. Scott and I decided that I should wear mine inside out.

When Scott disappeared to try and find out when the main show would start, Stevens took further pity on me. Why didn't I join the governor inside his campaign bus while we waited for the warm-up acts to finish? I did, and spent a relaxed twenty minutes with the Romney and Ryan families, surrounded by end-of-the-day detritus of dirty styrofoam coffee cups and snack wrappers. Ann Romney fixed me with a firm stare and assured me that her husband was going to win. The governor was more circumspect. He thought he could win. If he did, he looked forward to working with me; if he didn't, well, he'd see me around.

Three and a half years later, I saw him a couple of times at Harvard, where I was teaching and lecturing for a term after finishing up in Washington, relaxed and with some very good Trump jokes. For a while after the election, whenever I was at events where Paul Ryan – by then Speaker of the House of Representatives – was speaking and caught my eye, he used to tell the audience, tongue in cheek, that the British ambassador had been part of the 2012 Romney–Ryan campaign.

My time in Washington came to an end in January 2016. I had got into the habit of inviting a small group of well-informed, interesting political journalists to a round table breakfast for a private discussion of whatever was going on at the time. I held the last in the series just a few days before Susie and I left the city for good. For fun, since it was the beginning of an election year and our last gathering, I asked everyone to say who they thought would be the Republican nominee and who would be elected president in November (Obama would have served two terms and so couldn't run again). We were nine round the table. Seven thought Senator Ted Cruz of Texas would be the nominee, one went for the libertarian Senator Rand Paul and one for Donald Trump. As successor to Barack Obama, eight voted for Hillary Clinton and one for Cruz.

At that point even the experts couldn't see Trump winning: he was too flawed, unprepared, conflicted and unpresidential. Moreover, the Republican Party didn't want him as their candidate as they did not think he could win. In fact, right up to election night on 8 November, Trump himself didn't think he was going to win. As the world now knows, he lost the popular vote to Clinton by 3 million but became president because fewer than eighty thousand voters in the three critical states of Michigan, Pennsylvania and Wisconsin gave him a majority in the electoral college.

I was the one who voted for Trump at that last breakfast, not because I had any special intuition but because I felt the other runners were weak and he had already begun to attack them effectively. Moreover, it was already clear that he was doing well with his impression of being a man of the people who spoke their language, played to their fears and empathized with their sense of alienation from the political elites as they continued to pay the price of the global financial crisis of 2008.

Six months earlier I had received a phone call from Ed Llewellyn, then the prime minister's chief of staff, now Lord Llewellyn and ambassador in Paris, who was in a car with David Cameron in Singapore. They wanted my off-the-cuff sense of who the Republican candidate was going to be. I recall trotting out all the usual caveats, insisting that it was early days, but saying that my instinct was that it would be one of Jeb Bush, the former president's elder brother, Scott Walker, the governor of Wisconsin, or perhaps Chris Christie, governor of New Jersey. I knew all three and thought at the time that one of them might secure the nomination. But all crashed and burned early in the primary race, reminding me that political predictions are a mug's game. Neither Cameron nor Llewellyn was unkind enough to remind me of the conversation afterwards.

13

Business diplomacy

I was rarely demoralized during the four-plus decades I was in public service. The buzz, variety and stimulation of the work and the calibre and humanity of the people I worked with – of all nationalities – was too great for that. But I did sigh each time a new secretary of state arrived at the FCO and announced that ambassadors were going to have to start acting commercially. I had always regarded promoting the interests of British business as a key part of diplomatic work, to the point that early in my time as ambassador in Turkey I had to explain to London that helping British firms invest abroad was not exporting jobs but creating prosperity. But I did not appreciate being informed out of the blue, when ambassador to the US, that the Department for International Trade in London had determined a precise (albeit completely arbitrary) target for the growth in UK exports to our biggest market in the world for the coming twelve months and that my performance as head of mission would be judged by whether or not that target was met.

As ambassadors, we had significant assets which could

be deployed to help business. We had relationships, of course, judgement, and tactical advice on how to win contracts, though we always had to be careful not to favour one UK firm at the expense of another. We also had valuable real estate. More and more over the years, heads of mission have found ways of using their residences and the public spaces of their embassies and consulates not just to make friends, influence people and put up visiting VIPs but also to promote British business.

Sometimes that would involve – as it often did when I was in Washington – launching a new range of cars on behalf of a prestige UK brand. Sometimes, in both Paris and Washington, we would make the house and its amazing garden available to British fashion houses or financial services firms. Sometimes we would host a lunch or dinner on behalf of a British firm. In each case, the commercial organization would foot the bill, and – increasingly – make a contribution to the wear and tear of the property. If we were going to keep these extraordinary premises, it was only right that they earned their keep.

In Turkey, I was closely involved in helping BP get their Baku–Ceyhan oil pipeline built across Eastern Anatolia to the Mediterranean, ensuring that Vodafone was able to bid in a genuinely open competition for the mobile phone operator Telsim, supporting Airbus and Rolls-Royce in their (successful) efforts to break the stranglehold which US companies had always had on civil aviation, and plenty else.

In France, the UK's membership of the EU's single market meant that there was less need for direct intervention of this kind, though there were moments when the interventionist instincts of the French state needed a nudge to ensure that the rules were applied; and when the legitimate interest of both governments in their respective defence industries required the close involvement of ministers and officials on procurement and collaborative projects.

Sometimes that interest went beyond defence. The rail tunnel under the English Channel – 'la Manche' to the French – was underwritten by the two governments, even if the British side had always sought to emphasize the involvement of the private sector to reduce the cost to the public purse. Finally opened in 1994, it had taken a while to build.

Various schemes had been suggested by imaginative French engineers in the first half of the nineteenth century, but none was able to overcome government caution and the objections of the shipping industry. Urged on by great British engineers like Robert Stevenson and Isambard Kingdom Brunel, Queen Victoria's husband, Prince Albert – who suffered greatly from sea-sickness – took up the cause with the prime minister, Lord Palmerston, in 1856. Palmerston, reflecting an opinion which would have delighted some of his fellow Conservatives 150 years later, replied that the distance between Britain and France was already too short. He is reported to have added, for good measure, that HRH might have thought differently if he had had the good fortune to have been born in the British Isles (Prince Albert of Saxe-Coburg and Gotha had been born in Germany).

Once built, the management of the tunnel and of Eurostar, the train operating company, often attracted – or required – official interest. The French government, for example, saw no reason why Eurostar should feel free to order new trains from the German company Siemens when a comparable product was available from a French firm, Alstom. For the

UK, which no longer had any firms capable of making the train sets, it was a matter of allowing Eurostar to exercise its commercial judgement free of political interference. Usually, but not always, business logic prevailed.

Aerospace was another sensitive sector. Airbus – or rather its original parent company EADS – had begun life in the 1960s as an initiative of the French, German and UK governments as a means of challenging US domination of the civil aviation market. The British government pulled out of the project at the last minute in the 1970s, leaving British aerospace firms in the role of mere subcontractors. The UK achieved full partner status when British Aerospace plc took a 20 per cent stake in the parent company in 1979, only to sell out in 2006 for financial reasons. Overnight it became harder for the UK to apply leverage on business issues like workshare, but it remained one of the four European governments willing to provide repayable launch investment (RLI) as and when Airbus chose to develop new aircraft.

My role, sitting in Paris, was twofold. First, I had to try and ensure that Airbus continued to build substantial parts of their aircraft in British factories: the former British Aerospace plants at Filton, near Bristol, and Broughton in North Wales were particularly strong in the design and manufacture of wings and landing gear. As productivity and engineering quality began to fall behind the international competition, I did what I could to bring British politicians and top Airbus management together so that expectations could be managed, and remedies found.

On one occasion, I invited Louis Gallois, the chairman of Airbus' parent company, EADS, to breakfast with Peter Mandelson, then UK secretary of state for trade and industry, so that each could understand the other's issues. As we discussed whether more could be done to ensure that the UK's share of work was maintained, Gallois asked Mandelson to produce evidence to support his view that Airbus had had a viable commercial alternative to out-sourcing the manufacture of the aluminium wing panels for its next-generation aircraft to the Far East. The secretary of state couldn't – and returned home realizing that there were some important gaps in the briefing he had been given by officials.

It had become impossible to maintain the original 20 per cent workshare agreed when British Aerospace were partners, but we did a reasonable job of ensuring that as much as possible of the wing, landing gear and fuel systems business of what had become Boeing's only serious global competitor remained in the UK.

My second role was to help manage the often-fractious financial relationship between Airbus and the British govern-ment, represented by the DTI and the Treasury. The UK government was normally the most demanding of the four 'home' governments when negotiating the terms of RLI, even though – as I often pointed out – the huge commercial success of the single-aisle A320 family of Airbus aircraft had produced returns on investment above our wildest expec-tations. My argument was that, although the UK no longer had a direct financial interest in the success of Airbus as a business, we had every interest in it remaining willing and able to sustain the success of the UK's aerospace sector, where Airbus employed, directly, twelve thousand people and, indirectly, another hundred thousand.

In the US, the biggest single commercial problem I had to address was the fall-out from the April 2010 accident on the *Deepwater Horizon* oil-drilling platform which was operated in the Gulf of Mexico by Transocean, on behalf of BP. The blow-out killed eleven people and injured another seventeen. BP assumed virtually all the liability, including that of Halliburton, the oil services company which installed the concrete core which blew out after the well had been capped. Huge quantities of oil and gas were discharged – the total oil spill was estimated to be in the region of 4–5 million barrels before the leak was stopped in the middle of July.

BP's response got off to a bad start, underestimating the rate of spillage and with Barack Obama emphasizing the 'British' in BP's name (despite the company's investments at the time being substantially larger in the US than in the UK, or anywhere else) and the under-fire BP CEO Tony Hayward unhelpfully saying to a reporter: 'There's no one who wants this thing over more than I do, I'd like my life back.' To regain the initiative and, I would argue, because BP is a company which takes its corporate responsibilities seriously, the firm decided to accept responsibility rather than litigate.

It made funds available immediately for clean-up of the Gulf Coast and agreed to compensate anyone whose liveli-hood had suffered from the effects of the accident. Late in the day, they decided to end the distribution of funds by Ken Feinberg, a well-known attorney who had made his name *inter alia* by distributing compensation to the victims of 9/11, and seek a separate settlement with a group of plaintiffs' attorneys who were pressing a class action suit. As part of the process, BP were advised by their US lawyers to issue a new invitation to anyone who had suffered loss as a result of the oil spill to make a claim.

Some very dubious claims were lodged, and accepted by the local courts in Louisiana. When I complained to the White House and the Department of Justice (DoJ) about the miscarriages of justice, I was told that that was only to be expected if you went to court in 'the most corrupt state in the Union'. Meanwhile, DoJ was weighing up the penalties it would be applying under the Clean Water Act while the Environmental Protection Agency (EPA) debarred BP from being able to bid for public sector business, including supply contracts to the Pentagon – a long-established client. Initially telling me, and BP, that the ban was temporary and would be lifted within a week, it was retained for more than a year while the other negotiations took their course.

Throughout, I stayed in close touch with senior officials in the White House, the EPA and with the US attorney general, Eric Holder. At various moments it looked as though there were the makings of a deal with DoJ but they were never concluded since BP could only accept complete closure and the attorney general, a federal appointee, couldn't deliver the littoral states along the shore of the Gulf of Mexico which also wanted a share of the cake.

So concerned were London about the damage that was being done to BP, a flagship British company, that the UK government took the unusual step of submitting an *amicus curiae* brief in support of BP's bid to the US Supreme Court to stop the distribution of their money to undeserving and at times fraudulent claimants in Louisiana. The court declined even to take the case. That happens with over 90 per cent of the applications it receives but it was dispiriting to learn that the court had concluded that the documents inviting bids for compensation were drafted in such a way that there was no substance to BP's (or HMG's) complaint.

A settlement was finally agreed in 2016, at a total cost to BP of $65 billion. For purposes of comparison, I note that the 1989 *Exxon Valdez* tanker disaster, which probably did more environmental damage to the coast of Alaska than *Deepwater Horizon* did to the Gulf of Mexico, but did not cause any fatalities, cost Exxon $3.8 billion in clean-up costs and just $500 million in punitive damages, after the US Supreme Court – before the days of the Clean Water Act – upheld the company's complaint that the $5 billion fine ordered by the State of Alaska was excessive. The Union Carbide Corporation of the US paid just $470 million for the toxic gases released by its plant in Bhopal, India, in 1984, which killed at least 3,800 people and harmed half a million more.

The sad conclusion I drew from the experience of *Deepwater Horizon* was that, at least in the state of Louisiana but perhaps also in other parts of the union, it pays to litigate, not accept responsibility as a good corporate citizen.

Louisiana was not the only state where I felt the US judicial system left something to be desired. One of the sadder consular cases I had to manage during my time in Washington was that of Krishna Maharaj, a British subject and once successful businessman, who had been in jail in Florida since 1987 – including ten years on death row – after being convicted of two murders. Maharaj himself, his lawyers and his wife continued to assert his innocence. A former collaborator of Pablo Escobar, the late Columbian drug baron, has recently provided what Maharaj's lawyer calls irrefutable new evidence that he was framed and the men were killed on Escobar's orders. In September 2019 a federal magistrate who reviewed his case said 'no reasonable juror could convict' Maharaj in the event of a retrial.

The judge presiding over Maharaj's original trial was arrested for soliciting a bribe from an undercover police officer three days after the trial began. Six witnesses who would have sustained his alibi were never called. Despite overwhelming evidence that the original trial was neither fair not impartial, and that there is now 'new and material evidence… which would probably have changed the verdict of the court, and which the defendant could not with reasonable diligence have discovered and produced at the trial' (Rule 3.600 of the Florida Criminal Procedure), successive governors of the state of Florida have refused a re-trial. His Christian faith, and his devoted wife, somehow keep Krishna Maharaj optimistic that he will be released before he dies. As I write, he is over eighty years old, diabetic, lame and not due for parole until he is 101.

The status of the dollar as an international currency of choice allows the United States to act against other countries, their citizens and their businesses even when they are not subject to US laws. In Washington, I was frequently asked for help by British firms penalized by US regulators or law enforcement agencies for trading with countries like Myanmar, Cuba or Iran in contravention of US but not UK or international sanctions. Rarely were the indictments tested in court since the mere threat of the withdrawal of a licence to trade in dollars was usually enough to force a settlement, in exchange for a deferred prosecution agreement. I recall the chairman of one UK bank calling me up to complain about official 'extortion'.

The extraterritorial application of US laws and sanctions posed particular problems for the implementation of the 2015 nuclear deal with Iran. As part of the agreement, international (and EU) sanctions against Iran were suspended in exchange for Iran's verified compliance. But America's national sanctions – which related to other issues, including human rights abuses – stayed in place. So, when Secretary of State John Kerry came to London after the signature of the deal to try and persuade European banks and businesses to resume trading with Iran, so Tehran would feel it was getting the benefits to which it was entitled, he was told firmly that no one whose trade was dollar-denominated, or had business interests in the US, could afford to run the risk of doing so. Some said they would try to help if provided with a letter of comfort from the US Treasury, which declined to provide any.

After Donald Trump walked away from the JCPOA in 2018, and imposed additional sanctions on Iran, the Europeans tried to set up an arrangement of their own called Instex to provide a limited facility for the resumption of trade with Tehran. The US made clear that it was opposed to any attempt to help foreign firms get round the effect of its sanctions – which was one of several reasons why in 2019 Iran began to raise the stakes with deniable but highly effective attacks on shipping in the Straits of Hormuz, a US drone and Aramco's oil production facilities in Saudi Arabia.

Extraterritoriality has long been a bone of contention between the United States and other countries, including its closest allies. One of the few major arguments between Prime Minister Margaret Thatcher and President Ronald Reagan in the 1980s centred on America's – ultimately unsuccessful – attempts to stop a British engineering firm providing turbines for the transmission of Siberian gas to European markets. Almost a quarter of a century ago America's 1996 Iran and Libya Sanctions Act came close to falling foul of the UK's (and other European) protection of trading interests legislation before the Clinton administration, after the EU threatened to make a formal complaint to the World Trade Organization, decided to issue waivers to European companies affected by the new law.

This weaponization of the dollar's global role has also been an effective, if much resented, instrument of US foreign policy. Attempts to counter its effects, through such initiatives as Instex or the development of the international role of the euro, have had only limited impact. Those efforts are likely to continue, particularly if the United States persists with the unilateralist approach to foreign policy promoted enthusiastically – but not begun – by Donald Trump. As China's role and influence grows, the chances of the renminbi becoming a rival international currency are also likely to grow. Is it really in the interests of the US to see the global role of the dollar – which contributes significantly to the management of the trillions of dollars of US official debt – called into question by allies and competitors alike?

During the endless debate in the UK about the pros and

cons of Brexit after the 2016 referendum, there was plenty of – mainly misleading – talk of how new free trade agreements (FTAs) with the US and other important markets would make up for the economic cost to the British economy of leaving the EU single market. The reality was that as a member state of the EU, which doesn't have an FTA with the US, our single most important trading relationship was already with the US – where we were also the single biggest foreign investor. At the time of the referendum, Britain did twice as much trade with the US as with its next largest trading partner, Germany. Economists estimated that, if we were able to negotiate a comprehensive post-Brexit FTA of our own with the US, just 0.2 per cent was likely to be added to the UK's GDP over a decade.

As the months passed in 2020, it became clear – as many of us with experience of trade negotiations with the US had warned for years – that there wouldn't be a comprehensive deal by the end of the year. With the US we were negotiating as a single country, not with the clout of a twenty-eight-member state trading bloc – the EU – which was the negotiating partner of the US when we tried, and failed, during Obama's time to agree on a Transatlantic Trade and Investment Partnership. And Britain was dealing with a country which, for all Trump's political enthusiasm for Brexit, was more attached to the concepts of 'America First' and 'Buy American' than to genuine free trade.

Moreover, any deal the UK concludes with the US will have to cover agriculture, including the US desire to export chlorine-washed chicken and hormone-enhanced beef, which upsets consumer groups and would put UK farmers at a huge competitive disadvantage. Other tough nuts to crack with US negotiators will include financial services, public procurement, defence and pharmaceuticals.

By the summer of 2020 the Johnson government, reading the polls suggesting that Trump was likely to lose to Joe Biden in November, and realizing that FTAs were harder, and took longer, to negotiate than they had hoped, began to be less convinced that it would achieve its proclaimed objective of concluding a trade deal with the US by the end of the year.

It was also beginning to rethink its earlier hope that the cost of a no-deal end to the Brexit transition period would be lost in the much larger bill for the Covid-19 pandemic: too many first-time Conservative voters in northern constituencies which are likely to bear the brunt of the cost would be unimpressed. As concern grew in parallel that 'no deal' could lead to Scotland – which voted to stay in the EU by 62% to 38% in the June 2016 referendum – deciding, after all, to leave the United Kingdom, there were fresh signs by the late summer of efforts to reach some kind of trade deal with Brussels. But not with Washington.

14

After Washington (2016–20)

My diplomatic career ended on 17 January 2016, after a little more than forty-three years as a member of the UK's diplomatic service, and the FCO stopped paying my salary the day I left Washington.

Susie and I left Washington for a two-week, end-of-career holiday in Hawaii, the fiftieth state of the union, to which I had never felt I could justify paying an official visit during my four years as ambassador. We visited Pearl Harbor, the site of the attacks by the Japanese air force on 7 December 1941 which brought the United States into the Second World War. We stayed on four different islands; flew over dramatic coastlines, remote interiors and stunning waterfalls in small aircraft and helicopters; went whale-watching; and paid a visit to what was then the gently smouldering Kilauea volcano on Hawaii itself, known as the Big Island.

In Hawaii we became aware of important historical links to Great Britain. Why, we wondered, did the flag of the state of Hawaii include the British flag in the top left-hand corner, despite having never been a British territory? The reason, it turned out, was that Captain James Cook, the renowned British explorer, gave King Kamehameha a Red Ensign on one of his visits, probably in 1785, and the king then used it as his own flag until the end of the century. After disputes with the US at the time of the War of 1812 as to which flag Hawaii should use, the kingdom commissioned its own flag, incorporating stripes representing each of the eight islands of Hawaii but still with the British flag in the corner. The design has remained largely unchanged for the last two hundred years, despite Hawaii becoming a republic in 1894, a US territory in 1898 and then the fiftieth state of the union in 1959. Today, there are probably more visitors to Hawaii from Japan than from any other foreign country, but we found that the history, and the flag, contributed to a very warm welcome wherever we went on Hawaii's beautiful islands.

During my time as ambassador I had however managed a working visit to Alaska. The main purpose had been to meet the governor and local officials, and to visit BP's important Prudhoe Bay production facility on Alaska's North Slope, America's largest oil field, two hours' flying time north of Anchorage and inside the Arctic Circle. Susie and I also visited some of Alaska's natural wonders, including Glacier Bay National Park, where the ice has retreated 70 miles in the last 250 years but the wilderness and natural beauty remain awe-inspiring.

There too, Britain is part of the history. We never had particularly close links with the territory, although Captain Cook visited and some of the finest early exploration and charting of Alaska' glaciers was undertaken by the Scottish environmentalist John Muir. Until the middle of the nine-teenth century, Alaska was Russian, and traces of Russian influence are still visible in some of its architecture. But few Russians lived there and, after the costly Crimean War of 1853–6 in which Russia found itself opposed by the British and French navies, Tsar Alexander II decided that Alaska was too far away and too difficult to defend. As a result, in 1867, in exchange for $7.2 million (about $130 million today), almost 600,000 square miles of Alaskan territory were added to that of the United States.

This was not, of course, the first time that buying territory from a foreign government had helped make the United States what it is today. In 1803, in an even larger transaction known as the Louisiana Purchase, the United States paid France $15 million (about $345 million today) for a total of 828,000 square miles of land stretching from New Orleans in the south to what is now the border between Canada and the states of Montana and North Dakota in the north. In 1916 the United States was also able to purchase the Danish West Indies, which subsequently became the US Virgin Islands, from Denmark for $25 million (in gold).

Given the history, it is perhaps not wholly surprising that in 2019 President Trump should come up with the idea of buying mineral-rich Greenland, a self-governing Danish territory and the world's largest island, excluding Australia which is considered a continent. In 1946 President Harry Truman had offered Denmark $100 million for the same territory. But that was then; and the way Trump approached the subject as a real estate dealer wanting to negotiate led inevitably to a rebuff from the Danish prime minister – and a comment from the somewhat nationalist Danish People's Party that Trump's suggestion was 'final proof that he's gone mad'.

After Hawaii, and with the encouragement of some friends in Washington, both Republicans and Democrats, who had done it themselves, I went to the Kennedy School of Government for a semester. But it might not have happened. When I was getting ready to leave Washington at the end of 2015, Britain was having bureaucratic problems with the Iranian authorities over restoring relations to ambassadorial level after the trashing of the ambassador's residence by a Tehran mob in 2011; so I volunteered to return to Iran for a couple of years to unblock things. My thought was that the Iranians might be flattered to be offered a senior diplomat who had already served as ambassador to France and the United States, who knew their country and had actively lobbied the US Congress on behalf of the JCPOA nuclear deal back in 2015. I also thought that, since Susie's father was still widely respected in Iran for his philanthropy, having built a water works and hospital and endowed a university, she could help break down barriers; and that the Americans – who hadn't had a diplomat posted to Iran since 1979 – might welcome the idea of there being a senior British diplomat in Iran whom they knew well and who would be able to interpret and conceivably influence what was going on there.

The prime minister, David Cameron, liked this idea of 'diplomatic surge'. This was, after all, an opportunity for Britain to make itself more valuable to the US and perhaps offer constructive advice both to policy-makers in Washington and to those Iranians who wanted to reset their relations with the West. But it was too bold an idea for the FCO, who thought it could create difficulty for the Iranians in matching my seniority (not a view shared by US Secretary of State John Kerry, who knew his Iranian counterpart better than any other foreigner) and convey the wrong message to the Arab Gulf states who were getting nervous about Iran's growing regional clout and didn't want to see the UK showing them any favours (a more legitimate concern). So we dropped the idea, and I went off to Harvard for a rewarding and instructive three months before returning to the UK to pursue a new life outside government.

The Kennedy School kindly provided me with two positions – a fellowship at the Institute of Politics (IOP) and one at the Belfer Center for Science and International Affairs. It was the perfect halfway house between the intensity of being ambassador in Washington seven days a week and returning to the UK as a retiree looking for new ways of paying the mortgage.

At the IOP, I was one of six recently, or partly, retired public servants – and the only non-American. The idea was that we would talk about our careers, and share the experience we had gained with those wondering what to do with their own lives, or wanting to test their ideas of what they thought they wanted to do against reality. Each of us had six undergraduate 'liaisons' assigned to us whose role was to help us make a success of our fellowships, spread awareness of what we were doing, drum up publicity for our speaking events and come up with bright ideas for how we might contribute to Harvard life. My liaisons were all delightful, but I was struck by how it was those with the minority ethnic backgrounds, particularly those from South Asia, who seemed the most determined to make the best of every opportunity – including that of liaison.

My role comprised teaching a ninety-minute class once a week on foreign policy, and a session of 'office hours'– a kind of surgery when you make yourself available for anyone who wants to come and talk to you, about anything under the sun – two other days a week. In between times, I found myself giving after-dinner speeches at different Harvard houses, and teaching a class at a local public school. My group of 10- and 11-year-olds, who were overwhelmingly Black, wondered for a while what I was doing there but became seriously energized when we got into debates on issues like gun control and parental responsibility. The kids simply couldn't understand why there weren't laws preventing people buying assault weapons and other instruments of mass murder over the counter.

At Harvard, I addressed workshops and seminars with groups of students both inside and beyond the Kennedy School who were interested in European affairs, foreign policy and international law. With the Brexit referendum coming up in June, there was plenty of interest in assessments of how we had got ourselves to such a point, and what was likely to happen. On a couple of occasions I did a double act with Douglas Alexander, a former cabinet minister in the Blair and Brown Labour governments who had trained as a lawyer and had a remarkable command of the facts matched with a rare ability to explain them intelligibly.

My attachment to the Belfer Center was less structured, but every bit as enjoyable. There was a constant stream of foreign policy experts – many of them friends from Washington – coming through, and a number in residence while they wrote books or underwent detox from a gruelling stint in the White House or other part of the administration.

The dynamic director, Graham Allison, was a historian who at the time was writing a book, *Destined for War*, which considered whether what he called the Thucydides Trap – a tendency for war to become inevitable when an emerging power threatens the hegemony of an existing great power, as Athens threatened the power of Sparta 2,400 years ago – had any relevance to the current US response to the rise of China. (Answer: yes, so avoiding conflict wouldn't be easy.) Allison was surrounded by other hugely talented academics and I always enjoyed joining their lunchtime conversation, book presentations and general debates.

Cambridge, Massachusetts is bitterly cold in winter and could be stunningly beautiful when feet deep in snow and illuminated by the cold evening sunshine. But the welcome was unfailingly warm, the experience unforgettable. It even allowed me time to start jotting down some thoughts for the book my friends kept telling me I should write.

Across the Charles River from Cambridge lies Boston, the state capital of Massachusetts and one of the oldest cities in the country. It was also the home of John Kerry, the secretary of state and previously one of the two Massachusetts seniors in the US Congress. One Saturday when he was in town, he asked us round to dinner. Apart from a relaxed and delicious meal with John and his wife Teresa Heinz, I recall us revisiting the diplomacy that had led to the JCPOA signed with Iran six months earlier, to which Kerry had contributed so much; discussing whether Brexit might actually happen; and a long, private conversation about where Turkey now seemed to be headed.

Susie and I returned to the UK in May 2016, a few weeks before the 23 June referendum on whether or not the UK should leave the EU. The Sunday before the vote, we joined a few thousand people in Hyde Park at a final rally in favour of staying in – forming the letters IN so the aerial photographers flying above us were left in no doubt as to our purpose. As I looked up, I felt someone touch me on the shoulder. It was Ed Llewellyn, David Cameron's chief of staff. I found him much less confident about the outcome than I would have liked.

On the morning of Friday, 24 June, like millions of other Remainers across the country, I woke feeling physically sick at the result. Thirty-eight per cent of the electorate had managed to deliver a 52–48 per cent majority in favour of leaving the community we had finally joined – after years of being rebuffed – in 1973, four months after I had entered the FCO.

A first referendum on UK membership of the EEC had been held in 1975 and produced a 67–33 per cent majority in favor of staying in. Supporters of the decision to hold a fresh referendum in 2016 argue that the question was going to have to be put to the British people again at some point because of the decision of the EU to create a currency union which, if it was ever going to work, would have to be followed with fiscal and political union – a process from which the UK could not indefinitely stand aside. But when David Cameron made the commitment in January 2013 there was no pressure from the British people to make such a fundamental choice; the UK was very well served by the opt-ins and opt-outs, and the budget rebate, it had negotiated. Its problems of austerity and inequality were far more the result of the global financial crisis of 2008 than a consequence of our membership of the EU. And there were other member states as concerned as we were about "ever closer union".

To me, the decision to commit to a referendum was much more about the divisions within the Conservative Party – encouraged by overconfidence that, if the vote ever happened, the government would be able get its way as it had in 2014 on the referendum on Scottish independence. Bizarrely, Conservative high command seemed to have forgotten that it came very close to losing that vote and might have done so had it not been for the intervention in the last days of the campaign of former Labour prime minister Gordon Brown on the side of the No vote.

Moreover, I had always feared a nasty surprise: I had heard too many European friends reminding me that referenda were much more likely to reflect the mood of the country on a given day than a considered answer to the question on the voting form. I was also conscious that for years before finally announcing that he would be campaigning in favour of Remain, on the basis of the deal he had negotiated with Brussels, Cameron had made no secret of his euroscepticism; and his government had done little to remind the British people of the benefits of membership.

Once the campaign began I, like many others, was incensed by the dishonesty of the arguments peddled by Vote Leave about the extra money that would become available for the National Health Service, the ease with which we would negotiate new FTAs with the rest of the world and the disingenuous claims that nationals from other EU countries living and working in the UK were a drain on, rather than indispensable to the functioning of, the health and other social services. But I still hoped that voters would put their own interests, and that of the country, before beguiling notions of sovereignty and the nostalgically misleading view of the country's past peddled by Brexiteers.

Those hopes were dashed. Later that month I was asked to speak at a commemorative dinner attended by several hundred of my fellow alumni of New College, Oxford, where I had spent three happy years almost half a century earlier. I spoke about diplomacy, transatlantic relations and Britain's place in the world. I also spoke about Brexit. The gist of my remarks was that such a momentous decision had been taken, by such a small proportion of the population, and on the basis of such limited knowledge of what leaving the EU would actually mean for the country, that I thought we might find ourselves putting the issue back to the people for a confirmatory vote before the deed was done. A number of people, even at high table, made their displeasure felt and began to barrack.

After dinner, the judgement of my friends was divided between those who thought I'd gone a bit far and those who said thank goodness I had said what I did. I had not intended to provoke. I simply felt that, with my recent experience of what our closest and most important foreign ally, the United States, thought of Brexit, and what it would do to our global standing, I should say what I thought. Perhaps I had underestimated the number of highly educated Oxford graduates who went along with the arguments in favour of leaving; perhaps, having been out of the country for so much of the toxic debate leading up to the referendum, I was surprised that people used to polite differences of opinion in academic circles should, on this issue, disagree so aggressively. We were close to the end of a long evening lubricated by plenty of good wine. But here was a forceful reminder that Brexit was a more divisive issue for the people of Britain, whether in an Oxford college or on the shop floor of the Honda and Mini factories down the road (where Brexit is likely to mean the loss of a large number of jobs), than any since the rearmament debate of the 1930s.

Back in 2012, David Davis, one of the leading Conservative advocates of Brexit, had said in an interview, 'if a democracy cannot change its mind, it ceases to be a democracy.' But once the referendum was over, it became clear that the supporters of Brexit were not remotely interested in allowing the question to be put to the voters again, however much the terms of Britain's departure from the EU came to differ from the promises made during the campaign.

In July 2016, as Susie and I were still trying to sort out where we were going to live in London, Turkey again became the focus of our attention. Turks – most of them at least – could hardly believe their ears when they heard Prime Minister Binali Yıldırım announce in the early evening of 15 July that a *coup d'état* was underway. By the time it was clear early the next day that the putsch had failed, the government had announced that more than 250 people had been killed.

One of the early results of the botched coup was a rallying of support for President Recep Tayyip Erdoğan. It was natural enough that the AKP base should be there for him. But so too were the leaders of the other political parties and even leading non-political secular people known to have serious reservations about the direction in which he was taking the country.

By the time they all realized that the coup did not have the support of the top military leadership, that it seemed to be the work of a network owing allegiance to an ageing cleric living in self-imposed exile in Pennsylvania, and that it had failed, even Erdoğan's fiercest critics had concluded that the affront to Turkish democracy was unacceptable. As one business leader put it to me, 'we'd rather have a Putinist strongman we're used to than another Ayatollah Khomeini returning from exile and giving us an Islamic republic'.

The military saw things much the same way. Relations between the president and the top brass had improved significantly over the previous couple of years as both sides began to realize they had been played by the Gülenists in the *Ergenekon* and *Balyoz* trials described in Chapter 10, and the military grasped the extent to which their ranks had been infiltrated by the Gülen movement. Their enemy's enemy had become their enemy too.

Visiting Turkey a few weeks later, I found widespread anger that the West – with the UK a notable exception – had not moved more quickly to condemn the coup, and conviction that the US must have been at best aware of and at worst behind it. How could they not be, the argument ran, when Fethullah Gülen ran his network – renamed by the Turkish government as the Fethullah Gülen Terrorist Organisation – out of Pennsylvania without impediment and with the support of neo-conservatives long committed to the cause of 'moderate Islam'?

I could see why even level-headed people might take that view, but I didn't share it. Well before the coup, I had often alerted US officials to the damage which perceptions of Gülen's 'plotting' were doing to America's reputation in Turkey. On the night of the coup itself, watching events unfold on television in London, I took a call from a friend in the White House asking if I knew what was going on in Ankara because they didn't. Not a call that would have been made by someone pulling the strings of attempted regime change.

Unsubstantiated as it was, the allegation of US collusion became an obstacle to closer relations between Turkey and the US. Erdoğan said he was determined to bring Gülen back to Turkey to face trial for terrorist offences. Previous Turkish complaints about Gülen had never been followed up with a formal request for his extradition. This time Erdoğan appeared to be serious, although by 2017 and 2018 the Gülen issue was but one of many bones of contention between Turkey and the United States – the biggest perhaps being the decision of the US government to back the Kurdish YPG militia in Syria at a time when the Turkish authorities regarded the group as indistinguishable from the PKK. And, as one of my journalist friends in Turkey, who was less sure that Erdoğan really wanted Gülen extradited, put it to me: 'Sometimes there is only room for one imam in the mosque.'

Another Turkish commentator reminded me that it took America's closest ally, the UK, nine years to secure the return of Joseph Doherty, an IRA gang leader who had escaped from prison in Northern Ireland while awaiting trial for the killing a British army officer. What chance, he asked, was there of Turkey faring any better if it asked the US to send back Fethullah Gülen? He didn't know that the crime of which

Doherty was accused, and later convicted *in absentia*, had been the murder of my cousin Captain Richard Westmacott. Or that he had been released early as part of the Good Friday Agreement of 1998 – which I still hope could one day serve as model for a political agreement between the Turkish government and the PKK.

In fact, there are more unanswered questions about what happened on the night of 15 July 2016 than there is evidence of any foreign interference. How far were the president and his entourage aware of the plotters' intentions before the putsch began? Why did the government leak the information that hundreds of military officers suspected of being close to Gülen were going to be fired in the annual appointments round a month later? If the president escaped from the hotel where he was staying in Marmaris just fifteen minutes before a special forces team arrived to arrest or even kill him, where did he go, and how?

How much did President Putin – with whom Erdoğan had mended fences in June after Turkey shot down a Russian bomber close to the Syrian border in November 2015 – know in advance? Did he in fact offer Erdoğan the support of Russian special forces temporarily stationed on the Greek island of Rhodes just a few minutes' flying time from Marmaris? If tens of thousands of journalists, generals, academics, judges, policemen and diplomats had been Gülen sympathizers all along, why was nothing done to root them out sooner?

Some years later, an Iranian official told me that, according to his Turkish contacts, there had been strong support for the failed coup from Mohammed bin Zayed, Crown Prince of Abu Dhabi, and his close friend and Saudi counterpart, now Crown Prince Mohammad bin Salman. On the night of the coup itself, when it looked as though it might succeed, the Saudis were said to have sent a private message to the Emir of Qatar – which they had declared a pariah state – saying that it would be his turn next.

This struck me as far-fetched, but Turkish friends have since told me that there is a strong perception in government circles that Saudi Arabia and the UAE were indeed supportive of the coup. There had, of course, been bad blood between Turkey and some of the Arab Gulf states for some time, given Erdoğan's support for the Muslim Brotherhood, his good working relations with Iran and Qatar, and his talk of recreating the Caliphate in Istanbul – much too redolent of the old days of Ottoman Empire for the Arab nations which were under its rule for five hundred years until the end of the First World War.

True or not, the suspicion that Crown Prince Mohammad bin Salman of Saudi Arabia and Mohammed bin Zayed of the UAE were complicit could help explain the decision of the Turkish authorities to leak, bit by bit, the gory details of the murder of *Washington Post* columnist Jamal Khashoggi in the Saudi Consulate in Istanbul on 2 October 2018, to the considerable embarrassment of the Crown Prince.

Some conspiracy theorists suggest that Erdoğan emerged from the coup so much stronger, with declarations of support from around the world ringing in his ears, that it must have been stage-managed by the man himself. I would not go that far. But there are signs that the anti-Gülenist establishment, some of whom clearly knew that a further attempt to get rid of Erdoğan was being planned, were happy to let the plotters go ahead and fall into the trap being laid for them. Erdoğan played the part of victim to perfection and emerged from the drama stronger, and more popular than ever, calling the failed coup 'a gift from God'.

We may never establish the whole truth. Unfortunately, in the aftermath of the failed coup, Erdoğan seemed keener to crack down on his enemies than to celebrate the defeat of the plotters with a return to inclusive politics. The McCarthy-esque round-up of tens of thousands of public employees, journalists, academics and members of the armed forces alleged to be Fethullah supporters; the further restrictions on press freedom; the restructuring of the armed forces in ways that suited the AKP; and the president's refusal to include the Kurdish political party HDP in his initiatives to promote national solidarity, all pointed to a determination to consolidate his personal hold on power.

By November 2016 Erdoğan was responding that Turkey's critics could draw whatever red lines they wished – he would draw his own. For good measure, he reminded the world that Turkey had not willingly given up its title to the Dodecanese islands close to the Turkish coast, which were transferred from Italy to Greece after the Second World War, and that today's Turkey was barely a seventh the size of the Ottoman Empire which the West had dismantled at Versailles, Sèvres and Lausanne.

Even some of his supporters began to worry that wide-spread purges risked creating a dangerous degree of aliena-tion (think de-Baathification in Iraq back in 2003), and that the open, tolerant society so many Turks have striven to achieve in recent decades was giving way to a culture of fear and intimidation. Predictably, on 24 November the European Parliament voted overwhelmingly – in a non-binding motion – to freeze EU accession negotiations with Turkey; equally predictably, Erdoğan immediately threatened to reopen the flow of Syrian refugees waiting in Turkey to cross illegally into Greece for the chance of starting a new life in the EU.

As a secular democracy in a deeply unstable region, a country of 80 million increasingly sophisticated consumers, a NATO partner, a candidate for membership of the EU, and a crucial partner in the fight to defeat ISIL and bring an end to the slaughter in next-door Syria, Turkey matters. The remarkable degree of national solidarity sparked by anger at the effrontery of the coup plotters provided an opportunity to bring the country together, not drive people apart; to regain the momentum of reform and modernization it had enjoyed under the AKP a decade earlier. But it was not to be.

Instead, Erdoğan chose to press ahead with constitutional changes, creating a far more executive, directly elected presidency, and abolishing the role of prime minister. Unable to secure a majority in the National Assembly for these changes, he organized a referendum on 16 April 2017. Erdoğan obtained the result he wanted, by a majority of 51.5 per cent to 48.5 per cent. But the result was deeply controversial. Those who campaigned for a No vote were branded as traitors and supporters of terrorism. For the first time, unstamped ballot papers – more than 1 million of them – were deemed legitimate and there were widespread allegations of intimidation. Both the Organization for Security and Co-operation in Europe and the Council of Europe determined that the campaign had not been conducted fairly.

For all the complicity that once existed between the Gülen network and the AKP, the anger at those who sought regime change through violence in 2016 was widespread and lasting. Part of this was about disappointment that the bad old days of the military coups of 1960, 1971 and 1980 had not after all been consigned to history; but it was also that so many – Erdoğan, the judiciary, the police, even many of the liberal intelligentsia – were taken in by the infiltration of the institutions of the Turkish state and media by the Gülenists, and the false plots and dirty tricks they were able to launch against their rivals. They were finally seen through only in 2014, before they overbid by launching their failed coup attempt in July 2016.

One of the best analyses of the impact of the Fethullah Gülen network on Turkish society was written in 2014 by Professor Dani Rodrik, now a professor of international political economy at Harvard University, whose father-in-law, General Çetin Doğan, was caught up in the *Ergenekon* trials. Rodrik notes in *The Plot against the Generals*: 'The established narrative that painted the military as the villain not only made it difficult for well-meaning outsiders to comprehend the nature of these trials, it also made them unwitting accomplices in the fraud being perpetrated.' Rodrik went on, presciently: 'Just as the military's own transgressions in the past had undermined democracy, so the dirty war against the military and secularists [led by Gülen] would ultimately serve to empower a mafia within the state and condemn Turkey to an even darker authoritarianism.'

Friends sometimes ask me whether it was hypocritical of the British government to support Turkish accession to the EU, knowing that it was never going to happen. I don't think so. At the time, there were two big strands to the UK's policy towards the EU. One was the completion of the single market and the breaking down of barriers to trade, business, investment and people. The other was to consolidate the gains for democracy of the collapse of the Warsaw Pact, including through the enlargement of EU membership to other European countries which met the membership criteria.

Turkey was already part of the Western camp as a member of NATO, the Council of Europe and the European Convention of Human Rights. But it was not yet fully anchored to Europe. To those who argued that only 3 per cent of Turkish territory was in the continent of Europe, and the rest was part of Asia, I would reply that almost all of Turkey was closer to the heart of Europe than Cyprus, which the EU admitted – despite it still being a divided island – in 2004. And to those who argued that it was unrealistic to expect a country that was so large, so populous, so poor and so Muslim ever to be admitted to the EU, I replied that in that case the journey to meeting the criteria for membership would still have been worth it, and Turkey would be a better and more prosperous place for its people, its neighbours and its allies.

By the end of July 2016, Susie and I were back in the United States where I had been invited to speak at the Aspen Security Forum. The forum is an annual on-the-record gathering of foreign and security policy experts in the small town almost 2,500 metres up in Colorado's Rocky Mountains which was originally known for its silver mines and is now, in summer, an important conference centre and, in winter, one of America's smartest ski resorts. It was always worth attending, as much for the conversations with old friends in the lovely natural surroundings as for the readiness of senior government officials to take the stage and discuss the state of the world (and America).

Epilogue

I n June 2016, a little more than a third of the British electorate, but a majority of those who voted, opted for Brexit. Just six months later, 3 million fewer votes than were cast for his opponent, Hillary Clinton, sent Donald Trump to the White House.

Such are the vagaries of our democratic processes. Trump said Brexit had helped propel him to victory. It certainly felt as if, like the Leave campaign in the UK, he had been able to tap into feelings of resentment, alienation, inequality and economic stagnation among the middle classes, as well as frustration with the political establishment. This was fertile ground for campaigns to promote anger against immigrants and a backlash against the globalization which had helped generate worldwide economic growth and prosperity but had left behind many who had lost their jobs and security, felt that other countries were eating their lunch and feared their own were headed in the wrong direction.

Fertile ground too for those with a political agenda of their own to foment anger and fear, and to fuel prejudices, by using the new magic of social media to channel distorted or invented stories to the voters they were trying to influence. Some of it came from the increasingly sophisticated professional campaign teams harvesting data so they knew which groups to target with what they wanted to hear. Some, we are now beginning to realize, came from malevolent foreign powers able to use the freedoms of the democracies they wanted to undermine to spread lies, sow discord and weaken Western values, alliances and resilience – all at amazingly low cost.

In both the US and the UK, the angry, fearful and generally less well-off were attracted by populist messages of 'Take Back Control' and 'Make America Great Again' which tapped into nostalgia for times past. They were encouraged by other groups who had not lost out from globalization or the consequences of the global financial crisis of 2007–9 but saw a vote for Trump or Leave as a route to less regulation, lower taxes and greater personal wealth.

Democracies are having to fight back, while remaining true to their values. This isn't easy when data are increasingly packaged to influence rather than inform, and algorithms decide who receives what. More Americans now get their news from Facebook than from any other source, yet Facebook has been slow to accept that it has a responsibility to vet the material its users post of a racist, anti-Semitic or personally offensive nature. In the White House, Donald Trump watched Rupert Murdoch's Fox News and tweeted out its conspiracy theories and falsehoods as if they were fact.

By the summer of 2020, the president of the United States had been tracked by the *Washington Post* as having told 20,000 untruths since entering the White House in January 2017. Yet his standard defence of any criticism was to dismiss it as 'fake news' made up by a hostile and dishonest liberal media. He accused his political opponents of being corrupt, without evidence, while his family took advantage of Trump's presidency to promote their own financial interests in unprecedented fashion.

The contagion is spreading. The liberties with the truth which were taken during the 2016 referendum campaign in the UK would have been unthinkable a few years earlier. In July 2019 the Conservative Party chose as its leader, and by extension as prime minister of the UK, a man described in the *Financial Times* as having 'lied his way through life and politics'. During the 2019 election campaign the Conservative Party was happy to doctor an interview with Labour's shadow Brexit secretary, and to issue invented figures about the cost of Labour's spending plans, which it knew to be misleading but which served the purpose of creating a narrative that made people think worse of their opponents.

During the same campaign, Prime Minister Boris Johnson suppressed the publication of a report by the British Parliament's intelligence and security select committee that looked into allegations of Russian interference with the British democratic process, later shown to have included evidence that large sums of Russian money had been given to his party and to the Brexit campaign. Elsewhere in the EU, particularly in Hungary but also in Poland, democracy was under strain as elected politicians used their positions for personal gain, to suppress basic freedoms and to stymie the chances of others unseating them.

The more I looked at the US political system during my time in Washington, the more I concluded that the years had eroded some of the admirable principles set down by the Founding Fathers for the new republic they created after winning independence from Great Britain. The Federal Constitution of 1783 asserts that 'government is for the common good, not for the profit... or private interest... of any one man or class of men'. Yet more and more money flows into the political system as lobbyists and special interest groups seek to ensure that their people are elected, and their interests are pursued by those whose campaigns they have financed. Revenue for Washington lobbying firms rose from $100 million in 1975 to $3.47 billion in 2019.

In a critical ruling in the January 2010 case of *Citizens United* v. *the Federal Election Commission*, the Supreme Court determined that restrictions on corporate spending on electioneering violated the First Amendment's protection of free speech. The majority 5:4 opinion, led by Justice Anthony Kennedy, found that 'independent expenditures, including those made by corporations, do not give rise to corruption or the appearance of corruption'.

It opened the floodgates. Vast sums were raised and spent by political action committees which, while technically independent of individual candidate campaigns, provided substantial material support. At a meeting of the Aspen Security Forum, at which I spoke in 2014, the former Senate Majority Leader George Mitchell, a Democrat, said he thought the *Citizens United* decision was 'the biggest single blunder committed by the Supreme Court in its entire existence'.

Everyone learned to play by the new rules. By mid-2019 the normally hawkish Republican Majority Leader of the Senate, Mitch McConnell, was supporting the lifting of sanctions against the Russian aluminium company Rusal, owned by a number of pro-Putin individuals and entities, which wanted to invest $200 million in a new plant in his home state of Kentucky. (This was the same majority leader who in 2016 refused to allow hearings for President Obama's Supreme Court nominee in an election year, as a matter of 'longstanding tradition', and then did exactly that in late 2020 to give Donald Trump the third Supreme Court justice of his presidency.)

Earlier in 2019, the Federal Aviation Authority (FAA) was roundly criticized for being the last global air safety authority to ground the Boeing 737 MAX after two of the new aircraft had crashed in similar circumstances in Kenya and off the coast of Indonesia, killing a total of 346 people. Shortly before the FAA finally agreed to ground the planes, the president and CEO of Boeing, Dennis Muilenburg, telephoned President Trump to say his planes were safe. His company had given $1 million to help pay for Trump's inauguration festivities and had been authorized in 2018 – after intense lobbying of Congress – to carry out itself the bulk of the safety certification of its new planes hitherto done by engineers of the FAA.

Money talks. It affects elections, legislation, foreign affairs, air safety, energy policy and – of course – taxation. President Trump's tax reform bill, passed in December 2017, cut corporate tax from 35 per cent to 21 per cent, penalized those earning annual salaries of less than $75,000 and rewarded all earning more than $200,000. The rules applying to the real estate business were even more skewed in favour of the rich, thanks to the generous rules on depreciation and capital gains which lobbyists are paid handsomely to maintain.

Money has become the dominant feature of American

public life. That makes for bad law-making. Giving money to politicians, and charities, is also a handy way for shady individuals and enterprises to buy legitimacy and respectability. No wonder other countries sense hypocrisy when US prosecutors take action against foreign firms and individuals under the Foreign Corrupt Practices Act but fail to address the abuses going on nearer home.

Justice is also affected since, in forty-three of the fifty states of the union, attorneys-general are elected and have to raise funds for their campaigns. In his seminal *Democracy in America*, published in 1835, Alexis de Tocqueville observed 'the most weighty argument against the election of a chief magistrate is that it offers so splendid a lure to private ambition'.

Similarly, the growing tendency of British prime ministers to award cronies, relatives and donors with honours, lifetime titles and seats in the House of Lords weakens the right of British governments to suggest how others should behave. Not only with regard to corruption and influence-peddling, but also in respect of human rights, freedom of expression and rule of law – in both Johnson's Britain and Trump's America, journalists who ask inconvenient questions and judges who find fault with the government have been branded 'enemies of the people'. In October 2020 over 800 former British judges and law officers formally complained that abusive attacks on their profession by the prime and other ministers were endangering the personal safety of lawyers.

From the moment in April 2020 that it was clear that he would be the Democratic nominee to challenge Donald Trump, former Vice President Joe Biden was consistently ahead of the president in the polls. But Democrats were nervous because the polls had wrongly predicted that Hillary Clinton would win in 2016; and because Trump was increasingly clear that he would only accept the result of the election if he won.

In the event, he lost the popular vote by 6 million and the electoral college by the same margin as he had won it in 2016 – 306 delegates to 232, which he called 'a landslide' at the time. But he won 10 million more votes than four years earlier, and lost some states by small margins. And so, sure enough, rather than concede, he launched a series of wholly unfounded claims of voter fraud while beginning to prepare a fresh run for the presidency in 2024.

As alarming for American democracy as a president refusing to accept the outcome of the democratic process was the willingness of the Republican Party to go along with the fictions peddled by the outgoing president. Trump was far from the preferred candidate of the Republican establishment in 2016, much of which he spent insulting his fellow contenders for the nomination. But the Republican Party supported him unquestioningly after he became their candidate and have since loyally defended even his most egregious behaviour.

Why? Because in the November congressional elections, Republican candidates needed the votes of Trump's base. After 3 November, they refused to stand up for democracy, and the truth, out of fear of being called out by Trump in advance of the next time they will need the votes of his supporters. They needed Trump voters to turn out in January 2021 for run-offs determining two critical Senate seats in Georgia and the midterms – when the whole of the House of Representatives and one third of the Senate are again up for re-election – are just two years after the presidentials.

In Britain, three and a half years of uncertainty as to whether Brexit would actually happen were ended by the general election held in the UK on 12 December 2019. On that day, Boris Johnson, having replaced Theresa May as leader of the party in July, led the Conservatives to an overwhelming victory having persuaded a tired and frustrated electorate that a vote for his Conservatives, purged of Remainers and even Brexiteers not prepared to entertain the option of a ruinous no-deal departure from the EU, would 'get Brexit done'.

Which it didn't. Britain formally left the EU on 31 January 2020 – with a worse deal than the one Theresa May had failed three times to get Parliament to endorse. But nothing actually changed, and the detailed negotiations about Britain's future relationship with the EU, which only began after that date, were always destined to go down to the wire as the 31 December deadline for the end of transition approached.

The future of Britain's trading links with the EU and the rest of the world, and much else, will depend on how those negotiations conclude. There is no form of Brexit which will not be worse for Britain, in trading and economic terms, than the arrangement we enjoyed as full members of the EU, complete with opt-ins, opt-outs and a budget rebate. But even a thin deal will be less harmful than the option of no deal at all.

By mid-November 2020 there were signs that the close control over 10 Downing Street and Conservative Party policy exercised by a cabal of recycled Vote Leave activists was coming to an end when two of his closest advisers

– veterans of the Leave campaign – were finally shown the door by an exasperated prime minister. As I finished writing this book, it was not yet clear what kind of culture, and political operation, would take their place. But the sighs of relief, and hope that a semblance of normal service and civility would be resumed, were being felt throughout British politics, even as some of us listened with disbelief, and a degree of horror, as the former Conservative Party leader Iain Duncan Smith greeted the conclusion of the UK's trade and cooperation agreement with the EU just before the end of the year with the claim that Britain would now be 'dominating the world again'.

In the US, Britain, Turkey and a number of EU member states democracy is under attack, from both within as the independence of institutions and traditional checks and balances are weakened, and from without as organized criminals and opponents of individual liberty continue to sow confusion and discord.

A report published by Cambridge University's Department of Politics in October 2020 found the highest level dissatisfaction with democracy across more than 150 countries than at any time in the last quarter of a century.

Without serious efforts to address these disturbing tendencies, it is going to be increasingly difficult to suggest that the Western liberal model is one which others should seek to emulate. Why would China, for example – which has disregarded the international commitments it gave at the time of the handover of Hong Kong, abuses the rights of millions of Uighurs in Xinjiang province and is moving back towards the supremacy of the Communist Party and its president for life over the rights of its people – wish to opt for the kind of political reforms championed by liberal democracies? Not for the Chinese Communist Party the kind of humility which might be expected from a country which, however unwittingly, turned out to have played host to Covid-19, the most destructive virus the world has seen in a hundred years.

As soon as the referendum result came through in June 2016, it was clear that Britain was going to be wholly absorbed by domestic politics and Brexit for some time to come, leaving little bandwidth for, or interest in, foreign affairs. Some foreign policy experts argue that the government took itself out of mainstream foreign policy much earlier than that, when the House of Commons decided on 29 August 2013 that the UK would not join President Obama in making airstrikes against the Syrian regime in response to its use of chemical weapons.*

That was a critical decision, but I don't believe it was the moment when the UK walked off the stage. It is true that afterwards we left the diplomacy of Ukraine to the 'Normandy group' of France, Germany, Russia and Ukraine, while negotiations seeking an end to the calamitous civil war in Syria were taken over – after the arrival of Trump in the White House – by the unlikely trio of Iran, Russia and Turkey. But Britain remained active at NATO and the UN and was instrumental in negotiating, with others, the Iran nuclear deal of July 2015.

I do nevertheless believe that the referendum of June

---

* See Chapter 12, p. 258.

2016; the combination of declining defensive capabilities, about which the Americans were warning me in 2014 and 2015; diminishing public and parliamentary support for overseas military adventures; the total absorption of Britain's political machinery by Brexit for four years; and now the far-greater-than-average impact on our economy and society of Covid-19 have made Britain a less significant international player. Talking to old friends in Europe, North America, the Middle East and several Asian countries, I hear the same refrain: where have you gone? We need you, your expertise, your friendship and your diplomatic skills.

The problem was compounded by the decision of two successive prime ministers to try and be best friends with Donald Trump. His promises that, after Brexit, the UK would benefit immediately from a tremendous new FTA with the United States were pie in the sky. But they led Theresa May and her successor Boris Johnson to give top priority to aligning British policy with that of the Trump administration. Even before the new president had taken over, Theresa May's government turned its back on the Middle East peace process initiatives which had been developed, in close partnership with the UK, by President Obama's secretary of state, John Kerry. Britain also joined the Americans at the UN Security Council in tabling draft language on Yemen, placing the entire responsibility for the war on Iran and its Houthi proxies without mentioning the suffering caused by the bombing of civilian targets by the Saudi and Emirati air forces.

On issues where we disagreed, London tended to keep its views to itself. Only on Trump's decisions to move the US

Embassy from Tel Aviv to Jerusalem and to tear up the 2015 nuclear deal with Iran did the UK publicly distance itself from US policy.

In January 2020, Boris Johnson took a decision to limit the future involvement of the Chinese firm Huawei in Britain's 5G communications network, which stopped a long way short of the complete ban Trump and Pompeo had been demanding – and led to a bad-tempered phone call from Trump. By July new US sanctions on Huawei had left the UK government with little choice but to ban *all* future Huawei involvement in the 5G network, since Huawei would be more dependent than ever on Chinese technology. Washington was delighted, but the process showed that at least on this issue the UK was prepared to make its own decisions and not simply bow to US pressure.

The time to discuss Huawei had been a few years earlier before Western economies became so dependent on the company for much of its 3G and 4G, let alone 5G, telecommunications technology. Yet I recall a White House official telling me in 2014–15, with regret, that the crises of the day always ensured that there was never time at our bilateral summits for the kind of non-urgent, strategic discussion of China which both London and Washington knew we needed.

2021 offered the chance of a reset. The Brexit debate was finally over. Prime Minister Johnson, with a comfortable majority of eighty in the House of Commons, would be freer than in the past to select ministers on merit rather than on mere loyalty and readiness to go along with a no-deal Brexit. The world would be looking ahead to a more normal life post-Covid-19. And the British government, having announced in November 2020 a significant upgrade in defence spending, could be in a position to rediscover an appetite for foreign policy and the kind of multilateral approach which alone will allow members of the rules-based international order to stand up to malevolent players and trends. As the Chinese Communist Party continues its search for ways of countering the Western worldview based on individual liberty and national sovereignty, the need for a considered, collective Western response had never been greater.

It looked as though the main EU players wanted to keep working with the UK on foreign policy, defence, intelligence and cyber security, regardless of how the economic and commercial relationship ended up being reconfigured after Brexit – even though the UK government refused during the Brexit negotiations to agree to anything more ambitious than ad hoc cooperation in these critical areas.

Then there was the Biden factor. As long as Donald Trump was in power, his disregard for the truth, affinity for corrupt strongmen, unilateralist instincts and dislike of international institutions and alliances meant that meaningful cooperation with the United States was going to be difficult for the UK. President-elect Biden was going to be different. His instinct would be to work with allies, to seek consensual solutions.

But it would not be plain sailing. Biden believed that Brexit was a mistake, and, very conscious of his Irish roots, signalled early on his concern that no withdrawal agreement should be allowed to jeopardise the peace and stability brought about by the 1998 Good Friday Agreement. He told Boris Johnson that he wants to maintain a strong economic and commercial relationship with Britain, but was more realistic than Trump about the prospects of securing a comprehensive free trade agreement in the near future.

Encouragingly, Biden's first appointments were of people of experience, ability and integrity to key positions in the White House, State Department, Homeland Security and as director of national intelligence. He and those around him were keen to restore the very close foreign and security policy partnerships with close allies which had been a traditional feature of US foreign policy over many decades. This offers the possibility of working effectively with Washington, and other like-minded partners, on managing the rise of China, dealing with Vladimir Putin, revitalizing NATO, correcting the damage Trump has done to the Iran nuclear deal, and helping stabilize the Middle East. Biden's choice of John Kerry, a former secretary of state, as presidential climate change envoy offers the UK a perfect opportunity to help bring America back to the heart of global climate negotiations in the run-up to the COP summit in Glasgow in November 2021. Chairing the G7 in Cornwall, England in June 2021 offered another bonus – the opportunity to engage with Biden on his idea of a summit of democracies to start pushing back against authoritarianism. But the summit was unfortunately, if predictably, overshadowed by a row between Johnson and the EU, with whom Biden clearly sympathised, over the UK's attempt to unpick the very aspects of the Northern Ireland protocol which Johnson and his lieutenant, Michael Gove, had negotiated with Brussels, in the process confirming Washington's suspicions that Johnson was unsound on all matters Irish.

Covid-19 has reminded us that the sovereign nations of the world remain interdependent. When the province of Hubei in China was hit with the coronavirus, Jaguar Land Rover plants in Britain were threatened with closure, Apple ran short of parts for its iPhones and Chinese tourists cancelled reservations all over the world. As Henry Kissinger put it pithily in his slim but prescient volume *World Order* back in 2015, 'chaos threatens side by side with unprecedented interdependence'.

We can help each other out. In Colombia, foreign mediation played a significant role in bringing to an end the long conflict between the FARC rebels and the central government. In Afghanistan, volunteers with experience of difficult negotiations worked for years to find common ground between the elected government and the Taliban before the Trump administration reached a (fragile) peace agreement with the insurgents in February 2020. In Turkey, mediators have tried to find ways of bringing an end to the armed conflict led by the PKK, the Kurdish terrorist group demanding regional autonomy and cultural freedoms. Others have attempted, but failed, to resolve the last remaining territorial dispute within the EU – that between the Turkish north and Greek south of Cyprus – and the associated maritime border disputes between Turkey and Greece; and, perhaps most tragically of all, the unresolved issue of Israel and Palestine.

The need for diplomacy and experience has not been supplanted by new technology, social media and instant communications. In the US, senior government servants tend to be political appointees. They do not retire when their president leaves office. They go to the private sector – often a law firm or consultancy – or join one of the many world-class think tanks like Brookings, the Wilson Center, the American Enterprise Institute, the Atlantic Council, the Carnegie

Endowment for International Peace, all of which help to make the US a world leader in thought and comment on public policy. Then, when the country chooses a new president with whom they are politically affiliated, they are ready and willing to come back into government.

It isn't like that in the UK. Once civil servants – having served governments of all political persuasions as apolitical professionals – leave the public service, they go for good. Occasionally they are invited to brief new appointees, or parliamentary select committees. But this is rare, even if some of us take advantage of the knowledge, experience and relationships we have acquired in different parts of the world to help with private diplomacy, problem-solving or conflict resolution.

Of course I am biased, but it seems to me that there could be real advantage for the country in more effectively tapping into, rather than walking away from, the expertise of those who have honed their skills in what has traditionally been one of the best-performing governmental machines in the Western world.

I worry that recent attempts by the current UK government and its cheerleaders in the media to devalue and politicize the civil service and other institutions, including the judiciary and the BBC, may soon invalidate that claim. So the knowledge, experience, relationships, credibility – and independence – acquired by public servants in the course of the kind of career of which I have tried to give a flavour in these pages may yet be of value as Britain works out how best to rediscover its role, protect its interests, and make a difference for the better, in a post-Brexit world.

Acknowledgements

I never intended to publish a memoir or autobiography but I was encouraged to do so at the end of my career by friends, family members and former colleagues who thought there could be value in sharing my experiences and reflections with others. From a long list I hope Charles Anson, Bill Burns, Michael Beschloss, Martin Fletcher, Peter Foster, David Lough, Paul Richards and David Taylor won't mind being singled out.

The book began to take shape when, in January 2016, the Belfer Center for Science and International Affairs and the Institute of Politics (IoP) at Harvard's Kennedy School of Government each awarded me a fellowship for a semester to write, think, teach and learn while I decompressed from fourteen years of non-stop engagement as British ambassador to three fascinating countries – Turkey, France and the United States. I had an office, a computer, some time and the most stimulating company. I am hugely grateful to Graham Allison, then head of the Belfer Center, and Maggie Williams of the IoP, for the opportunity. At Harvard I also had the good fortune to be encouraged and advised by Douglas Alexander, Paula Dobriansky, David Ignatius, Steve Hadley, Beth Myers, Joe Nye, Deval

Patrick, Dan Poneman, David Sanger and Wendy Sherman.

The first result was a booklet published in 2017 by the Atlantic Council entitled *Turkey's European Journey – A Ringside View*, and I am indebted to the Council for their permission to reproduce much of that short publication in the chapters on Turkey.

After returning to London just before the 2016 Brexit referendum, many people pressed me to finish the job. Friends I had made as ambassador in Washington continued to provide encouragement and wise counsel. They include Tony Blinken, Tom Friedman, Phil Gordon, Vali Nasr and Frank Wisner while Peter Baker, Dan Balz and Steve Erlanger have helped keep me up to date on domestic American politics. In Turkey old friends who should remain anonymous have made valiant efforts to keep me informed about a country where I spent a total of eight years as a diplomat, where we have a home, and for which I wish the best possible future.

Many of the friends I made in Iran back in the 1970s have either passed away or had to leave the country – which in many cases has made it easier for us to stay connected. To them, and to those still there, living in difficult and dangerous conditions – including a handful of government officials for whom I developed both affection and respect – thank you. I am indebted also to friends elsewhere in the region – in Afghanistan and Iraq, particularly the Kurdistan region – who always made me welcome and have been kind enough over many years to help me understand what's really happening in their complex countries.

Thanks too to the many wonderful colleagues in the British and other governments from whom I learned so much and who, in thousands of different ways, helped me do the job, and made the adventure so challenging, rewarding and enjoyable.

I could not be more grateful to Georgina Capel for agreeing to be my literary agent and for providing invaluable wisdom and practical advice to a neophyte author. Huge thanks also to her husband Anthony Cheetham of Head of Zeus for publishing my book. My editor at Head of Zeus, Richard Milbank, has provided an extraordinary blend of enthusiasm, practical advice, helpful suggestions, patience and kindness without which *They Call it Diplomacy* would never have seen the light of day. Thanks are also due to Matt Bray for the cover, to Adrian McLaughlin for his typesetting, and to Clémence Jacquinet and Anna Nightingale for all their hard work on the production and editorial side.

Finally, tons of love and gratitude to my family for putting up with, and supporting me throughout, this peripatetic life, especially to my wife Susie who not only lived much of this story with me but over four long years offered invaluable corrections, suggestions, and memory-jogging.

Index